FV.

St. Louis Community College

Forest Park
Florissant Valley
Meramec

Instructional Resources
St. Louis, Missouri

GAYLORD

moral dilemmas of feminism

Thinking Gender
Edited by Linda Nicholson

Also published in the series

moral
dilemmas
of

**PROSTITUTION,
ADULTERY, AND
ABORTION**

feminism

LAURIE SHRAGE

ROUTLEDGE

NEW YORK LONDON

Published in 1994 by

Routledge
29 West 35th Street
New York, NY 10001

Published in Great Britain by

Routledge
11 New Fetter Lane
London EC4P 4EE

Copyright © 1994 by Routledge

Printed in the United States of America on acid-free paper.

Library of Congress Cataloging-in-Publication Data

Shrage, Laurie, 1953–
    Moral dilemmas of feminism : prostitution, adultery, and abortion
    Laurie Shrage.
        p. cm. — (Thinking gender)
    Includes index.
    ISBN 0-415-90550-8 — ISBN 0-415-90551-6
    1. Feminist theory—Moral and ethical aspects. 2. Feminism—Moral and ethical aspects. 3. Feminist ethics. 4. Sexual ethics. 5. Adultery—Moral and ethical aspects. 6. Prostitution—Moral and ethical aspects. 7. Abortion—Moral and ethical aspects.
    I. Title. II. Series.
    HQ1190.S45 1994
    305.42′01—dc20   93-48107
                                                      CIP

British Library Cataloging-in-Publication Data also available

For Dan

Contents

Preface

When I was a graduate student (1977–82), I occasionally participated in the abortion rights efforts of the San Diego County Chapter
of NOW (National Organization for Women). As part of this group
of activists, I helped to organize a talk by Margo St. James, founder
of the prostitutes' civil rights organization called "Call Off Your Old
Tired Ethics" (COYOTE).[1] In the early to mid 1970s, St. James had
begun organizing a grassroots campaign for the decriminalization of
prostitution. Several years later, the California state NOW endorsed
the idea of decriminalization, and began to lend support to the efforts
of prostitutes' rights activists. Yet many of the local NOW women
with whom I had worked were uneasy with the new alliance between
feminists and prostitute advocates. Some were especially uncomfort-
able with St. James—a former prostitute—who promoted prostitutes'
rights in essentially the same terms as feminists promoted women's
rights. Indeed St. James was seeking support among feminists, and
many feminists were extremely troubled about giving it to her. I had
not planned on attending St. James's talk, but was eventually enlisted
to join a group of critics who were hoping to expose the flaws in St.
James's feminist reasoning.

In a combative frame of mind, I went to hear St. James speak. She
argued that the same rights to which feminists appeal to defend legal
access to abortion—privacy and the right to control one's own body—
justify removing laws against prostitution. For just as the government
has no right to intervene in the reproductive decisions of women,
according to St. James, it has no right to intervene in their consensual
sexual behavior with other adults. Moreover, St. James claimed that
the behavior of the typical prostitute was consensual—that is, rational
and uncoerced. At least she pointed out to us that to assume that the

prostitute's behavior is inevitably coerced, as some feminists do, is just as patronizing and condescending as treating the behavior of a woman who seeks an abortion as inevitably coerced. In other words, she maintained that the prostitute's actions are typically no more irrational acts of desperation than the actions of a woman who has an abortion. Furthermore, given that exchanging sex for money can be rational for women, a woman's choice to do this should be guaranteed by her right of bodily sovereignty, just as her choice to have a medically induced abortion is guaranteed by this right.

St. James then ably explained how the criminalization of prostitution is responsible for most of the troubling consequences of prostitution, just as the criminalization of abortion was responsible for many of the injuries women risked to have illegal abortions. She also emphasized the gender inequalities manifest in existing statutes prohibiting prostitution and their enforcement, for these statutes generally empowered public officials to harass, arrest, and punish sexually "delinquent" women. Strengthening her analogy between abortion and prostitution, St. James argued that just as laws restricting abortion are aimed at controlling women's reproductive capacity, laws restricting prostitution ultimately aim to control women's sexuality. These laws together imply that women have no authority to make life-and-death decisions pertaining to their reproductive labor, and that women have no right to profit economically from their sexual labor. Furthermore, St. James alleged that just as legally permitting abortion does not degrade human life, but reaffirms the value of voluntary motherhood and responsible reproduction, legally permitting prostitution does not degrade women, but reaffirms the value of sexual expression and economic freedom for women. For St. James, to think that selling—and therefore permitting the selling—of sexual services degrades women is to buy into sexist double standards of sexual morality that limit women to sexual abstinence or amorous sexual self-sacrifice. In short, St. James concluded from her analogy that laws prohibiting prostitution are just as obstructive to women's pursuit of sexual expression and economic opportunity as laws prohibiting abortion.

To the disappointment of some of my NOW companions, I found St. James to be rather persuasive. At least, I was persuaded that St. James had identified some serious inconsistencies in feminist theorizing about sex, more than I was convinced of the adequacy of her analysis of prostitution. For how can we support legal access to abortion so that women, as MacKinnon has recently put it, can have sex with men on the same terms that men have sex with women, but not support decriminalized prostitution so that women can have sex with men and charge for it, and so be more economically independent?[2]

Moreover I suspected that St. James was right in arguing that feminists were wrong to represent prostitution as the ultimate form of gender exploitation and subordination. Nevertheless, I found it difficult to accept that prostitution might offer some women sexual liberation and economic empowerment. There had to be other feminist perspectives on prostitution besides these two alternatives, and other ways to defend abortion rights that would not engender the difficulties of the standard liberal defenses.

Soon after getting my Ph.D. for writing a dissertation on a somewhat sterile topic in analytic philosophy, I began reading case studies, histories, and ethnographies of prostitution. Perhaps with more knowledge of the lives of prostitutes, a better feminist analysis would emerge. My initial attempt to forge an alternative feminist approach to prostitution was written up in an article titled "Should Feminists Oppose Prostitution?"[3] In that paper I argued that prostitution was neither a subversive sexual practice nor an inherently oppressive one. Rather my analysis framed prostitution as a contingently oppressive practice—oppressive due to the way it has been shaped by historically and culturally specific forces.

Some of that paper survives in this book, though it has been reworked and expanded. In the decade and a half that I have been thinking about prostitution, feminist debates have been significantly influenced by a number of intellectual movements, especially postmodernism, lesbian and gay studies, critical race studies, and postcolonial theory. Postmodernist ideas have forced us to recognize some of the ideological aspects of our own intellectual discourses, and to be more critical of claims to authority. Lesbian and gay studies has exposed many of the heterosexist presuppositions that structure our thinking on sexuality. Writings on critical race theory, especially by women of color, have challenged the analyses and political priorities of an earlier generation of predominantly white academic feminists. And writings about the remnants of colonialism in our contemporary world by Third World scholars have rendered visible many of our Western conceits. All of these areas of scholarship are especially relevant to the ongoing development of a feminist sexual politics.

This book explores alternative ways to theorize about prostitution and abortion—ways that can support a critical and self-aware feminist politics. I begin though with a third moral issue—the issue of adultery—in order to illustrate some philosophical problems with sexual moralities that essentialize human behavior. I argue that codes of sexual and reproductive behavior, even revolutionary ones, need to reflect an appreciation of human difference as well as similarity. Building upon the insights of cultural anthropologists, who more than other scholars have been concerned to explore the full range of human possibilities, I begin to formulate an anti-objectivist, "interpretive" (hermeneutical) and pluralist approach to feminist ethics. Applying this approach to questions about legal access to abortion and sex commerce, I try to avoid the reductionism and ethnocentrism prevalent in much feminist and American moral philosophy, and to develop practical policy proposals that will benefit women.

In the first two chapters of this book, I consider how interpretive approaches to human behavior differ from objectivist approaches, and I consider the importance of knowledge of human diversity for ethics. I then examine feminist "discourse" or "communicative" ethics and feminist "care" ethics, and argue that their reductionist methods ultimately lead to ethnocentric moral reasoning. Building upon the work of Clifford Geertz and Charles Taylor, I develop an anti-reductionist, anti-objectivist approach to moral analysis. Using the topic of adultery, I especially emphasize how semiotic critical tools and methodologies can enable moral analysis. I argue that moral analysis should aim to identify the cultural presuppositions that form the background to social action in order to generate evaluative and comparative judgments about human practices that are relatively less parochial, and which can provide a basis for political compromise.

In chapter 3, I develop this approach further by applying it to the controversy over abortion. Utilizing feminist ethnographies of pro-choice and pro-life women, and a cross-cultural study of abortion practices, I attempt to probe the social origins of attitudes to abortion in American society. After identifying some idiosyncratic cultural principles that condition our beliefs about abortion, I propose some political and policy compromises on this issue that feminists can support.

In chapters 4, 5, and 6, I attempt to illustrate and refine an interpretive and pluralist feminist ethics by taking up the issue of sex commerce. Using ethnographies and histories of women's lives, in this case the lives of prostitutes, I compare prostitution in ancient Babylon, medieval Europe, colonial Africa, and contemporary Nepal. I argue that together these case studies allow us to see the cultural distortions in previous feminist accounts of prostitution, and can help us develop less provincial analyses of sex work in our society. Moreover, I formulate an account of prostitution that highlights race as well as gender as a significant aspect of the social organization of prostitution in the U.S. and elsewhere. I end my discussion by advocating a policy of socialist and feminist regulationism in regard to prostitution.

In chapter 7, I consider and discuss the relativistic implications of my interpretive and pluralist accounts of prostitution and abortion. I try to show that if we understand relativism in terms of particular interpretive strategies for avoiding ethnocentrism, then cultural relativism will not lead to critical paralysis or universal toleration. Thus I reject pluralist accounts that try to appropriate and reconstruct notions of objectivity. By briefly considering the topic of commercial and medically assisted access to pregnancy ("surrogate motherhood"), I try to show that interpretive and thoroughly pluralist accounts can generate new feminist strategies of resistance.

I would like to thank Dan Segal and Pat Lin for their constant willingness to discuss the topics in this book with me, read drafts of chapters, and for repeatedly directing me to relevant and helpful materials. I would also like to thank Sandra Bartky and Philippa Levine for their interest in my work, their ongoing encouragement, and their insights on parts of this project. Other colleagues who read and commented on earlier drafts of parts of this book include David Adams, Jim Bogen, Linda Nicholson, Edward Park, Darrel Moellendorf, Terry Winant, David Schneider, Ernestine McHugh, Nathan Tierney, Sheila McCoy, Marilyn Pearsall, Tom Moody, Wayne Wooden, Sonia Blackman, Per Dahlin, and Mary Mahowald. Colleagues whose ideas and advice have contributed to my work include Ann Garry, Lourdes Arguelles, Dick Arneson, Rita Manning, Virginia Warren, Alison Jaggar, Betty Farrell, Wynne Furth, Lorraine Code, Norma Almodovar, Naomi Zack, and Dorothy Wills. These people and others have had a considerable influence on me, and thus I am not sure I would exonerate them of all responsibility for what I have written, which is typical in these kind of acknowledgments. By writing this book, I have been able to appreciate how academic scholarship is a collective enterprise.

I am especially grateful to Linda Nicholson and Maureen MacGrogan. Their interest in my work and professional support allowed me to concentrate my efforts on this project. Linda's influence as a philosopher has been important for me, as her work challenges some strains of provincialism in feminist philosophy. I am also grateful to Alison Shonkwiler of Routledge, who helpfully answered many tedious questions without appearing to find them tedious.

I would like to acknowledge all the help I have received from students in my Philosophy of Love and Sex classes and my Issues in Gay and Lesbian Studies class. The dialogues and discussions that have taken place in these classes forced me to rethink some conventional feminist wisdom on human sexuality.

I am indebted to the members of the Pacific Division of the Society for Women in Philosophy, Moral and Political Philosophers of Southern California, Pacific Division of the American Philosophical Association, Huntington Library Seminar in Women's Studies, Cal

Poly Pomona Campus Forum, and the Philosophy Department and Women's Studies Program at Cal Poly SLO for providing me with opportunities to present some of the work in this book and get valuable feedback. For the same reason, I am indebted to Iris Young, who organized the Feminist Ethics and Social Policy Conference at the University of Pittsburgh (1993). I would also like to thank Cal Poly Pomona for supporting this book by granting me a needed sabbatical, and by supporting me with various CSU research grants. I would especially like to recognize the Dean's Office in the College of Arts and the Faculty Development Center for their contribution to creating supportive environments in the CSU system for faculty research.

I am very much beholden to Mili Dawai, who has always cared for my children as if they were her own. I am also beholden to my children, whose delightfulness and exuberance always make it possible to take rewarding breaks from my writing. My daughter Hannah (six years) kept asking me what my book was about, why I was writing it, and if we would get to keep it when it was done. I found responding to these questions more challenging than some that I address in this book. And my son Nathaniel (two years) kept asking me the longest question he could muster whenever he found me at work in my loft office: "'Allo Mom, what you doing up there?"

My partner Dan Segal must be credited here for knowing how to organize our lives so that we can both take on the challenges of writing books, for taking on a significantly greater share of household work when I am in the frenzy of writing, for planting some seeds of ambition and courage, for correcting my errors about social science, for always being available to pursue and evaluate ideas, and for doing all this with relative calm, patience, humor, and creativity. It is to him that I dedicate this book.

1

Eschewing Ethnocentric Ethics

Cinematic and Philosophical Takes on Adultery

In a film titled *Ju Dou,* a woman seduces her husband's nephew. This act, so starkly described, might strike my reader as despicable (depending on who you are), but consider the social context in which this affair takes place. The general context for this cinematic act of adultery is 1920s pre-Communist China. The principals in the story include an elderly dye mill owner (Jinshan Yang) who, at the film's opening, has just acquired his third wife (Ju Dou). She is a rather young bride, and her purchase has cost him a considerable sum. Jinshan, though advanced in age and previously married, brings no biological offspring into this marriage. Indeed, we soon learn that the point of this new marriage is to create a much desired male heir for the Yang family. Jinshan's previous wives are no longer alive at this point, and one minor character in the film alleges that he tortured them to death when they failed to carry out their customary reproductive duties.

This allegation becomes quite credible when, not long into this film and the marriage it depicts, we see Jinshan forcefully subject Ju Dou to his rather bizarre and violent sexuality. Later on we learn from Ju Dou that "he's sick," "that he's not human, not a man," and that "he can't do it." All, it seems, that he can do is torture the women he tries to impregnate. And, in scenes where he is raping Ju Dou while she is tied up and muffled, he tells her "I bought you, now obey me," and "when I buy an animal I treat it as I wish and you're no better than an animal." But he also tells her that if she gives him a son he will be her slave.

As divorce or escape do not seem to be options for Ju Dou, eventually she seeks to interrupt the sexual and physical abuse of herself by

1

getting herself pregnant by other means. (How self-conscious her actions are at this point remains somewhat unclear.) Fortunately, in her husband's household lives his nephew (Tianqing), a man in his forties whom Jinshan adopted when he was orphaned as a child. Jinshan somewhat ruthlessly exploits Tianqing's labor in his dye mill and, because Jinshan does not want extra "mouths to feed," he has never provided Tianqing with his own wife. Consequently, Tianqing is understandably weary, miserable, lonely, and, most importantly, sexually unfulfilled. And consequently, he begins to fixate on his uncle's new bride. He also begins to sympathize with her plight, as he hears her screams at night, and he knows about his uncle's sexual history. For a short time, though, he becomes a bit of a voyeur, and she an exhibitionist. Perhaps impolitely observing his uncle's wife offers him a refuge from his toil and loneliness. Conversely, accepting and then inviting her nephew's attention, and eventually seducing him, offers her a refuge from her abusive husband. These actions also generate the solution to Ju Dou's problem. That is, Tianqing can impregnate her, and he does.

Ju Dou takes a critical perspective on the marital customs followed in the filmmaker's society. It does this, in part, by showing how these customs create intergenerational conflict. For example, Ju Dou achieves narrative closure when Tianqing is killed by his own son (Tianbai) for dishonoring his mother. The film emphasizes both the oppressive aspects of conventional marriage and the potentially subversive and liberatory force of adulterous behavior. Consequently, instead of the usual moralistic treatment of adultery that we get in many American pictures (e.g., Fatal Attraction), in Ju Dou, as Caryn James has written, "adultery is explicitly presented as heroic resistance to outmoded traditions."[1]

In an influential paper on adultery, Richard Wasserstrom considers whether the moral prohibition against all extramarital sex can be given a philosophical defense.[2] To defend this absolute prohibition one must demonstrate that acts of adultery are inevitably evil or harmful. Wasserstrom explores the steps of several purported demonstrations and concludes that the essential wickedness of adultery is extremely difficult, if not impossible, to prove. Wasserstrom reaches this conclusion because he recognizes that the evilness we see as inherent to adulterous behavior may only reside in this behavior when it occurs in the context of particular marital norms and practices. Moreover the marital norms with which we are most familiar are neither universally established nor historically invariable. If acts of adultery are only contingently, and not necessarily, evil, then wherever the relevant contingencies are not met, adulterous behaviors may exhibit more neutral (or even positive) moral characteristics. Yet before Wasserstrom can draw this relativistic and skeptical conclusion, he must show that adultery is contingently and not inherently a bad thing.

To demonstrate that moral badness is an accidental and not essential property of adulterous acts, Wasserstrom does not appeal to the foreign cinema, but rather he appeals to the philosopher's reflective imagination and cultural memory. He remembers that in our recent past (the past of contemporary Americans), there was an exotic group, which we shall refer to as "the sixties counterculture." The sixties counterculture was relatively peculiar in that it purportedly condoned nonmarital and extramarital casual sex (sex without any serious social purpose, such as procreation, marital bonding, etc.). By promoting sex with nonmarital partners, through "open" style marriages or by eschewing formal marriage altogether, members of the sixties counterculture challenged the marital and sexual norms of their larger society. Wasserstrom examines the countercultural practice of open marriage and uses it to show that extramarital sexual behaviors need not exhibit the characteristics that are generally thought to render them morally bad: deceptiveness, disloyalty, and social disruptiveness.

In an open sixties-style marriage, one can engage in adultery without the usual deception because to participate in an open marriage is to grant each spouse the right to be "open" sexually to nonmarital partners. Moreover each spouse can (and is perhaps encouraged to) communicate openly about her/his extramarital involvements, as well as other sexual interests, and so there is no need to actively deceive one's spouse about one's affairs. Furthermore, neither spouse is vulnerable to passive deception—the deception that occurs through acts of omission—for these marital customs create an expectation of extramarital sexual behavior, rather than an expectation of sexual monogamy. And finally, one can commit adultery in this type of marriage and avoid a deeper type of deception that Wasserstrom identifies: that of deceiving either one's lover or spouse about the state of one's romantic sentiments or the health of one's marriage. One avoids this type of deception because sex with the nonmarital partner can be casual—i.e., free of emotional involvement and social commitments. Thus, to have extramarital sex does not entail being romantically involved with someone other than one's spouse, nor does it entail being committed to an ongoing marriage-like relationship with someone other than one's spouse. Of course, being in an open marriage involves believing in the possibility of casual sex, and so long as all parties involved belong to this sixties culture and have this belief, nobody is deceived.

In an open sixties-style marriage, one can engage in extramarital sex without being disloyal to one's partner for one has not promised to be sexually faithful. In other words, faithfulness, loyalty, or fidelity in an open marriage are not seen as a function of making and carrying out an implicit or explicit vow of sexual exclusivity. And in an open six-ties-style marriage, one can engage in adulterous behavior without the socially disruptive consequence of destabilizing the institution of marriage itself, as long as institution we have in mind is the open kind.

Of course, adulterous behavior may weaken the foundations of "non-open" marriage. But to pursue this line of argument in defending the prohibition against all extramarital sex, the moral philosopher must show, according to Wasserstrom, that the social institution of sexually monogamous marriage is worth preserving, especially if it means sacrificing other goods. To show this, the philosopher must understand the institution's practical advantages and disadvantages (i.e., its personal and interpersonal benefits), which may require, Wasserstrom suggests, that she compare American marital practices with those of other cultures and subcultures. Until such examination yields a more generalizable and complete understanding of sexually monogamous marriage and its relationship to other human goods, this instrumental defense of the prohibition against adultery, accord-ing to Wasserstrom, remains "seriously incomplete."[3]

Wasserstrom is certainly correct that, if one's philosophical defense of the prohibition against adultery appeals to the damage adultery causes to a particular social institution, then one's defense needs to include a moral appraisal of the allegedly vulnerable institution. If someone argued that educating slaves threatened the practice of slav-ery, this would hardly be taken to count as an argument against the practice of educating slaves. The more difficult issue is how we morally evaluate a social institution. How, for example, did various societies (and moral philosophers) come to appreciate the moral evils of slavery? And was their appreciation fostered by a deeper under-standing of the institution's practical consequences or through less rationally explicable historical changes, such as in the application of the category "human" and in our assignment of properties to the members of this category? Did rational philosophical reflection and the refinement of practical reasoning promote the enlightenment of modern society on the question of slavery?[4]

Similarly, how can we gain a deeper understanding of the practical benefits or harms that ensue from the practice of sexually monoga-mous marriage? And must our moral judgments about adultery (at least our philosophically defensible ones) await the outcome of some larger sociological, anthropological, or psychological investigation into our culturally entrenched marital practices? If they must wait, then should not our moral evaluations of other activities await similar investigations of the societal institutions they threaten? If the correct answer to these questions is "yes," then much of what goes on in the area of normative moral philosophy and applied ethics can be accused of premature theorizing. In the next section I shall address the need for moral theory to assess the practical value of certain human practices and institutions in the course of providing guidelines for moral judgment. In other words, I shall address the question of how practical knowledge of human affairs—to be gained in part by the human or social sciences—is related to the enterprise of moral philosophy. Following this discussion, I will attempt to formulate the central aims of this book.

Human Diversity and Moral Theory

What is the relationship between practical reason and practical knowledge? How much practical knowledge of human institutions and practices must we have in order to determine what institutions and practices are good? And is the knowledge we gain about human institutions and practices informally by living our own lives sufficient for this purpose? Although this is sometimes all a moral theorist seems to have to go on—her own limited and quirky set of experiences—it may not be sufficient for the purposes of moral theorizing. For, just as the theater critic needs to have seen an abundance of plays before she can generate serious art criticism, the moral and social critic probably should be exposed to a great deal of social life before she can construct authoritative moral analyses.

On the "traditional" picture of moral philosophy—that is, the intellectual tradition we have inherited from our European Enlightenment ancestors—skill in practical reasoning is not proportional to practical knowledge or experience. Alasdair MacIntyre describes this picture well in discussing Kant:

> Practical reason, according to Kant, employs no criterion external to itself. It appeals to no content derived from experience . . . It is of the essence of reason that it lays down principles which are universal, categorical and internally consistent. Hence a rational morality will lay down principles which both can and ought to be held by *all* men, independent of circumstances and conditions, and which could consistently be obeyed by every rational agent on every occasion.[5]

Those who subscribe to this picture may even fear that "content derived from experience" will bias the outcome of practical reason and, if they do, then perhaps they will see adeptness in practical reasoning as inversely proportional to practical experience. In other words, the moral thinker is probably better off, on this view, if she retreats from the world than if she immerses herself in it. Retreating from the world is allowable because, according to this picture, the moral dimensions of behaviors are apparent by directly reflecting on the behaviors themselves, not by situating these behaviors in their cultural and historical contexts. For instance, on this view, the moral thinker can assess the moral dimensions of the adulterous actions cinematically depicted in *Ju Dou,* and those imagined and projected back into the sixties by Wasserstrom, without knowing much about 1920s China or 1960s America.

Yet when we compare radically diverse adulteries such as these, we see that they are not easily reducible to one another. We see, that is, that there are moral dimensions to these actions that we may miss by failing to understand the human institutions and societies in which the principal characters participated. For this reason and many others, some philosophers, including MacIntyre, have begun to repudiate the Enlightenment picture of practical reason. Without going into all the reasons for rejecting this picture of practical reason, for my purposes it will simply do to note that if we reject it, we have no reason to think that we can think or reason well about practical affairs when we are ignorant about the diversity of human practices.

In her essay "Why Philosophers Should Become Sociologists (and Vice Versa),"[6] Kathryn Pyne Addelson joins MacIntyre in encouraging philosophers to dispose of their Enlightenment notions about practical reason and moral theory. And once properly disposed of, we can no longer legitimate the armchair moral theorizing that these notions encouraged. For this reason, Addelson challenges us to learn more about social life, and to do this in particular by appropriating the anti-Enlightenment methods of a school of thought in contemporary sociology known as "symbolic interactionism."

To demonstrate the usefulness of symbolic interactionism, Addelson contrasts the critical methodologies of this school with those of more positivist social science. She states,

> The Enlightenment world was one of objects and concepts that could be objectively observed and neutrally reported. In contrast, the postanalytic philosophers and the symbolic interactionists agree that the human world is a world not of objects but of action and interpretation.[7]

By differentiating these two conceptions of the human sciences, Addelson suggests that it is not enough simply to reject Enlightenment notions of practical reason; moral philosophy should also reject Enlightenment conceptions of scientific knowledge. The Enlightenment model of practical knowledge, as Addelson notes, is one where the methodologies and tools for analyzing the human world are similar to those employed for scientifically analyzing the so-called natural world. By contrast, on a post-Enlightenment model—exemplified in the work of symbolic interactionists—we adapt the critical tools and concepts employed for the analysis of language or symbolic forms to describe human beings and the worlds they create. I will briefly describe each model and its implications for how the social sciences can assist moral philosophy.

Some moral philosophers—even some "postanalytic" ones—who seek to ground their theories on social scientific knowledge about particular human practices assume an Enlightenment model of how the social sciences operate. On this view, coming to know about humans and what they do involves becoming familiar with available objective, scientific, neutral and detached third person descriptions of people and their behavior. On this positivistic model, the moral philosopher who approaches the social sciences can expect to be presented with numerically expressed sets of empirical data, as well as various causal conjectures or theories about human behavior that these data support or challenge. It is then the moral philosopher's job to discern the moral and political significance of the best theories. This is the model that Wasserstrom assumes when he urges us to compare the objective benefits of one form of marriage with another, rather than merely chauvinistically clinging to the form that American society conventionally sanctions. Such a model offers us the hope that we will be able to settle, in some unbiased fashion, which form of marriage is superior to all others. Should it turn out that sexually monogamous marriage is an inferior marital institution, then its infringement and upheaval through acts of adultery cannot be a serious moral crime. This model of social analysis *qua* "objective science" is popular not only with philosophers, but many social scientists as well.

The kind of social scientific understanding that Addelson recommends for filling out and grounding our ethical theories is derived from anti-positivist and anti-objectivist conceptions of knowledge. On an anti-objectivist account, human creations and human behavior reflect meanings and purposes that are neither exposed nor well understood through objective description. Human creations and behaviors are more like texts that require interpretation. Thus, instead of a positivist approach that tries to reach a perspective on diverse phenomena somewhat beyond a mere human one in order to generate more objective understanding, an "interpretive" or hermeneutical approach tries to see from within diverse human perspectives in order to understand the intentional and symbolic character of human phenomenon. Addelson identifies this approach with the work of symbolic interactionists, but it is, I believe, best developed and elaborated in the work of symbolic cultural anthropologists, such as Clifford Geertz.[8] Also, the key elements and philosophical implications of this post-Enlightenment school of social analysis have been systematically described by Charles Taylor and Hans-Georg Gadamer.[9]

Invoking a comment of Max Weber, Geertz claims that people are suspended in "webs of significance" that people have created.[10] An interpretive approach to social analysis involves probing the webs that inform what people do, rather than attempting to establish some neutral ground from which to observe what they do. When we investigate the webs of significance that inform human action, we engage in what Clifford Geertz—borrowing a term from Gilbert Ryle—has called "thick description." The enterprise of thick description does not reduce human phenomena to abstract behavioral laws; instead, it unpacks them in terms of the shared symbols and meanings around which the phenomena of human life are organized. Since different cultures share different symbols and meaning, they organize human life differently. Thus, the enterprise of thick description requires, as Geertz writes, that we attend to "the degree to which [the] meaning [of human behavior] varies according to the pattern of life by which it is informed."[11]

For Geertz, then, the analysis of different patterns of life, or different cultures, should not be treated as "an experimental science in search of law but an interpretive one in search of meaning."[12] In this way the work of the social analyst is much like that of the literary critic, for it involves, according to Geertz, "sorting out the structures of signification ... and determining their social ground and import."[13] Like literary analysis, social analysis involves perceiving textual and intertextual meanings, with the exception that the objects of analysis are not the canonized works of an indigenous elite, but rather the daily performances and customs of ordinary people. The enterprise of thick description attempts to capture the symbolic import of these ordinary social performances and customs by seeing them in relation to the cultural contexts and communicative systems in which they occur.

Geertz's interpretive model of how the social sciences operate does not permit us to imagine that we can objectively compare different human practices. This is not to say that we do not compare human practices, or that there is no knowledge to be gained by comparing them. Rather, on this model we understand that the human institutions we may compare are often irreducible or incommensurable and, therefore, we cannot judge these institutions without first understanding them in the terms that those who participate in them understand them. When we come to understand another group's practice in its own terms, we will be able to appreciate better its distinctiveness, and we will also have greater insight into the distinctiveness of our own practices. According to Geertz,

> Understanding a people's culture exposes their normalness without reducing their particularity ... It renders them accessible: setting them in the frame of their own banalities, it dissolves their opacity.[14]

It also exposes the non-normalness of our own practices; that is, it allows us to see that there are multiple ways to be normal, rendering "the normal" less familiar. In short, though we cannot reduce different practices to a single framework for the purpose of objective comparison, by comparing different practices we gain knowledge of how phenomena are socially constructed.[15]

Wasserstrom's appeal to the sixties counterculture and its perspectives on marriage exemplifies, at moments, an interpretive approach to social analysis. For Wasserstrom's discussion compares the marital practices of an another "culture" with our own, and describes these "alien" practices in terms of a shared belief system among those who participate in them. But Wasserstrom strays from this model when, after reconstructing the countercultural perspective for interpretive purposes, he appears to adopt or privilege this perspective. He does this when, after de-exoticizing their marital customs, he entertains the idea that the countercultural beliefs and practices regarding marriage and sex may be more rational or objectively superior to the dominant culture's. Wasserstrom slips back into positivism because, although he sees the distinctive peculiarities of the dominant culture's marital practices—e.g., their tendency to link sex and romantic love—he fails to see the distinctive peculiarities of the counterculture's practices—e.g., their tendency to promote sexual interactions outside of ongoing social relationships. He sees the peculiarities of the dominant culture by viewing it from the perspective of the counterculture, but he fails to see the peculiarities of the counterculture because he does not attempt to view it from other social and cultural locations.

In this way, Wasserstrom's analysis obscures a distinction that interpretive theorists draw between understanding the practices of other agents by *reconstructing* their point of view and understanding the practices of others by *adopting* their point of view. Understanding the practices of other agents by reconstructing their point of view or, in Charles Taylor's words, by recovering their self-descriptions, is what interpretative analysis aims at. According to Taylor,

> The interpretive view ... avoids the two equal and opposite mis-
> takes: on the one hand, of ignoring self-descriptions altogether,
> and attempting to operate in some neutral "scientific" language; on
> the other hand, of taking these descriptions with ultimate serious-
> ness, so that they become incorrigible.[16]

Though Wasserstrom sees the dominant culture's rationalizations about sex and marriage as corrigible, he takes the sixties countercul-ture radicals' views about sex and marriage far too seriously to make a judicious comparison between them and other human possibilities.

At some level, then, there is an inconsistency (a gap, if you will) in Wasserstrom's text. For if we can evaluate the cultural practice of sex-ually monogamous marriage from the perspective of the countercul-ture, then we should be able to evaluate the practice of open marriage from the perspective of the dominant culture (and the perspectives of still other societies). Yet Wasserstrom appears to neglect or dismiss the latter project because he identifies too closely with the countercul-tural perspective on sex and marriage. This identification leads him to believe that the dominant culture's marital practices may be objec-tively inferior to others. And if the dominant culture's marital prac-tices are defective, then the dominant culture cannot provide a reliable perspective from which to evaluate the moral properties of adultery. Nevertheless many philosophers who sympathize with the domi-nant culture, or other marginal cultures, might regard as defective Wasserstrom's use of the sixties counterculture to evaluate the moral properties of adultery precisely because they repudiate the marital practices of this marginal social group.[17] In a similar fashion, some might regard pre-Communist China as a defective context for evaluat-ing the moral significance of adultery because they find the marital practices of this society to be inferior to those elsewhere.[18] That is, these theorists may hold that while adultery in this context is not exactly bad, in this context adultery is not exactly adultery, and this is because the marital practices in which the adulterers participate are not exactly what marriage should be. If is it legitimate to hold this, then it is legitimate to hold that adultery in the context of an open marriage is not exactly adultery either, and thus what may be true of "adultery" in an open marriage is not true of "genuine" adultery. And if the latter is a legitimate claim, then Wasserstrom's countercultural thought-experiment may simply be beside the point when it comes to determining the moral properties of adultery. In short, by treating a particular cultural ideology as incorrigible, Wasserstrom initiates a process that is ultimately, for his purposes, self-defeating.

But working from within the interpretive framework, where Wasserstrom's sixties thought-experiment belongs, Wasserstrom's conjecture that the dominant marital practices in the U.S. could be objectively defective is not legitimate. Nor would it be legitimate, on this model, to treat either the dominant marital customs in pre-Communist China or the marginal marital practices in the sixties U.S. as somehow yielding marriages that are less genuine or real. For these analytical moves assume that there is a single transcultural ideal of marriage that each culture more or less realizes. And on an interpretive model, this is a questionable assumption.[19] For to assume that there is some transculturally determinable best form of marriage to which all cultures should aspire is to assume that all marital practices are commensurable. But this is just what an interpretive approach denies.

If Wasserstrom had worked more consistently within an interpretive model, he would not have undermined his sixties thought-experiment. Moreover, had he stayed within an interpretive framework, he would not have needed to postpone further moral consideration of adultery while awaiting a definitive verdict on marriage from the social sciences. For in an interpretive approach, no definitive, objective, transcultural decision on marriage will be forthcoming from the social sciences. What will be forthcoming are imprecise translation schema between more or less incommensurable marital institutions—of the sort Wasserstrom has pursued between dominant and marginal social groups—and these schema will allow tentative transcultural moral judgments about marriage and its rules. But before I consider further how interpretation enables the moral analysis of adultery, I will attempt to formulate the central aims of this book. In doing this I will consider and reject some other recent approaches to morality.

Interpretation and Feminist Theory

My project in this book is to explore what feminist moral and political analysis might look like if we take a post-Enlightenment approach to practical reason and an interpretive approach to social analysis. In particular, I will focus on the much-disputed issues of abortion and prostitution to see if these approaches will lead to a more informed, self-conscious, and robust feminist sexual politics. I am also interested in whether post-Enlightenment and interpretive approaches to social and moral theory can handle the diverse perspectives of women on controversial issues like abortion and prostitution in nonethnocentric ways. As will soon become apparent, I believe that adopting such approaches will enrich feminist theorizing and help achieve these aims. Indeed, many feminist moral and political theorists have already adopted some of the key elements of post-Enlightenment and interpretive approaches—such as the rejection of socially detached, generic rational selves—but have not fully dealt with their implications for feminist theory and politics. In this section I will consider two alternative post-Enlightenment, but anti-pluralist and thus anti-interpretive, approaches to feminist moral theory, which I believe do not meet the dual aim of sustaining a critical and self-aware feminist politics and of avoiding imperialist ethics.

Seyla Benhabib has developed a neo-Kantian feminist and post-Enlightenment approach to ethics—which she calls "interactionist universalism"—based on the communicative or discourse ethic developed by Jürgen Habermas.[20] Though this communicative approach rejects positivistic models of human knowledge, it differs from a hermeneutical approach in some significant ways. First, the communicative approach is essentially what Charles Taylor refers to as a "reductionist" or "formalist" approach to ethics. It attempts to reduce the myriad standards invoked in ordinary ethical judgments to some single, formal standard for the purpose of developing a rationally defensible, secular morality. In other words, interactionist universalism continues the Enlightenment project described by MacIntyre of attempting to find "an independent rational justification of morality,"[21] though the justificatory strategies offered take a post-Enlightenment turn. Second, communicative ethics rejects the idea that human practices, and the terms in which they are constituted and understood, are incommensurable.

Discourse ethics joins the Kantian idea that genuine moral rules are those that rational agents understand as universalizable to the contractarian idea that legitimate state authority encompasses only those constraints on liberty to which rational beings would universally consent. The result is a merging of two historical philosophical projects—the project of discovering a secular justification of morality and the project of discovering the most just form of political government. From this merger we get a procedure for justifying ethical rules of conduct that itself embodies ideals of political justice. More specifically, for a discourse theorist, universalizability is a procedure that brings multiple moral subjects into an ideal conversation: a discursive interaction between equally informed interlocutors free of communicative barriers, the aim of which is to achieve universal agreement.

Benhabib, however, modifies the aim of this procedure to that of universal participation, recognition, and understanding. For she is concerned that discourse ethics, in stressing universal rational agreement, may assume a single model of human rationality and selfhood, much like its Kantian and contractarian Enlightenment ancestors. Thus Benhabib reformulates the basic idea of discourse ethics in a way that emphasizes the historical and cultural embeddedness of the moral conversationalists who join in ideal dialogue, and also who define the procedural rules that constrain their dialogue. On Benhabib's view, the rules of conduct that are universally valid are those that would be generated by a discursive procedure that, while always debatable, is at the current historical moment the one most widely perceived by culturally diverse moral subjects as just and rational. When adhered to, this communicative procedure serves to foster, not universal agreement, but the mutual understanding and respect that is necessary for creating just human relationships and institutions.

Since Benhabib's ideal conversation is capable of critically engaging the very constraints imposed on it, the procedure does not beg many of the moral issues it is set up to resolve, unlike other versions of this theory. Her procedure also recognizes the heterogeneity and historical specificity of the voices that enter moral conversation. And it tries to achieve inter-subjective understanding, not by erasing either the differences between the moral conversationalists or the social particularities of their vision, but by requiring that participants in the dialogue be able to acquire multiple points of view. According to Benhabib,

> In ethics, the universalizability procedure, if it is understood as a reversing of perspectives and the willingness to reason from the other's (others') point of view, does not guarantee consent; it demonstrates the will and the readiness to seek understanding with the other and to reach some reasonable agreement in an open-ended moral conversation.[22]

The agreement achieved here is perhaps best construed as a political compromise between different, interested perspectives rather than intellectual acquiescence to the same set of propositions.

Unfortunately however, Benhabib offers us little help with what is involved in competently recreating other, and possibly radically different points of view (i.e., in the "reversing of perspectives"). What sort of knowledge of "the other" must one have, and how is one to acquire it? Does the moral conversationalist have enough resources from her own life, or must she consult the experiential and intellectual resources of others, especially radically different others? Will science, especially the so-called human sciences, help here? If so, should not the post-Enlightenment moral analyst assume an interpretive rather than a positivist conception of knowledge in the social sciences? Yet on an interpretive model, human activities are often incommensurable, and thus the communication between diverse others, though not impossible, is often less than ideal. That is, if the participants in an ideal conversation must possess a single set of terms and categories with which to explain their activities and practices, then the conditions for this dialogue, on an interpretive approach, will often not be met.

Benhabib's apparent belief in the unproblematic nature of "reversing perspectives" seems to belie a positivist conception of knowledge of the other, which is inconsistent with her post-Enlightenment aims. For example, Benhabib states that she does not accept "the radical incommensurability of conceptual frameworks," but instead holds that "the understanding of the past as well as of other cultures which are our contemporaries proceeds like a hermeneutic dialogue."[23] Unfortunately, these claims make little sense since hermeneutical or interpretive social science is science that aims to provide tools for understanding incommensurable cultural concepts and practices. But if one assumes the commensurability of conceptual frameworks, the task of reversing perspectives becomes an unchallenging and trivial enterprise. And since reversing perspectives becomes relatively unproblematic, her ideal interlocutors have or can easily acquire the practical knowledge of others they need to engage in practical reasoning—that is, they probably won't need the help of either a hermeneutical or positivistic social science.

However Benhabib's assumption that conceptual frameworks are commensurable takes for granted a significant degree of cultural homogeneity, and thus may obscure important differences between ourselves and cultural others. And her confidence that practical reason can proceed without a great deal of exposure to the variety of human practices and belief systems reflects a Kantian view of practical reason. In short, Benhabib's communicative ethics belie the Enlightenment conceptions of human selves and human reason contained in the Kantian and liberal theories from which interactionist universalism is derived. She does have one extremely important insight, though, and that is that the aim of moral analysis should be tentative political agreements between different and interested agents rather than intellectual homogeneity. This insight can and should be disconnected from the formalist apparatus she has developed.

To give an example of the difficulty Benhabib's approach finds itself in, consider the following conversational situation with which feminist moral theorists are concerned. Suppose a moral interlocutor is a member of an economically or otherwise privileged social group, and needs to competently recreate the perspectives of members of groups that are socially oppressed. Uma Narayan has argued that one's experience of one type of oppression may enable a theorist to fill gaps in her knowledge about a type of oppression she has not experienced.[24] Yet, she warns, this ability to extrapolate from one's own oppression may not afford the level of comprehension of the other required for the universalist's project. As Narayan states:

> It is a commonplace that even sympathetic men will often fail to perceive subtle instances of sexist behavior or discourse. Sympathetic individuals who are not members of an oppressed group should keep in mind the possibility of this sort of failure regarding their understanding of issues relating to an oppression they do not share. They should realize that nothing they may do, from participating in demonstrations to changing their lifestyles, can make them one of the oppressed. For instance, men who share household and child-rearing responsibilities with women are mistaken if they think that this act of choice, often buttressed by the gratitude and admiration of others, is anything like the woman's experience of being forcibly socialized into these tasks and of having others perceive this as her natural function in the scheme of things.[25]

Narayan well observes that men who try to see things from a woman's perspective (i.e., "in reverse") do not always get the full picture. And it is far from clear what a male moral conversationalist needs to do here to get the more complete picture of sexist oppression.

Benhabib is certainly right to insist, contra other proponents of communicative ethics, that including everyone imaginable in the imagined conversation and giving one vote to every voice, is not sufficient to guarantee that those who adopt a discourse ethic will not end up validating their own culturally and historically ingrained moral common sense. Benhabib rightly requires that interlocutors in a democratic moral conversation must also be able to recognize the distinctiveness and uniqueness of each voice. Yet Benhabib appears over-optimistic and naive about the ability of interlocutors to do this. Revealingly, in one of the few instances where Benhabib illustrates how her universalizability criterion works, she finds the practices of social others more problematic than those of her social familiars. Indeed, her reversing of perspectives in this instance seems no more than superficial. In her illustration, she considers the marital custom of polygamy—once practiced by Mormons and common in many Arab and African countries—and she argues that

> The practice of polygamy . . . should not be condoned by the state. Members of . . . [the Mormon or orthodox Muslim] sect should not be able to gain *legal recognition* for their practice of polygamy, although the state should not persecute those who practice polygamy as long as the equal consent of the adult males and females in their various practices is secured.[26]

A polygamist might respond by asking whether monogamy is always consensual and whether the state should persecute those who practice it without the consent of all participants. Significantly, Benhabib does not question whether the marital practices that are culturally familiar to her are consensual. Her omission here is perhaps a reflection of her cultural biases. As members of a predominantly Judeo-Christian society, we automatically infer the consent of those who participate in our Christian and Jewish custom of monogamous marriage for this custom accords better with our culturally specific notions about human desires, equality, and fairness. Yet, we infer the consent of married and about-to-be-married individuals even though Judeo-Christian monogamy prohibits same-sex marriages and, according to some feminists, renders the wife a vessel for reproduction and commits her to life of unremunerated domestic labor. More exactly, those who identify with the dominant culture in Western industrialized societies usually assume that such customary marital institutions are engaged in freely, while many lesbians and gay men, and some feminists do not (especially those who find themselves "trapped" by these customs and the expectations they raise). In short, our judgments about the consensual or coercive nature of human practices often reflect our gender identities and affectional orientations, as well as our cultural locations.

Given that our judgments about the voluntary nature of different marital customs are often culturally biased, what does Benhabib do to reverse perspectives before concluding that polygamy fails her universalizability criterion? Has she, for example, examined polygamy from the perspectives of its participants, many of whom are Third World women of color? Some of these participants have articulated a defense of polygamy on the grounds that it creates a communal family where work that might otherwise be dumped on one wife can be shared in a sisterly fashion with other women.[27] As Narayan states, "Western feminists, despite their critical understanding of their own culture, often tend to be more a part of it than they realize."[28] Is not Benhabib obscuring the voices of actual Third World women in her universalist condemnation of polygamy, while constructing an imagined dialogue for First World feminist purposes? At the very least she seems not to have appreciated how difficult is the task of appreciating the other's distinctness and uniqueness.

Rather than consult the actual testimony of polygamists—through ethnographic and other sources—she offers her own image of the polygamist moral interlocutor. She imagines her polygamist interlocutor and defender of polygamy as someone who is unwilling to question the conventional teachings of his (her image is, I think, gender-specific) religion or society. She states:

Such a conversation will likely end by appealing either to the ultimate veracity of the one true teaching, the correct interpretation of the work of the Koran, or maybe even to the fact that women are naturally inferior to men and thus must be protected by them and must submit to their authority. Now, as a defender of communicative ethics I know that those who adhere to a conventional morality have a cognitive barrier beyond which they will not argue; that they will invoke certain kinds of reasons which will divide the participants of the moral conversation into insiders and outsiders, into those who share their presuppositions and those who do not. Because the adherents of such moralities are willing to stop the conversation and because they have to withdraw from the process of reflexive justification in order not to let their world-view crumble, their position is not comprehensive and reflexive enough. They cannot distance themselves from their own position and accept that it may be right not to practice polygamy on moral grounds.[29]

Certainly the defense of polygamy offered by some Third World women described above does not fit this conversational description. Yet, I do not deny that some defenders of polygamy may appeal to cultural and religious doctrines not shared by all. I do not believe that by doing so this it means that they are stuck behind a "cognitive barrier" or that they are opting out of the conversation or that are not "reflexive enough." If Benhabib were forced to defend the practice of monogamy, would not she at some level have to appeal to presuppositions not shared by all—presuppositions about the purpose of marriage, about romantic commitments, ideals of friendship and equality, and so on.[30] If she argues that monogamy could be defended on grounds that all could accept—Muslims and Jews, Mormons and Christians, and even all atheists—then I would like to see those grounds. If she argues that these are grounds that Muslims and Mormons would accept only when they are "sufficiently reasonable and reflexive," when they have overcome their "cognitive barriers" and have engaged in postconventional thinking, then I would ask how we know whether those advancing the grounds are free of cognitive limits and conventional thinking? We often do not see our own cognitive barriers because the conventions with which we are most familiar are often invisible to us, and hence they may not be taken up as the subjects of endless moral conversation. That is, instead of closing moral conversations, we just do not begin them on some issues, and thus maintain the illusion that we are reflexive, postconventional, and cognitively superior.

In sum, Benhabib's modified discourse ethic appears to lead to the same ethnocentric validations as its other theoretical variants. While conjuring up a formal procedure for testing the universal validity of practices and norms affords one a powerful rhetorical position for critiquing patriarchy—an advantage that feminists should not easily dismiss or give up—it also provides a rhetorical position that easily leads to results at odds with feminist aims. As Narayan states:

> If [Western feminists] fail to see the contexts of their theories and assume that their perspective has universal validity for all feminists, they tend to participate in the dominance that western culture has exercised over nonwestern cultures.[31]

Similarly, believing that we have reversed perspectives when we really have not can have the same results. In short, without a more serious understanding of what is involved in the "reversing of perspectives," the transcultural moral judgments Benhabib's formal criterion generates will be biased in favor of the discourse theorist's own culture.

Many feminists have turned to an ethics of care, in order to avoid many of the problems associated with formalist approaches that take justice (or utility) as their guiding concept. Thus, I shall briefly consider whether an ethics based on the idea of care can help us avoid ethnocentrism in ethics. Care ethics asks us to conjure up our best models of caring for others in order to make ethical judgments. While this is not a procedural ethics in the formal sense, an ethics of care does offer us an informal procedure to guide moral analysis. By offering us rough guidelines rather than universal principles, care ethics strives to avoid the narrow and artificial formalizations of moral dialogue characteristic of traditional ethics. However, though not formalist in approach, an ethics of care is inevitably reductionist. That is, it reduces all the standards that may be invoked in moral debate to one basic standard—that of care. This to me is its most serious drawback, and one most likely to engender ethnocentric thinking.

Care ethics has contributed significantly to our understanding of morality by expanding the horizons of moral analysis and focussing on less "public" human relationships. In care ethics, relationships between parents and children, between siblings, between friends, lovers, and even humans and pets become models for larger social relationships, and they represent in themselves important dimensions of morality.[32] Moreover, an ethics of care provides moral analysts a richer language for describing moral concerns and their resolution. For it allows us to appeal to our feelings of love, admiration, and responsibility for others, as well as emotionally-free considerations, in formulating and responding to moral concerns. Moreover, the moral praiseworthiness or contemptibleness of many things we do is only explicable in these terms (e.g., being a good or lousy parent, sister, friend, spouse, teacher, and even citizen).

Yet a system of ethics framed in terms of care raises the following explanatory dilemma: should we care for others because recognizing our connection to others requires that we respond to their needs, or do we recognize our connection to others and respond to their needs because they deserve our care? This dilemma is very similar to one that is confronted by Christian moralists: is something morally good because God commands it, or does God command something because it is morally good? If the former, then we get an authoritative picture of morality; if the latter, then there must be a nondivine criterion of moral goodness. Some Christian moralists have navigated around these equally unattractive alternatives by arguing that morality is neither a function of divine decree, nor of God-independent standards. Instead, morality is a function of God's love for humanity. Since human beings are not always able to feel God's love for the whole of humankind, we experience the demands of morality as decrees. But even if we do not feel God's universal love for humans, we are supposed to love and venerate God. Thus we should fulfill the demands of morality in recognizing God's greater love for all.[33]

Similarly, is the obligation to care based on the mere fact of our connectedness to other people and things, or is it based on the characteristics of whom or what we are obligated to care for? If the former, then we must care for everything to which we are connected, and if the latter then we must determine some relationship-independent basis upon which others deserve or do not deserve our care. Sandra Bartky demonstrates the unattractiveness of the first alternative with her example of

> Teresa Stangl, wife of Fritz Stangl, Kommandant of Treblinka. Teresa, anti-Nazi and a devout Catholic, was appalled by what she knew of her husband's work; nevertheless, she maintained home and hearth as a safe harbor to which he returned when he could.[34]

Certainly in caring for her husband Fritz, Teresa fails to care for the people he tortured. If we take care theory to its logical extreme, we might ask if we are obligated to care for insects that spread disease because they belong to the ecosystem of which we are a part? And in caring for them, do I not fail to care for the beings they infect? These examples suggest that we need a connection-independent, or care-independent, standard for determining whom and what to care for (i.e., we need to choose the second alternative above). But what might that be, and would not any such standard diminish the fundamental importance of preserving connections to others, and the centrality of the notion of caring, that care ethics is based on? Patrocinio Schweickart suggests that someone who would guide her actions by an ideal of care would not care for people who are cruel and uncaring.[35] But cruelty is not merely the lack of caring, it is a distinct standard or consideration in itself. Fritz does not deserve Teresa's care not merely because he is uncaring but because he is cruel. And some people who are merely uncaring may be worthy of care, especially if by receiving it they could become more caring. In short, to avoid caring for the Fritzes we know we need more than a mere ideal or ethic of care.

Perhaps care theorists can base the obligation to care not on connection itself, nor on some connection-independent criterion, but on connection plus something else—perhaps love. But if we are talking about human love, and not God's love, this may constrict the objects of our care too much. Some care theorists seem to base our obligation to care on connection plus awe or profound respect for the entirety of things to which we are connected,[36] but this won't help us with Nazis and insects for they are part of, if indeed the downside of, this entirety. Of course, Christians can deal with Nazis through divine reprimand (God loves and forgives, but He is also punitive) and with insects through humanity's stewardship over nature, but how will care theorists handle them?

In sum, care theorists have this basic problem—that of defining the boundaries of our care. If they define them too widely, then our moral obligations may include fulfilling the needs of Nazis and insects; and if they define them too narrowly, then our moral obligations may extend only to our own loved ones. Moreover, if care ethics asks that we conjure up ideal models of caring for others, we need to ask where these ideals come from. These ideals, probably, are culturally and historically conditioned. Yet, how will an ethics concerned with recovering our own culturally shaped ideals help us to care across cultural boundaries, if indeed our moral obligations extend that far? Does the practice of polygamy, for example, violate the conditions of conjugal care, or do parents who circumcise their children—either boys or girls—violate our standards of parental care? How can we avoid ethnocentric caring where the socially powerful impose their ideals of care on the less powerful social groups?

A care ethicist might respond that recognizing and responding to the needs of others involves that we try to, in some sense, get inside them and experience the world from their point of view. In this way we can respond to the needs of others as they define them. Perhaps this is part of being "engrossed" with someone, to use Noddings's term. That is, following an ethics of care might involve the sort of reversing of perspectives that Benhabib recommends. Yet responding to the needs of others as they see them appears to require not merely that we invoke another's point of view but that we adopt the other's point of view. Yet adopting the other's point of view—as Wasserstrom does with the sixties counterculture—may not allow us to be sufficiently critical in our moral judgments. As Sandra Bartky has pointed out, care-giving women who adopt the points of view of those they care for may need to take an uncritical stance toward practices and ideas that are inimical to women and others, and that compromise their own values.[37] Moreover, Bartky shows that because responding to and meeting the needs of others often requires adopting the points of view of those we care for, care-giving tends to be not only self-sacrificing, but also self-effacing.

In short, how can we care for others without making either the mistake of ignoring the points of view of those we care for, or the mistake that Taylor identifies as "taking [the other's self-] descriptions with ultimate seriousness, so that they become incorrigible"? A care ethics that commits the first error may simply revert to Christian missionism in a secular disguise.[38] For such ethics may encourage us to think that our love and connection to others justifies our intervening in other people's lives and societies to meet the needs we think they have. A care ethics that commits the second error may lead to our uncritical indulgence of the prejudices of others. To avoid these errors, we need to appeal to moral concepts other than care, so that we can recover points of view without adopting them, and so that we can better define the boundaries of our care. That is, we need other moral standards so that connections are not seen as more basic than other considerations, and so that we can determine which connections are significant.

The upshot is that we need to avoid the reductionism characteristic of both care ethics and other more formalist approaches to ethics that impoverish our moral vocabulary. Feminist moral philosophers, for the most part, have missed this aspect of care ethics. For example, in describing her preference for the anti-formalist care approach to ethics over the more traditional and mainstream formalist approaches, Virginia Warren offers the following story:

> Years ago, there was an ad for Kotex napkins that showed a picture of a little girl and said, "Remember how simple life used to be?" What I want to tell students after they've been introduced to mainstream ethics is the opposite: "Remember how complicated life used to be? Well, it still is." An ethics of care is messy—because life is.[39]

But care ethics is actually fairly tidy, in that moral guidance rests on a single fundamental notion, that of ideal caring. We need to pluralize our moral standards, not reduce them, in order to complicate moral analysis in ways that life is complicated. Care ethics offers us one language in which to render intelligible moral choices and judgments, but the moral universe we inhabit is not monolingual.

Reductionism vs. Pluralism

Charles Taylor has argued for an approach to ethics that recognizes a plurality of goods. Some of the goods he mentions are integrity, charity, liberation, happiness, rationality, justice, equality, commitment to family, self-expression, sensitivity, and religious worship.[40] Each of these goods provides us with what he calls a "language of qualitative contrast," that is, a discursive apparatus for marking distinctions between higher and lower, better and worse ways of living.[41] By allowing us to articulate what Taylor calls "distinctions of worth,"[42] a language, in this sense,

> does not only serve to *depict* ourselves and the world, it also helps *constitute* our lives. Certain ways of being, of feeling, of relating to each other are only possible given certain linguistic resources.[43]

We can, and often do, order and prioritize the multiple goods we acknowledge in terms of some higher good. Taylor calls these second-order goods "hypergoods,"[44] and some that have been part of our intellectual traditions are utility, universalizability, respect for the universal dignity and rights of humankind, and piety. Moral theorists and actors may privilege different hypergoods, but there are no "hyper-hypergoods" that can provide us with a neutral basis for emphasizing a particular hypergood over others (which may explain why philosophical defenses of such ultimate principles often represent the best specimens of contorted philosophical reasoning). Reductionist approaches to ethics are those which select a particular hypergood as a framework for all discriminations of moral worth. Such approaches lead to what Taylor calls "ethics of inarticulacy."[45] Reductionist approaches render us inarticulate because they require that moral justification take place only at the level of hypergoods—in the allegedly less subjective, second-order languages of qualitative contrast—and thus we are denied the vocabulary to speak about many distinctions of worth in terms of which our lives are constituted.

Care ethics and procedural ethics lead to this kind of inarticulacy. Though ideals of care and universalizability enable many kinds of moral explanation, they reduce incommensurable goods to a single good, and thereby collapse, obscure, or rule out many distinctions of worth that render our lives and those of others intelligible. Moreover, reductionist approaches lead to ethics that are ethnocentric. Using the notions Taylor has developed, the reason for this can be made more evident: because all moral debate occurs at the level of hypergoods, reductionist ethics do not seek to understand the goods in terms of which others make sense of their activities. For example, in morally evaluating a practice like polygamy, the procedural ethicist does not attempt to recover the moral vocabularies in terms of which polygamists depict and also experience polygamy. In this way she does not genuinely "reverse perspectives," and her moral accounts end up validating her own cultural sensibilities.

Taylor illustrates what is involved in genuinely reversing perspectives by considering the practice some anthropologists identify as "human sacrifice":

> Understanding [a radically different society's] religious practices would require that we come to understand what they see themselves as doing when they are carrying out the ritual we have provisionally identified as a "sacrifice," what they seek after in the state we may provisionally identify as "blessedness" or "union with the spirits." (Our provisional identifications, of course, just place their action/states in relation to our religious tradition, or ones familiar to us. If we stick with these, we may fall into the most distorted ethnocentric readings.)[46]

The provisionally identified ideals of "blessedness" and "union with the spirits" serve to constitute the activity of sacrifice, and need to be considered in any moral account of it. These provisional ideals do not represent "cognitive barriers" or thinking which is "not comprehensive or reflexive enough," to borrow Benhabib's words, any more than our own culturally and religiously based ideals reflect these intellectual limits. Thus to ignore the ideals of those who practice human sacrifice, while tacitly appealing to our own, results in ethnocentric transcultural judgments.

Reversing perspectives does not mean that we adopt the ideals of the other in lieu of our own. Indeed it is by considering the ideals behind, for example, the practices of infanticide and circumcision, that we better understand the ideals of "care" and "nurture" reflected in our own parental practices. Similarly, by considering the ideals behind the practice of polygamy or even bride capture, we better understand the ideals of "equal respect" and "self-determination" reflected in our practice of monogamy. Cross-cultural comparisons between often incommensurable practices and goods allow us to see what is genuinely distinctive about both the things we and other people do and the distinctions of worth that we and others make. In short, these comparisons engender the kind of critical self-awareness that "critical theory" aims at in its critique of contemporary industrial societies.

Once we gain some critical self-awareness and understand the incommensurability of certain practices and goods, we may then formulate, in our languages of qualitative contrast, transcultural judgments about them which have been to some extent ethnically "decentered." Of course, the provisionality of our identification of goods, the non-orderability of hypergoods themselves, and the cultural and historical embeddedness of both goods and hypergoods means that we may often get conflicting transcultural judgments about the same practices. Some of these conflicts may be resolvable by appealing to more goods and hypergoods and then seeing, on balance, where things lie. But some conflicts may not be ultimately resolvable, and we must accept that sometimes there will be multiple, equally good human alternatives. Also, not all transcultural judgments need be in conflict with other transcultural judgments, since appeals to different hypergoods can occasion some convergences of judgment.

Reversing perspectives in the way that Taylor advocates is pretty familiar to social theorists who work within an interpretive model of human action. Cultural anthropologists, for example, have invented numerous imaginative, "re-familiarizing" labels for practices of others that are confusing, if not disturbing, to us. For example, an anthropologist who has studied the practice of infanticide cross-culturally recommends that the practice be described, in some cases, as "post-partum abortion."[47] Similarly, some anthropologists who have studied sex and gender initiation rites have found that what may look to us, in some cases, like incestuous homosexual fellatio (e.g., the ritualized sodomy that occurs typically between uncles and nephews in some societies in New Guinea) may be more accurately described as "penis-feeding."[48] And finally some anthropologists who have studied belief systems about witchcraft and magic have found that these belief systems may be better described as being about "bad luck" and "misfortune," rather than the former more exotic notions.[49] What reductionist approaches to ethics fail to recognize is that even our identification of moral issues—homicide, suicide, infanticide, incest, abortion, adultery, bigamy, and so on—reflects particular cultural and historical perspectives. This is to say that the objects of our analysis, as well as the linguistic and conceptual tools we use, are artifacts of particular human contexts, and they may shift when we move to other contexts. In other words, phenomena that are outwardly similar, such as certain behaviors of adults with children, may require different descriptions. If the things humans do are constituted, in part, by the categories they use to think and communicate about them, then these categories need to be provisionally identified when we theorize about our activities. Anything less will result in distorted ethnocentric moral analyses.

In his critique of reductionist social science—science which for the most part ignores the historically and culturally specific categories people use to make sense of their activities—Taylor argues that its appeal is based on a particular picture of the human subject. This is a picture of a self that avoids intellectual error by taking a detached, dispassionate, indifferent view of things. Universalist approaches to ethics inevitably assume some such picture of the self as a free agent that gains knowledge and empowerment by avoiding all things peculiar to it and other selves in order to gain clear, prejudice-free and dogma-free, universal vision.[50] For example, Benhabib's attempt to "situate the self" nevertheless requires that moral interlocutors not "invoke certain kinds of reasons which will divide the participants of the moral conversation into insiders and outsiders, into those who share their presuppositions and those who do not."[51] This means that Mormons and Moslems must cast off the very beliefs and ideals that make them Mormons and Moslems. Given this requirement, interactionist universalism actually reaches inter-subjective agreement by erasing the social particularities of different interlocutors and the cultural distinctiveness of their voices and perspectives.[52] In other words, discourse ethics must inevitably turn moral conversationalists into generic rather than situated selves, whenever it ignores the things that divide people into insiders and outsiders, i.e., the goods they recognize.[53] If feminists are genuinely going to reject the unencumbered, detached, atomized self, we need to reject all reductionist, universalist approaches to ethics.

Maria Lugones and Elizabeth Spelman describe what is required to reverse perspectives and to avoid treating others as generic selves. They suggest that, while feminists should be sensitive to the practices that divide women, or people in general, into "insiders" and "outsiders," as Benhabib is, we should not strive to erase the differences upon which these statuses are built. For it is possible to include both "insiders" and "outsiders" in a single conversation without dissolving the distinctions between them. According to Lugones and Spelman,

> At first sight it may appear that the insider/outsider distinction disappears in the dialogue, but it is important to notice that all that happens is that we are now both outsider and insider with respect to each other. The dialogue puts us both in position to give a better account of each others' and our own experience. Here we should again note that white/Anglo women are much less prepared for this dialogue with women of color than women of color are for

dialogue with them in that women of color have had to learn white/Anglo ways, self-conceptions, and conceptions of them.[54]

It is clearly time for white/Anglo women, and especially white/Anglo feminists, to acknowledge and learn the self-conceptions of others. Furthermore, Maria Lugones and Elizabeth Spelman state

> If white/Anglo women are to understand our voices, they must understand our communities and us in them ... [and] undergo the very difficult task of understanding the text of our cultures by understanding our lives in our communities. This learning calls for circumspection, for questioning of yourselves and your roles in your own culture. It necessitates a striving to understand while in the [un]comfortable position of not having an official calling card (as "scientific" observers of our communities have); it demands recognition that you do not have the authority of knowledge; it requires coming to the task without ready-made theories to frame our lives. This learning is then extremely hard because it requires openness (including openness to severe criticism of the white/Anglo world), sensitivity, concentration, self-questioning, circumspection. It should be clear that it does not consist in a passive immersion in our cultures, but in a striving to understand what it is that our voices are saying. Only then can we engage in a mutual dialogue that does not reduce each one of us to instances of the abstraction called "woman."[55]

As I think is evident in Benhabib's treatment of polygamy, interactive universalism does not promote the self-questioning and circumspection required for nonethnocentric dialogue with others. Moreover, it has not developed theoretical resources for understanding—without passively adopting—the communities, cultures, and sometimes incommensurable perspectives of others—the kind of understanding needed to avoid treating selves as abstract, generic others. By contrast, an interpretive and pluralist approach to ethics and politics is much better able to realize the goals that Lugones and Spelman have articulated. For an interpretive approach does not provide us the illusion of "having an official calling card"—a universalizable procedure—and it requires that we understand people in the context of the communities and cultures that have shaped us and give meaning to our lives.

One reason feminist theorists may be loath to adopt an interpretive-pluralist approach to ethics is that it may commit us to the philosophical doctrine known as "moral relativism." For to accept an interpretive model is to admit that human actions cannot be given objective, neutral descriptions, and that therefore appropriate, knowledge-enhancing descriptions can vary from one social context to the next. If the moral characteristics of actions are linked in some way to the descriptive categories under which they are subsumed, and if knowledge-enhancing descriptions of actions can vary in accordance with social contexts, then so too can the moral characteristics of actions.

I will admit, unlike some moral pluralists, that an interpretive approach commits us to some form of relativism.[56] Yet this approach need not commit us to what Bernard Williams has called "vulgar relativism"[57] or to what Taylor has called the "incorrigibility thesis."[58] Vulgar relativism is the normative view (and indeed even universalist view) that we must be tolerant of the behaviors and practices of others, because they may reflect values that are different than ours, and there is no way to adjudicate between competing values. The incorrigibility thesis commits us to the view that we must judge others only in terms of their own values and perspectives and, if we do this, then we cannot show them to be "wrong, confused, or deluded."[59]

Williams prefers what he calls "distance relativism,"[60] which holds that it is intellectually useless to try to universally retrofit or prefit one's moral standards and vocabularies to remote historical and cultural contexts. Nevertheless, he argues that we can judge others in terms of our values when conformance to their competing way of life is a real possibility for us. Taylor argues that the very incommensurability of practices and goods prompts us to employ our languages of qualitative contrast for making transcultural judgments of superiority. Yet if we have recovered the perspectives of others without adopting their perspectives, and have genuinely decentered some of our culturally ingrained notions, then our transcultural judgments will be relatively free of cultural distortion, i.e., relatively free of ethnocentrism. According to Taylor, "Really overcoming ethnocentricity is being able to understand two incommensurable classifications."[61] In short, if we understand relativism in terms of interpretive strategies for avoiding ethnocentrism, then relativism need not imply a paralysis of critical judgment or universal toleration.

Another way of putting this, perhaps, is that, as natives of particular cultures we are all mystified: we take our own self-descriptions (descriptions of activities and practices that are constitutive of ourselves) as representing reality. It is only by comparing self-descriptions that we see their parochial character, and reach a better understanding of "reality," or better ways of making the world intelligible. On this view, then, relativism involves a process of cross-cultural comparison that provides the moral theorist with the sort of exposure to human affairs that can engender serious criticism. It frees her criticism of the sort of distortion and naiveté that is present in the critic who has seen only one play and one human way of playing.

The Back-to-Aristotle Movement

Though MacIntyre is one of the most outspoken critics of Enlightenment approaches to ethics, he appears to shy away from radically pluralist approaches to ethics, unlike Taylor. For he sees the acceptance of some forms of pluralism as a postmodern hangover caused by our appreciation that the Enlightenment "project of providing a rational vindication of morality ha[s] decisively failed."[62] The turn to pluralism merely indicates that we appreciate the failure of the project without understanding the illegitimate assumptions that got the project started.

MacIntyre argues that the Enlightenment project got started when thinkers began to recognize an ethical sphere of existence distinct from the spheres defined by theology, law, and art. This ethical sphere, according to MacIntyre, pertained primarily to conduct in marriage and sexual matters. With the recognition of this new realm of life, a problem arose for Enlightenment thinkers concerning how to validate ethical rules of conduct. This problem became an especially intractable one, because the ethical injunctions these thinkers sought to validate were ones inherited from ancient and medieval philosophical, religious, and cultural traditions. And the basic intellectual framework of these traditions was a teleological one: life and the things in it had purposes over and above human ends. Moral injunctions functioned as practical guides to help humans realize these purposes. Unfortunately, the Enlightenment thinkers rejected the ancient and medieval teleological framework of these moral injunctions, but retained belief in the moral injunctions themselves. The impossible task, then, that Enlightenment thinkers attempted was to prove these injunctions correct without any appeal to divine or natural purposes—the framework in which these injunctions made sense.

MacIntyre recommends that, rather than continue the enterprise of justifying the injunctions of morality without a teleology, we should take apart the project itself. Perhaps it was a mistake to reject the teleological framework of premodern thinkers, MacIntyre suggests. Indeed, having examined the contours of this Enlightenment intellectual enterprise, MacIntyre argues that we now have a choice: to accept the failure but validity of the project, or to accept the failure and invalidity of the project—a choice, as MacIntyre imagines it, between Nietzsche or Aristotle. MacIntyre opts for Aristotle.

MacIntyre opts for an Aristotelian ethics in which being a good or moral person is a function of the particular social roles we assume. More specifically, it is a function of developing the character or virtues of those who fulfill their assigned or assumed roles well. To understand the complexities of these social roles and characters, and what it means to fulfill them well, MacIntyre suggests that we treat our lives and those of others as narratives. By studying these narratives, we learn about different roles, including some of those for which we have been recruited. Without understanding these roles and the social expectations they raise, we cannot make sense of the behavior of others or learn how to behave ourselves.

Moreover, narratives have purposes or ends toward which they move, and in this way are teleological in structure. Moreover, these purposes and ends exist over and above individual human ends: they are ones shared by and constitutive of different human communities. When these formative and historically embedded ends of the narratives we collect are in sight, the characters and deeds they describe become more intelligible to us. From this very rough account of MacIntyre's account of ethics, we can see to some extent that MacIntyre's teleological framework is basically an interpretive one. Moral understanding and insight comes from understanding principles internal to the stories we tell, and not from external and objective redescriptions of the characters and their actions. Moreover the characters, and their social roles and actions, are embedded in divergent ways of life that shape them in distinct ways. It is this plurality of lifeways, and the incommensurable moral ideals reflected in them, that interpretation seeks to articulate. Importantly, the pluralism interpretivists endorse is not a pluralism of abstract moral rules whose adoption stands in need of justification, but the pluralism of lifeways into which we are born, and upon which we may critically reflect. It is a pluralism that recognizes a multiplicity of moral ideals and practices constitutive of these lifeways.

Pluralism of the sort Taylor advocates is not a post-Enlightenment condition that needs to be treated. However, a fuller appreciation of this pluralism requires not merely the conceptual tools of premodern traditions, but the comparative human sciences of our postmodern and postcolonial world. That is, in order to avoid ethnocentric readings of the narratives we study or create, and in order to avoid essentialist pictures of human nature or human ends, we need to collect the narratives of radically different others. Thus, the choice is not between Nietzsche or Aristotle. For the teleological analysis interpretation embraces needs to avoid the essentialism of Aristotle as much as the nihilism of Nietzsche. We need a genuinely postmodern, rather than a premodern, approach to issues about human conduct and behavior.

The danger of ethnocentrism inherent in the virtue ethics approach that MacIntyre's writings have encouraged is perhaps clear in the following remark. In considering the relevance of the fact that some societies practice "infanticide" to the question of abortion, virtue theorist Rosalind Hursthouse states

> We should not automatically assume that is impossible that some
> other communities could be morally inferior to our own; maybe
> some are, or have been, precisely insofar as their members are, typ-
> ically, callous or light-minded or unjust.[63]

Regrettably, without knowledge of the purposes and convictions that
are constitutive of another society's practice of "infanticide," we are
likely to attribute faults of character to entire human communities.
To avoid such ethnocentric attributions, it is not sufficient to engage
in literary investigations of the virtues as they were conceived by premodern others, as MacIntyre encourages. We also need to consult
ethnographic investigations of the virtues as they are conceived by
contemporary human others. In sum, to avoid the ethnocentric and
colonialist mentality of premodern and modern Western thinkers, we
need to find the good in characters and habits created by cultural and
historical others.

I will consider further some theoretical implications of interpretive
and pluralist approaches to ethics in the last chapter of this book. But
before I do this, I will explore in some detail several interpretive
accounts of particular matters of conduct—especially conduct pertaining to marriage and sexuality—the "traditional" preserve of morality.
In the next chapter I will continue my investigation of interpretive and
pluralist approaches to adultery. In chapter 3, I will consider interpretive and pluralist approaches to abortion. In part of that chapter, I use
an interpretive approach to consider the relevance of infanticide to
abortion, and to unravel the abortion debate in American society in a
way that I hope preempts the arrogant dismissal of entire human
communities and subcommunities. In chapters 4, 5, and 6, I will
attempt to formulate an interpretive and pluralist account of prostitution, a topic that has vexed many feminist theorists and activists. In
chapter 7, then, I will consider some theoretical issues raised by my
examples of interpretive moral analysis.

2

Interpreting Adultery

People with "Bad Eyes"

When I was traveling in Iran many years ago, I was told by my Persian companion not to express admiration too strongly for the belongings of the people we would visit. For the polite host in this society will be obliged to offer any guest the objects upon which the guest bestows compliments. Of course, the polite guest must refuse such offers. However, sometimes it becomes a matter of honor for the host to insist upon the offer. The guest must then judge the sincerity of her host's insistence. If she judges incorrectly and refuses, she may insult his honor. If she judges incorrectly and accepts, she may deprive him of property he would like to keep. People who manifest a habit of casually accepting offers without thoroughly testing their sincerity may eventually find their own honor challenged—that is, they may gain a reputation for having "bad eyes."

Since my Persian companion understood the difficulty I would have recognizing what was at stake in these kind of encounters, he cautioned me to try to avoid them altogether. But it was not possible for me to avoid all such awkward encounters with our Persian hosts, for sometimes our hosts initiated such encounters by presenting objects for our admiration. Failure to express admiration in these circumstances could also be socially awkward. Moreover, the visit of a foreigner was likely to prompt such presentations, as indigenously produced objects were often shared particularly for the visitor's benefit. Also, a host may genuinely want to make some sort of gift to a foreigner, in honor of her visit. Thus a foreigner may find herself negotiating very complicated social situations, and often without knowing all the rules. For the inexperienced and non-ethnographically

31

trained visitor like myself, social clumsiness is inevitable. As it happened, sometimes my actions in these encounters caused surprise or amusement, and once they caused general hilarity when I accepted an offer of food after being asked only once, "Would you like ... ?" But such reactions allowed me to figure out, eventually, that I had accepted an offer too readily or refused one too emphatically. Fortunately my foreign status prevented such situations from becoming too awkward, as peculiar behavior like mine was expected from foreigners. That is, my foreignness may have prevented my being perceived as a person with "bad eyes"—at least, I hope it did.

Clifford Geertz states that we begin our efforts in thick description "from a state of general bewilderment as to what the devil is going on."[1] To understand what is going on in the situations I described— and to understand the culture to which these situations, the people in them, and their reactions belong—Geertz argues that we must become familiar with "the imaginative universe within which their acts are signs."[2] For Geertz, acts are signs because they articulate with "socially established structures of meaning."[3] Geertz illustrates this idea by borrowing and elaborating an example from Gilbert Ryle. Suppose a person squeezes one of her eyes shut. She may be involuntarily responding to a speck of dirt, she may be initiating a conspiracy, or she may be creating a parody of someone initiating a conspiracy.[4] Numerous interpretations are possible, but such interpretations are possible only in reference to a background of shared meanings or social conventions about winking.

Similarly, to understand whether the responses of my Persian hosts to my actions represented mere involuntary physical reflexes, a reply to my behavior, or a parody of my behavior, one needs to be clued in to a background of shared meanings in terms of which these responses can be read as signs. On the occasion, for instance, where I induced general laughter by readily taking food offered to me, other people present began to mimic my behavior. For the rest of the evening whenever anyone was offered anything, the person offered the item would promptly take it, causing further giddy and riotous behaviors. An adequate and thick description of these behaviors should not treat them as mere taking and offering behaviors, nor as mere involuntary physical reflexes, but as parodies of my taking behavior. But to understand them as such, we need to understand the cultural conventions that rendered my taking behavior on this occasion an object for parody.

For example, we need to understand that, in the culture in which I found myself, there exists a taboo against readily and casually accepting certain types of offers. Someone who violates this taboo can be marked as a person with "bad eyes." To understand, perhaps, why such a taboo exists, we need to know that, in this social world, politeness and honor require making sincere-appearing offers of one's belongings to others. Because of this, many offers may be made under duress—that is, when a person cannot afford to be making such offers. This is obvious to persons who are properly socialized, and thus it is also obvious that the polite and honorable response to an offer is to wait until it is made again and again—enough times so that one can be confident that the offerer is not merely trying to be polite.

To stress the obviousness of the impropriety of my behavior in these situation is to acknowledge that the meanings that shape social interaction are not mental ghosts that are privately glimpsed, rather they are discursive forms that are publicly shared. Charles Taylor also notes the public availability of these meanings, and states:

> the set of ideas and norms constitutive of negotiation themselves
> . . . must be the common property of the society before there can
> be any question of anyone entering into negotiation or not. Hence
> they are not subjective meanings, the property of one or some
> individuals, but rather inter-subjective meanings, which are consti-
> tutive of the social matrix in which individuals find themselves
> and act.[5]

Inter-subjective meanings, Taylor states, are constitutive of social reality itself.[6] Geertz, too, emphasizes that these meanings belong to a social, shared, public, and inter-subjective world rather than subjective one. He states:

> to say that culture consists of socially established structures of
> meaning in terms of which people do such things as signal conspir-
> acies and join them or perceive insults and answer them, is no
> more to say that it is a psychological phenomenon, a characteristic
> of someone's mind, personality, cognitive structure, or whatever,
> than to say that Tantrism, genetics, the progressive form of the
> verb, [or] the classification of wines . . . is.[7]

The structures of meaning in terms of which Persians make judgments about politeness and honor are not locked away in the inner reaches of their consciousnesses to where there is only privileged and private access. Rather these inter-subjective meanings are formed, transmitted, enforced, and established in a social world to which there is public access. As Geertz notes, the semiotic tools for the study of culture merely elaborate the Wittgensteinian doctrine that there are no private languages—that meaning is a function of public conventions rather than private intentions.[8]

Taylor draws a distinction between inter-subjective meanings and "common meanings." Common meanings occur

> when there is convergence between the subjective beliefs, aspirations, of many individuals . . . Common meanings are the basis of community. Inter-subjective meaning gives a people a common language to talk about social reality and a common understanding of certain norms, but only with common meanings does this common reference world contain significant common actions, celebrations, and feelings. These are objects in the world that everybody share. This is what makes community.[9]

For example, common meanings can come about from a convergence of opinion on how much of a nuisance people with "bad eyes" represent, and some collective acknowledgement or even celebration of this convergence. In the U.S., there may be common meanings regarding whether a minority sexual orientation (or adultery/casual sex) is desirable, or whether abortion is a fundamental right. Taylor's comments above suggest that by isolating inter-subjective and common meanings, we can analytically differentiate cultures and communities, though, given the amorphous and overlapping nature of these entities, the mechanism we have is necessarily imprecise. Basically, people who share inter-subjective meanings may be said to share "a culture," while people who share some common meanings may be part of an emerging or waning community—one that might be built, for instance, around tolerance or intolerance for particular members or practices of a larger society.

The distinction Taylor is drawing between inter-subjective and common meanings is similar, though not identical, to a distinction some social scientists make between cultural and social principles.[10] Cultural principles, like inter-subjective meanings, form the background for social interaction. They are the inherited property held in common by the members of a society that enables communication and interpretation. For instance, that honor involves making offers of one's belongings to others, and that sincerity is expressed by insisting that one's offers be accepted, are cultural principles that can render the responses of my Persian hosts intelligible to me and my actions meaningful for them. By contrast, social principles do not capture background meanings but describe patterns of, or prescriptions for, behavior—for example, that Americans, relative to Persians, treat offers of food and sex casually, or that in America there are prescriptions against eating dogs, killing neonates, and most forms of adult/child genital contact. Yet to understand these prescriptions and patterns of behavior, it would seem that we need to understand the cultural principles that inform them. This is just what an interpretive account of human behavior tries to do: it attempts to study human action in terms of its social origins—origins that derive from socially established structures of meaning—rather than in terms of the biological, ecological, or universal causes that are invoked by objectivist accounts. Even though objectivist accounts usually recognize common meanings and social principles, they are driven to locate the sources of human action outside human inventions and conventions of meaning because they ignore inter-subjective meanings and cultural principles.

When we analyze social action on an interpretive approach then, we are interested in probing the inter-subjective meanings and cultural principles that render social practices meaningful to those who participate in them. These principles are implicit in the communicative acts of social actors, but they are also implicit in the interpretations and readings that others give these acts. In a sense, all communication is interpretation for it involves knowledge of the inter-subjective conventions that make discourse meaningful. As Geertz states, "You can't wink (or burlesque one) without knowing what counts as winking . . ."[11] In short, we construct social practices and our interpretations of them in reference to the same conventions of meaning. In this way, what an ethnographer does in constructing interpretations of people's behavior is not so different from what social actors do constantly in everyday life.

Moreover the ethnographer's data, on an interpretive approach, are the interpretations, or misinterpretations, that others construct about social discourse in the social world they inhabit. According to Geertz, "What we call our data are really our own constructions of other people's constructions of what they and their compatriots are up to . . ."[12] Ethnographic inscriptions are thus interpretations of interpretations, and interpretations of interpretations of interpretations—that is, second order, third order, and so on, interpretations.[13] The primary difference between ethnography and the first order interpretation that people ordinarily engage in is that, in ethnography, what we learn from one interpretive situation is then utilized in some form both to construct interpretations in radically different social contexts and to construct scientific and philosophical theories about human beings, society, culture, good and just social institutions, and many other subjects of great interest. As Geertz notes, in ethnography, "small facts speak to large issues, [e.g.,] winks to epistemology . . . because they are made to."[14] In the next section I will begin to consider how small facts about sexuality contribute to our understanding of large issues of morality.

Sex As Social Text

By recovering other people's first order interpretations, or what Taylor refers to as their self-understandings, we probe the inter-subjective and common meanings that render their actions intelligible and familiar. This process may also expose, to some degree, the cultural principles that inform social action in our own societies, and the shared beliefs that form the basis for particular communities. And by gaining the cultural distance necessary to expose these principles, we render our own customs somewhat less familiar. For instance, by analyzing the sexual and marital practices of the sixties counterculture, Wasserstrom was able to defamiliarize our mainstream customs pertaining to sex and marriage, as well as render more intelligible some countercultural ones.

More specifically, Wasserstrom observed that, in the pre- and post-sixties social order of American society, sexual attraction and romantic love are believed to imply each other, whereas in the sixties counterculture, this mutual implication is denied. In both cases, a belief in the possible connection between the two must be negotiated in social action, either by denying it or affirming it. That is, one can try to make a point of disconnecting sexual attraction and romantic love, by treating sex casually, or one can fail to contest the conventional implications of one's behavior. But the connection between sexual attraction and romantic love is part of the inter-subjective background of meaning, and therefore neither countercultural nor mainstream individuals can afford to ignore it in negotiating sexual encounters. In the same way, neither Persians nor their foreign guests can ignore the socially established association between casual taking and having "bad eyes" in negotiating gift offering encounters, though they may contest the presuppositions and implications that this association carries. Sometimes the process of contestation leads to the forging of new communities, which can also be sites where cultural meanings are transformed.

Through public challenges to some of the socially established meanings of sex, and through the acknowledgment of these challenges by ritualized performances of "casual" sex, various collectivities or communities were formed in parts of America in the sixties. Whether casual sex in these communities had a different meaning from that in the dominant society, given the inherent tendency of the dominant society to dominate, is a matter for more microscopic—to borrow Geertz's term—ethnographic analysis.[15] Nevertheless, to explore further the implications of Wasserstrom's analysis, I will grant him this assumption. Moreover, if Wasserstrom's interpretation of casual sex in the counterculture turns out to be invalid, it may still be valid for some sexual transactions in the dominant culture. For although there is less acceptance of casual sex in the mainstream culture of American society, sex can have different degrees of seriousness. And, as Wasserstrom shows, the seriousness of a particular agent's engagement may depend, in part, on the agent's gender.

Drawing from the ethnographic observations of a cultural native, (i.e., himself), Wasserstrom probes some of the webs that surround sexual negotiations in the dominant culture of American society. He states:

> If you were a girl, you showed how much you liked a boy by the degree of sexual intimacy you would allow. If you liked him only a little you never did more than kiss—and even the kiss was not very passionate. If you liked him a lot and if your feeling was reciprocated, necking and, possibly, petting were permissible. If the attachment was still stronger and you thought it might even become a permanent relationship, the sexual activity was correspondingly more intense and intimate . . .[16]

But—drawing from my own native knowledge here—a boy could, and was often expected to engage in sexual activities without feelings of affection for his partners, and without evidence of his partners' affection for him. However, given that his potential female partners were not similarly disposed, a boy would often make an insincere expression of affection in order to initiate a sexual encounter. Indeed, it was part of the girl's job in a sexual negotiation to discern the degree of the boy's sincerity or seriousness: the seriousness of the encounter for her would simply be taken for granted.[17]

These behavioral norms show, according to Wasserstrom, that the importance of a correlation between sexual intimacy and feelings of love and affection was taught by the culture and assimilated by those growing up in the culture. The scale of possible positive feelings toward persons of the other sex ran from casual liking, at one end, to the love that was deemed essential to, and characteristic of, marriage, at the other. The scale of possible sexual behavior ran from brief, passionless kissing or hand-holding, at one end, to sexual intercourse, at the other. And the correlation between the two scales was quite precise. As a result, any act of sexual intimacy carried substantial meaning with it, and no act of sexual intimacy was simply a pleasurable set of bodily sensations . . . [Sexual activity] was not like eating a good meal, listening to good music, lying in the sun, or getting a pleasant back rub.[18]

As a consequence of the cultural patterning involving gender, sex, and romantic interest that Wasserstrom carefully observes, sexual interactions represent social texts that call for interpretation. Typically, the cultural principles that govern negotiation enable competing readings of our outward social transactions, and individuals within a society may contest alternative interpretations (i.e., inter-subjective meanings are not determinative of beliefs or behavior, they merely render them meaningful). Yet the inter-subjective meanings operative in a situation may make some readings appear more natural or inevitable, and thus all readings do not carry equal authority. A reading that depends on a mere subjective rather than inter-subjective belief is one that is likely to carry less authority.

For example, just as the publicly shared conventions regarding offers of food and other items in Iran make it difficult for Persians to treat such offers casually, the meanings Americans share regarding sexuality make it difficult for American women (and men who care about them) to treat sex casually. That is, sexual transactions for members of American mainstream culture cannot be as casual as dining or sunbathing, even if individuals privately intend them to be. As Gayle Rubin puts it, "Sexual acts are burdened with an excess of significance."[19] In American society, sexual acts are susceptible to particular authoritative readings that involve ascriptions of romantic desires and affection.

Rereading Adultery

Like sexual acts generally, adulterous sexual acts are susceptible to particular readings in our mainstream culture. In this section, I will try to comprehend some of these possible readings and their moral significance. I will also consider whether and how we can challenge such readings of our experience without creating, in Taylor's words, "a field for the exercise of ethnocentric prejudice."[20]

The sense we make of adultery is a function of the social customs pertaining to marriage as well as sex. In the dominant culture of American society, marriage is constituted by principles that include the following: (1) marital partners should be romantic partners, and (2) faithfulness, loyalty, honesty, and respect between romantic partners (and thus marital partners) require, and are demonstrated by, sexual exclusivity (among other things). Principle (2) follows from (1) together with the presuppositions that (3) romantic love implies sexual love, and sexual love implies romantic love (at least for women), and that (4) romantic love is exclusive.

Now given this background of inter-subjective meanings, adulterous acts in American society will generally signify to others a failure of romantic love between marital partners. Accordingly, these acts will also signify faithlessness, disloyalty, dishonesty, and disrespect. In almost any language of qualitative contrast that we invoke, or in terms of many of the goods we recognize, these conditions score pretty low. This is not to say that all extramarital sexual acts are inevitably low or bad, but that whenever they occur in a context where sex and marriage are constituted by the principles described above, adulterous acts will be constructed as qualitatively inferior in certain ways.

Yet, in these very same contexts—the context of American mainstream society—adulterous sexual acts can also convey the need for and the possibility of greater sexual fulfillment, and the possibility of greater personal freedom and happiness. These messages stem from the background beliefs implicit in the dominant culture that sexual fulfillment is related to sexual variety and novelty, that personal freedom is a function of sexual freedom, and that personal happiness is a function of sexual fulfillment. As personal freedom, fulfillment, and happiness are recognized goods, the actions that manifest them are qualitatively superior to others. In short, acts of adultery can be judged in terms of incommensurable goods, and these goods may yield conflicting judgments of moral worth.

At this juncture in our theorizing about adultery, we have at least two options. One option is to weigh the goods of romantic love, faithfulness, loyalty, honesty, and respect against those of personal freedom, fulfillment, and happiness by invoking some higher good. On an interpretive model of human action, this option is viable, as long as we recognize that the explanatory strategy it offers cannot resolve all potential conflicts. For "hypergoods" are multiple, incommensurable and nonorderable, and thus may generate conflicting advice. Another option we have is to contest one or more of the background presuppositions that give rise to an association between particular acts and particular goods (or their reverse). For example, we might contest that sexual fulfillment requires sexual variety, or that marital partners be romantic partners. In taking this option, we need to be careful not to privilege, naively or uncritically, our own culturally idiosyncratic assumptions over those of others. That is, we need to avoid ethnocentrically rereading or redescribing the activities of others.

In concluding his analysis of adultery, Wasserstrom elects the second strategy. He considers the argument that adultery in American society, if not in all societies, involves betrayal and dishonesty, and responds:

> [T]he argument leaves unanswered the question of whether it is desirable for sexual intimacy to carry the sorts of messages

> described above . . . It might, for instance, be the case that substantially more good than harm would come from a kind of demystification of sexual behavior—one that would encourage the enjoyment of sex more for its own sake and one that would reject the centrality both of the association of sex with love and of love with only one other person.[21]

Here Wasserstrom is contesting the background presuppositions that sexual and romantic love are connected, and that romantic love is exclusive. Yet how can we contest these presuppositions in a non-chauvinistic way? As I argued in the last chapter, Wasserstrom appears to be challenging these presuppositions nonchauvinistically by invoking the perspective of the sixties counterculture, but then he treats the countercultural perspective chauvinistically by uncritically privileging its sexual and marital ideals.

The option Wasserstrom selects has certain dangers. To invoke this strategy is to see certain moral problems as mere artifacts of the cultural customs in which they are entrenched. It is to view, for example, the problem of having "bad eyes" as a mere artifact of the cultural assumption that honor dictates sharing one's property with those who admire it. Often such conclusions are a result of cross-cultural comparison. We see that having "bad eyes" is not a problem in American society because, though other people may covet one's property, nothing in American culture requires that we indulge or assuage their envy (there may be certain exceptions in situations with children). Similarly, Wasserstrom observed that, in the (perhaps mythical) society of the counterculture, adultery was not regarded as problematical. Thus he suggests that the moral problems raised by adultery may be mere artifacts of the cultural assumptions that connect sex and romantic love. Yet this strategy involves challenging the social realities of others, and thus is easily susceptible to ethnocentrism.

In challenging the presuppositions behind particular readings, we are challenging inter-subjective meanings: beliefs that are the property of entire groups and not merely one or more individuals. However, though these presuppositions are collectively shared, they are not static, and indeed they may be constantly undergoing historic transformation. For example, the presuppositions which once made human slavery appear morally acceptable in some societies have undergone some transformation. Thus we might ask: what kind of transformation of inter-subjective meanings might have a positive impact on our sexual practices? Or we might ask the more cynical question: can we really demystify sexuality, or do we only end up substituting one mystification for another? Stuart Hampshire appears to believe the latter:

> Just as there is no ideally rational arrangement of a garden, and no
> ideally rational clothing, so there is no ideally rational way of
> ordering sexuality and there is no ideally rational way of ordering
> family and kinship relationships . . . As raw food has to be cooked
> and changed in accordance with learnt custom, natural sexuality
> also has to be trimmed and directed in accordance with some cus-
> toms or other. When ideally natural arrangements are sought in,
> for example, clothing or in sexual practices, the result is one more
> fashion, later seen as characteristic of a particular period and of a
> particular place.[22]

For Hampshire, casual and serious sex would be simply sexual "fashions" linked to particular societies at particular times. But certainly
in comparing slave and nonslave labor systems, we should not treat
each as "one more fashion . . . characteristic of a particular period
and of a particular place." Perhaps we need to avoid the extremes of
Hampshire's simplistic relativism and Wasserstrom's crude positivism.

To avoid crude positivistic reasoning, we need to admit that inter-
subjective meanings are not capable of objective demonstration or fal-
sification, and yet they are relevant to understanding the social
institutions they define. Admitting this means that we cannot entirely
escape mystification by resorting to some ostensibly objective procedure, though we can develop critical self-awareness, and ethnically
less distorted vision, by comparing alternative social realities. To
avoid simplistic relativistic reasoning, we need to recognize that
though our social realities are incommensurable, i.e., not reducible to
each other or describable in the same terms, they are not incomparable. That is, there are higher languages of contrast that can be
invoked to make ethnically-decentered, qualitative, transcultural judgments between practices that are radically different.

Taylor calls these higher languages: "languages of perspicuous contrast." According to Taylor,

> it will almost always be the case that the adequate language in
> which we can understand another society is not our language of
> understanding, or theirs, but rather what one could call a language
> of perspicuous contrast. This would be a language in which we
> could formulate both their way of life and ours as alternative pos-
> sibilities in relation to some human constants at work in both. It
> would be a language in which the possible human variations would
> be so formulated that both our form of life and theirs could be per-
> spicuously described as alternative such variations.[23]

Once two radically distinct practices are put in the terms of such a
language, we may see, according to Taylor, that one practice scores

successes that command the attention of those who practice the other.[24] For example, according to Taylor,

> there is a definite respect in which modern science is superior to its Renaissance predecessor; and this is evident not in spite of but because of their incommensurability . . .
>
> What we have here is not an antecedently accepted common criterion, but a facet of our activity—here the connection between scientific advance and technological pay-off—which remains implicit or unrecognized in earlier views, but which cannot be ignored once realized in practice. The very existence of the technological advance forces the issue. In this way, one set of practices pose a challenge for an incommensurable interlocutor, not indeed in the language of this interlocutor, but in terms which the interlocutor cannot ignore. And out of this can arise valid transcultural judgements of superiority.[25]

While technological control may not be an ideal that all societies share, nevertheless it is an ideal whose successful realization different societies can appreciate. In terms of this ideal, modern Western science is superior to its historical predecessors and perhaps non-Western competitors. Yet Taylor realizes that this does not show that the society in which modern science developed is superior to others, or that technological know-how is the only criterion in terms of which knowledge systems can be compared. It may be that modern science has achieved a greater sense of "mastery over" nature, while other sciences can achieve a greater sense of "harmony with" nature. But this is just to say that other nonethnocentric transcultural judgments of superiority are possible, and that the jury is not in yet on this one (and may never be). Perhaps, the process of expanding our knowledge and understanding does not require a verdict in these cases, but requires only our ability to formulate and support provisional transcultural judgments of superiority.

In comparing slave and nonslave systems of labor, monogamy and polygamy, or casual and serious sex, what successes of each can we point to that might command the attention of cultural others? Taylor challenges us to identify these successes, even though we must recognize that radically different others may not give great importance to the criteria in terms of which the identified successes are measured. That is, Taylor challenges us to identify these successes before and without identifying some hypergood (universal and equal respect, happiness, care, etc.) that all should hold even if all do not. For we identify antecedently held hypergoods in the hope that their fulfillment by a practice could not only be appreciated by others but could convince others of the ultimate goodness of the practice, and perhaps convince them to accept the practice. But Taylor is suggesting here that moral conflict be resolved through an appreciation and understanding of incommensurable practices, and not necessarily or exclusively through agreement on the terms of description—i.e., not through, what we might call "categorical colonialism."[26]

In chapter 1, I noted that Seyla Benhabib had a similar insight— that the aim of moral analysis should be tentative political agreements between irreducibly different others rather than intellectual homogeneity. But contra Benhabib, I would argue that an understanding and appreciation of the virtues of incommensurable practices offers a sufficient basis for these political agreements, and these political compromises do not require finding some criteria held in common, or a procedure followed in common, as Benhabib suggests. Indeed by relying on the former basis for political compromise and eschewing the imperatives of categorical colonialism, we are much less likely to deliver ethnocentric judgments. For this reason I suggested in chapter 1 that we need to separate Benhabib's insight here from her formal apparatus.

Nancy Davis draws a useful distinction between "strategies of rapprochement" and "strategies of compromise."[27] Rapprochement involves attempting to find values that disputing parties hold in common as the basis for fashioning political policies that each can endorse. Compromise involves fashioning political policies that give each disputant part of what she wants, without giving any party all of what she wants. Davis argues that those who aim for rapprochement will not find policies that compromise "satisfactory if one believes that failure to achieve rapprochement is a sign that a compromise is unprincipled or unstable."[28] However, while compromises are in principle unprincipled, they need not be unstable if they are generated from sincere but not simple-minded relativism. Such relativism requires that we understand, though not necessarily accept, the self-descriptions of the other disputants so that we can make nonparochial judgments about their practices. Reaching such compromises should be the aim of moral analysis.

Taylor's challenge to identify ideals that might not be embraced by all cultures but whose successful realization can be appreciated by radically different societies is important and interesting, for judgments involving such ideals might offer possibilities for compromise. Moreover, successfully meeting Taylor's challenge may help us through the dilemma of choosing between the colonialist impulses of even sophisticated versions of moral universalism or the promiscuous chauvinism and impotent tolerance of simple-minded relativism. Yet what might some of these ideals be? Taylor has suggested one—the capacity to provide a technological payoff—but this ideal will not help us compare slave and nonslave systems of labor, polygamy and monogamy, or casual and serious sex. But consider the following possibilities. Not all societies may give importance to the peaceful resolution of conflict among both individuals and groups of individuals, but all societies may be able to appreciate another society's accomplishments in this area. Similarly, not all societies may give great importance to freedom from oppression, and those that do may define "oppression" differently. Some define it in terms of social and political oppression, and other in terms of the oppression of physical embodiment and separation from an eternal, spiritual reality. Nevertheless the success of some in realizing their ideal of freedom from oppression may command the attention of others.

One small caveat needs to be entered here in response to Taylor's challenge. In identifying the hypergoods that, though not shared by all, are capable of appreciation by all (or many) when successfully realized, we need to be careful not to engage in unwarranted reductionism. This might happen if we place an arbitrary and formal restriction on the number of such hypergoods we recognize in this regard, which there is no reason to do once we have accepted the provisionality of transcultural judgments of superiority.

The upshot of this discussion is that if Wasserstrom wants to entertain countercultural sex as demystified sex, he should ask the following question: are there any ideals whose successful realization by casual sex could turn the heads of radically different others, even though these others might not give great importance to those ideals? Wasserstrom should also inquire after the cultural ideals to which competing sexual practices may aspire, especially ones that casual sex may fail to realize and may even infringe. To pursue questions such as these, we need to consider more than the countercultural and dominant cultural norms about sex. For these norms that Wasserstrom invokes may fail to reflect the perspectives of women and other marginal social groups on sex.

For example, some theorists have noted that for many women in American society, sex divorced from ongoing social relationships, and sex divorced from romance, is unappealing. In other words, many women do not share the same ideals of unburdened sex and sexual freedom that many men appear to have. Thus, rather than offering to women the possibility of unburdened sex or sexual freedom, casual sex merely offers to women the possibility of conforming to male sexual norms without the usual social sanctions. The practice of casual sex offers American men no real new possibilities since, in our contemporary society, men are generally allowed to treat sex casually; though, by permitting women to do the same, it may make available to men more potential sexual partners. However, could the successful realization of the ideals of unburdened sex and sexual freedom by a variety of casual and often impersonal sexual transactions be appreciated by others, if those others are women? In the next section I will explore further how the fulfillment of particular ideals can command the appreciation of others, and therefore figure into relatively less ethnically chauvinist transcultural judgments.

Sexual Libertarians and Sexual Romanticists

The second option we were exploring above—of rereading the actions of others in terms of possibly less mystifying categories—raises for us the question posed in the first option. Are there higher goods that we can call upon to assign weights to lower goods, and even to contest the culturally idiosyncratic or distorted ideals upon which particular readings rest? And how do we call upon these higher goods in ways that are not ethnocentric, reductionist, or universalist?

Steven Seidman has developed a sexual ethic that attempts to identify some culturally entrenched hypergoods that have some limited universal appeal, in order to resolve moral disagreements without engaging in universalism or ethnocentrism.[29] Seidman, like Wasserstrom, first distinguishes in American society two broadly distinct sexual cultures. Unlike Wasserstrom he does not conceptualize these cultures as discrete groups existing at particular historical moments (sixties vs. pre- and post-sixties): rather, he conceptualizes them as two internally consistent ideologies that have been in tension in the recent past of American society. One of these ideologies is the romanticist ideology, whose adherents approve sex for social bonding. The other is the libertarian ideology, whose adherents approve sex for bodily pleasure as well as other ends.[30]

According to Seidman, sexual romanticists believe that sexual and amorous longing are essentially connected. They also hold that a person should have one relationship, among her/his social relationships, that is more special, more significant, more intimate than the rest. A relationship will have this status if and only if a person reserves for it exclusively her/his deepest expressions of friendship and love, and therefore her/his sexual activities. Also, sexual romanticists generally believe that marital relationships ought to have this special, intimate status.

According to Seidman, sexual libertarians believe that human sexual activity need not be encumbered by worthy or socially redeeming aims (e.g., bonding, procreation, health, etc.). Instead, sexual activity can have many aims, including the mere production and enhancement of bodily pleasure. Moreover the aim of sensual pleasure is achievable autonomously from the aim of social bonding, and thus good sex can occur (and for some only occur) outside of significant social relationships. In other words, on this view, aesthetic evaluations of sex may sometimes preempt moral ones. For sexual libertarians, then, sex has no essential connection to emotional intimacy, and just as sex need not be redeemed by love and marriage, neither love nor marriage need be redeemed through sexual exclusivity.

Unlike Wasserstrom, Seidman does not see one sexual ideology as potentially representing mystification and the other as potentially representing rationality. For Seidman, neither sexual culture can be dismissed in some positivist fashion:

> Judgment[s] to the effect that a[n] entire cultural pattern is narcissistic, anomic or immoral for whatever reason (e.g., promiscuous, product of "high" rates of divorce or illegitimacy) do not exhibit the minimal level of respect and knowledgeability of social difference that I take to be a condition of a moral judgment. Dismissive judgments of a whole way of life presuppose some absolutist standpoint that is, in certain key ways, external to the social patterns being evaluated. Such global critiques devalue a way of life to the point of sanctioning its elimination and stigmatizing those who participate in it. Totalizing critiques strike me as authoritarian and dangerous. By failing to accord any legitimacy to a social pattern, and thus failing to grasp its adaptive aspects, these absolutist moral judgments function as dangerous hegemonic strategies.[31]

Recognizing how ethnocentric arrogance and absolutist conceit can legitimate imperialist ends, and also recognizing the equal impotence of crude cultural relativism to guide reasonable social policies, Seidman fashions a "pragmatic" approach that avoids these extremes. He states,

> We must begin, then, with the forms of life that moral agents have created. This means acknowledging observable differences and according sexual variation at least a minimal level of legitimacy. A pragmatic sexual ethic renounces the task of making global judgments. It strives only to provide guidelines ... It seeks less to impose a moral order from the high ground of expertise or moral authority than to contribute to an ongoing conversation about private and public life.[32]

Both romanticist and libertarian sexual cultures are forms of life that moral agents have created. Thus Seidman looks to them to extrapolate some moral goods that may be used to guide legal policies, and individual moral judgment and choice in American society but not necessarily in others. In doing this, Seidman rightly attempts to avoid some of the essentialist assumptions about sexuality underlying the sexual ideologies from which they are derived.

From sexual libertarians, Seidman extracts the principle of consent:

> We—contemporary adult Americans—would agree, I think, that no matter what our disagreements over particular sexual practices and arrangements, a necessary condition of their moral legitimacy is that they be based on free choice, and that the parties to the exchange should have voluntarily agreed to it . . .[33]
>
> I believe that we need a concept of consent to function as a general norm. The notion of consent provides one basis for a very general moral classification of sexual practices that would seem to be consistent with widely shared liberal cultural traditions in the United States. For example, an appeal to a notion of consent allows us to proscribe acts of sexual coercion such as sexual abuse and rape. Similarly, the norm of consent renders sex between adults and children illegitimate, even if the issue of the age of consent can be legitimately contested.[34]

From sexual romanticists, Seidman extracts the principle of responsibility:

> [R]esponsibility suggests an awareness that what one does influences the world of objects—human and otherwise—and that one has a moral obligation to consider these consequences in deciding on whether and how to act. Deployed as a normative standard, responsibility implies a pragmatic ethical standpoint. Acts or practices carry no intrinsic moral meaning but get their moral significance from their consequences or impact on the individual, society, and the world of natural and cultural objects.[35]

Seidman has developed a basically interpretive approach to ethics in which moral goods are recovered from the self-descriptions of others: they are the goods we recognize to explain the world to ourselves and others. Moreover, insofar as there is variation in sexual norms, Seidman recognizes a plurality of incommensurable sexual goods. Furthermore, in saying that acts have no intrinsic moral meaning, Seidman appears to acknowledge the possibility that there may be no ideals or criteria in common between distinct sexual cultures that enable unitary interpretations of sexual acts. Actually he does equivocate somewhat on whether the ideals of consent and responsibility are commonly shared by both groups,[36] or whether they each represent an ideal of one group that, while not given central importance by the other, would (in Taylor's words) command the attention of the other when successfully realized. If these ideals are conceived in terms of the latter model, then Seidman may have demonstrated how moral judgments about sexuality can escape authoritarianism, ethnocentrism, or helpless relativism.

While Seidman has avoided some of the flaws evident in other accounts, it is not clear that his account can resolve the moral conflicts between different groups that Seidman seeks to resolve. For example, in applying Seidman's standard of responsibility to adultery, we might be led to see as morally inferior those acts of adultery that occur in the context of a conventional, mainstream (non-open) marriage in American society. For in this context, an act of adultery signifies to others the failure of romantic love within marriage and, with this failure, it conveys disloyalty, faithlessness, dishonesty, and disrespect. Because of what it implies about the state of a relationship, an adulterous act can cause third parties (spouses, children, friends, and relatives) a great deal of emotional pain. Seidman's standard of responsibility requires that we consider these consequences. But within this same context, acts of adultery can imply a need for, as well as the possibility of achieving, greater personal freedom and fulfillment. Which consequences should be given greater weight?

Seidman's standard of responsibility might do better when applied to acts of adultery within an open marriage, where adulterous acts do not carry the same messages. On Seidman's view, "acts and practices do not carry intrinsic moral meaning," and thus we can evaluate adultery differently in this context. Since the marital partners in this situation generally aim to contest the conventional messages carried by adulterous sex, adultery does not have its usual consequences. However, though the marital partners may contest the conventional meanings of adulterous acts, can we be sure the nonmarital lover, or the children, parents, and friends of the adulterers will be able to contest the negative, and potentially hurtful, messages?

Applying Seidman's standard of consent to adultery is equally difficult. For example, it would probably lead us to view as morally inferior those acts of adultery in a conventional, mainstream marriage in American society, if we consider the sexually faithful spouse a party to the adulterous exchange. For, in the typical case, the adulterous transaction is imposed on the faithful spouse without that party's consent. But should we consider the faithful spouse a party to the extramarital exchange, and how do we determine whether that party has given consent? (Has the wife who looks the other way to maintain her marriage and, therefore, social standing given her consent?)[37]

Applying this standard to acts of adultery in an open marriage is somewhat easier, since we presume that partners in an open marriage implicitly give consent to their spouse's adultery. We also usually presume that their nonmarital sexual partners consent to the adulterous sex, though if they are misled about the casual nature of its meaning, their consent may not be "informed."[38] Also, while children may not be direct parties to an adulterous exchange, they may be indirect parties, and thus failure to be open with children about the sexual commitments in an open marriage, and perhaps gain their tacit consent, may represent some form of unjust manipulation.

Paradoxically, Seidman's standards may work best when they are applied to adulterous actions in an entirely non-American context, even though they were not meant to be applied there. For they do help to explain why we are not offended by the actions of the wife in *Ju Dou*. In this film, the marriage depicted did not involve the wife's consent (by our standards of consent), and neither did the marital sex depicted appear to have the wife's consent (i.e., by our standards it was rape). By contrast, the adulterous film sex at least involved the consent of the sexual partners, if not that of the husband and later the adulterous pair's own son. Moreover, in this society, marital partners are not assumed to be romantic partners, and thus the adultery depicted did not have some of its more "ordinary" consequences, i.e., failure to maintain a romantic attachment. Yet it did have the consequence of interrupting both the wife's and her lover's exploitation by the husband, and thereby resisting the oppressive social institutions that sanctioned the husband's exploitation (I suppose it is really the filmmaker here who resists these institutions by depicting this case of adultery in a movie). Moreover, since the wife and her lover were romantic partners, while she and her husband were not, the adulterous sex in the film was redeemed by a deepening of a significant social bond: in this way the movie appeals to our romanticist tendencies. And finally, the marital sex in this film was clearly painful for the wife, while the adulterous sex appeared pleasurable—a fact that appeals to our libertarian leanings. In short, Seidman's approach allows us to make culturally sensitive judgments about adultery, not by applying the ideals of all Americans to American adultery, but by applying our languages of qualitative and perspicuous contrast to the incommensurable practices of others. Of course, these judgments would be freer of ethnocentrism and more self-aware if we had recovered pre-Communist Chinese views on sex and marriage, and on consent and responsibility, before evaluating the superior and inferior qualities of this instance of adultery.

Seidman anticipates some of the problems involved in applying his standards of responsibility and consent that we encountered above.

For though Seidman appears to propose responsibility as a universal American value, he acknowledges that the potential or actual effects of practices that responsible agents must consider cannot be assessed from some universal American perspective, nor even from the perspectives of sexual libertarians or romanticists alone. He states:

> If, as I have argued, we evaluate the morality of an act by its consequences, from whose vantage point do we assess the effects? ... It seems reasonable that in assessing the morality of a practice, the agent will initially consider its consequences in light of his or her own values and interests. Yet this represents a limited moral standpoint and contains an authoritarian logic: a logic of identity which may easily translate into one of domination. The moral agent needs to acknowledge sexual and social diversity ... The moral agent should consider the standpoint of the other as potentially different from his or her self and evaluate the consequences of behavior from that vantage point as well. The consequences of behavior for different groups or populations who are differently situated or socially positioned with regard, say, to class, gender, sexual orientation, or race, would perhaps vary considerably.[39]

If there are so many ways of viewing the consequences of actions, how does Seidman's standard of responsibility resolve moral conflict?

How, for example, might differently situated and positioned agents assess the consequences of adultery? If Carol Gilligan is right and women tend to be concerned with maintaining relationships in resolving moral problems, then women are likely to see the consequences of adultery in terms of its effects on the romantic and familial relationships involved. If men are socialized to take a more atomistic approach to morality, then they may be likely to see the effects of adultery in terms of the personal freedoms and pleasures gained and lost. Those with particular ideals of religious worship may see the effects of adultery in terms of their relationship with God, or in terms of their spiritual development. And persons with a stigmatized minority sexual orientation, and who see the sexual and marital practices of American society as oppressively restrictive, might see mass acts of adultery and casual sex as effecting a destabilization of hegemonic social institutions. And given that these different ways of seeing structure social reality itself, the same activities will not only appear to have, but will actually have different consequences for different agents. According to Seidman,

> casual sex may have had a set of meanings and consequences for gay men in the 1970s that was very different from those for hetero-

sexual women ... To assess the morality of sexual practices I
would argue that we need to understand the meaning and consequences of that act for those individuals or populations implicated
by that act.[40]

Seidman suggests here that a gay man (in the pre-AIDS 1970s), whose
personal life was confined primarily to a gay male sexual libertarian
community, might engage in casual and extramarital sex (presuming
his "marital" partner was also a gay man) without harming his other
social relationships and the people in them.[41] By contrast, a nongay
man or lesbian woman, whose private life involved sexually romanticist women, could not similarly avoid causing harm to others and
his/her relationships with others, while engaging in casual or extramarital sex.

Thus (middle-class?) American heterosexuals and lesbians need to
be aware of the predominantly romanticist sexual culture in which
they operate when they participate in sexual activities and institutions, and when they make moral judgments about the sexual behaviors of middle-class American heterosexuals and lesbians. Yet, when
they evaluate the behavior of others or propose social policies that
would affect others, American heterosexuals and lesbians need to take
into account alternative sexual ideologies. Similarly, American gay
men in the 1970s needed only to consider the predominantly libertarian sexual culture in which they operated when they negotiated sexual
encounters and institutions, and when they morally evaluated the sexual behaviors of other American gay men at the time. But when they
evaluate the sexual behavior of heterosexuals, lesbians, or gay men in
the 1980s and 1990s, or propose social policies that would affect
them, American gay men need to take into account romanticist and
possibly other sexual ideologies.

Beyond Consent and Responsibility

In addition to libertarian and romanticist sexual ideologies, we
should consider those that are based on sexist and racist (and heterosexist, classist, ageist, etc.) premises. These ideologies structure not
only the perceived and actual consequences sexual behaviors have for
different individuals, but also their perceived causes. For example a
husband's adultery may be perceived as the failure of his wife to
please him, while a wife's adultery may be perceived as her failure to
avoid temptation. Similarly the adultery of a person of color may be
explained in terms of some pernicious racial, ethnic, or national
stereotype. In contexts where such readings of adultery carry author-

ity, it may be less important to determine whether the sexual activities involved are consensual and responsible than it is to challenge the cultural ideals or prejudices that underlie these authoritative readings and structure the social choices we have.

For example, in a society where men are thought to be entitled to sexual satisfaction in marriage, a man may see his choices in terms of getting sexual pleasure from his wife or getting it from some other woman. If this is a society that sees women as perhaps capable of sexual pleasure but not necessarily entitled to it, a woman may see her choices in marriage in terms of giving or failing to give sexual pleasure to her husband. Of course she may choose to commit adultery, and sometimes her choice may be perceived as a consequence of her husband's failure to sexually satisfy her. But where it is predominantly held that she has no right to expect a high level of sexual satisfaction, then she may still be held uniquely blamable for the adultery. On the contrary, her husband's adultery may be more "understandable" and tolerated in this social environment. Unless we can appeal to the ideals of equal entitlement and equal respect, we have no goods in terms of which to challenge such understandings of adultery.

For feminists, it may be less significant that a husband and his nonmarital lover consent to their adulterous sex (and that his wife knowing her place in this system of meanings tolerates her husband's sexual activities), than that the system itself is unfair to women. And it won't help to argue that what's really wrong here is that the wife really doesn't consent, for once we start second-guessing another's consent in these situations, then we are engaging in the kind of authoritative rereadings of another person's experience that Seidman seems to oppose. What's gone wrong here is Seidman's pragmatic apparatus itself: by privileging the standards of consent and responsibility, Seidman has depleted our vocabulary of the ideals we may need to invoke to contest sexual ideologies that socially disempower women and members of other stigmatized groups. While romanticist and libertarian ways of life may command our appreciation, sexist and racist ones may not command the same degree of respect. We need, therefore, to avoid the sort of pragmatic reductionism that Seidman proposes, as it leads ultimately, in Taylor's words, to an ethics of inarticulacy, and also to an insufficiently critical sexual politics.

To show that Seidman's problems are not limited to adultery, let me consider a somewhat more controversial sexual issue. Seidman supports his pragmatic sexual ethic by arguing that it explains our concerns about cross-generational sex. He claims that our intolerance for sexual activity between adults and children stems from our belief that children are too vulnerable to adult sexual authority, and too insufficiently knowledgeable about sex to give genuine consent.[42] Yet, while children are not sufficiently knowledgeable about what foods to eat, and are vulnerable to adult authority in these matters, we do not believe that children should either abstain from eating, abstain from eating with adults, or abstain from eating what adults want them to. We do not believe that children should entirely avoid adult eating habits because we believe this would be bad for them. Similarly, if we believed that abstaining from sex (with adults or other children) was bad for children, we would probably not be concerned to obtain their consent in order to impose it on them.

In this regard, consider the following example. Mothers who breast-feed their children and parents who circumcise their infant sons in the U.S. are generally not concerned with whether their children are capable of giving consent to these activities. For they assume that human breast milk and circumcised penises are beneficial, and per-haps even required, for normal human development or—in the case of circumcision—the development of a particular ethnic identity. In short, our concern with adult/child sex is primarily based upon our evaluation of the safety and benefits of sexual activity for children, and not upon our opposition to either the coercion of children or paternalism toward children.

Though many American parents are happily paternalistic toward their children, Seidman's emphasis on the importance of consent sug-gests that paternalistic interference is a problem where children are concerned. Here he invokes the basically liberal idea that we should not define the good, but allow each person as much as possible the freedom to realize the good as s/he sees it. He then states that the con-cept of consent "compels us to view acts in relation to the meanings of those engaged in the acts."[43] However because he is unsure that children will be able to define the good in sexual matters, he regards them as incompetent to give consent, and regards our perception of this incompetence as underlying our unwillingness to have adults force sex upon them. But, as I stated above, it is not the incompetence of children to give genuine consent but our belief in the likelihood of their being physically and psychologically harmed by sexual activity with adults that underlies our perception that children are exploited in sexual activity with adults. By invoking consent to articulate our concerns about adult/child sex, Seidman "compels us to view acts in relation to the meanings" that liberals give those acts, and thus actu-ally obscures many of the meanings that parents give to adult/child sexual activity.

Had Seidman applied his standard of responsibility here, and assessed the consequences of adult/child sex from the point of view of many American parents, he might be better able to articulate our concerns about adult/child sex. To fully articulate these concerns we may also need to appeal to ideals of care and nurture, to the ideal of protecting the weak against the strong, to ideals of childhood innocence, to some ideal of mature sexual desire, and perhaps some other ideals. These ideals too stem from "forms of life that moral agents have created." Yet even articulating how adult/child sex infringes all of these ideals is not sufficient to yield nonparochial judgments about this practice.

It is not sufficient in moral analysis to merely articulate our concerns in ways that are satisfying to us—to "capture our intuitions" as moral theorists often say, as if these intuitions were culturally neutral.[44] To avoid ethnocentrism and authoritarianism, we need to understand the ways our ideals may distort the realities of others. Regarding adult/child sex, we should also attempt to recover the ideals and beliefs of adults who seek children (usually adolescents) as sexual partners, and also of adolescents who have engaged in cross-generational sex, both in our own society and elsewhere. By this I mean we should consult not the solitary adults who unreflectively have sexual contact with a child, but communities of adults (and adolescents) who tolerate and support adult/child sex.[45] We should consult these communities because the ideals and beliefs that form the background to social action and that condition both the perceived and actual consequences of social action, are inter-subjective not subjective meanings, as Taylor has emphasized. By recovering the self-descriptions of those who believe in adult/child sex, we critically reconsider the dominant ideologies that are used to stigmatize this practice, as well as the sexual practices of others. In brief, we should not condemn or approve adult/child sex from the "high ground" of consent and responsibility, but attempt to understand it by recovering the background of self-descriptions both of adults who provide primary care for children and oppose it, and of adults and adolescents who tolerate and support adult/child sex. Once we have done this, we are in a better position to make judgments about the superiority or inferiority of this practice.

3

Fetal Ideologies and Maternal Desires: A Post-Enlightenment Account of Abortion

Excavating the Abortion Controversy

Feminism is characteristically conceived in terms of a politics of equal entitlement: whatever men are entitled to, so are women. Nowhere has this feminist politics of entitlement more vehemently played itself out than in the conflict over abortion in the U.S. Thus we hear that if men have a right to pursue sexual pleasure, then women should have the same right. Or we hear that if a society guarantees to all a right to privacy, to bodily sovereignty, or even to be selfish with one's property, then it must grant these same rights to women: in short, it must grant women the right of reproductive choice.

Recently, many theorists, including some feminists, have become dissatisfied with rights-based approaches to abortion. Some theorists are challenging not only the particular liberal and libertarian notions of equality, privacy, and autonomy on which some abortion defenses turn,[1] but the Enlightenment concept of individual rights itself. For example, Mary Poovey argues that individual rights are

> a dead end for supporting abortion on demand for two reasons: first, because the appeal to individual rights *in the absence of* an interrogation of the metaphysical assumptions behind the idea of rights leads almost inevitably to a proliferation of those considered to have rights—in other words, to a defense of fetal personhood; second, because appeals to this metaphysics obscure the fact that both the metaphysics and legal persons are always imbricated in a system of social relations, which, given the existence of social differences, are also inevitably politicized.[2]

Historically, Poovey's first point is quite accurate: from the moment doctrines about the rights of "man" were articulated, feminists like Mary Wollstonecraft and slaves like Toussaint L'Ouverture claimed individual rights for women and African slaves. Indeed, the idiom of rights became quite powerful for affirming the personhood of women and slaves, that is, for finding within our cultural definitions of these subjects a basic core of distinctly human qualities upon which rights are predicated.

As we have seen in the pro-life movement, the idiom of rights has become an extremely powerful one for articulating our cultural notions regarding the distinctly human qualities of fetuses and, thus, for grounding claims to their protection. Fetuses are said to be potentially capable of reason, of sentience, of language acquisition, even if they do not already possess these qualities.[3] Can feminists who have celebrated the expansion of the legal and moral category of "person" to women and other oppressed subjects now consistently narrow the category to exclude fetuses? Or, a question that Poovey's second point raises, can feminists who have drawn our attention to the socially constructed nature of the categories of "person" or "woman," now insist on objectively drawing the line of the former at fetuses? And if we accept or argue for the naturalness of this line, how can we contest the supposed naturalness of particular definitions of gender? As Judith Butler has well demonstrated, freeing feminism of its Enlightenment metaphysics exposes many theoretical inconsistencies and obstacles for feminists.[4]

The defense of abortion in terms of rights not only leads feminists to theoretical inconsistencies, it also renders us unable to articulate the concerns we may have about abortion. For example, recognizing abortion as a woman's basic right makes it difficult for us to articulate our concerns about the abortions chosen by women because the fetuses they are carrying are female, or the abortions risked by women because they don't want to postpone or diminish their partners' sexual pleasure. For if it is a woman's fundamental moral right to choose abortion, then it will seem inappropriate to question her reasons.[5]

Though feminist theorists are beginning to appreciate the problems inherent in liberal rights-based defenses of abortion, we are also well aware that these defenses form the basis of the majority opinion handed down in *Roe v. Wade,* the Supreme Court decision that gave women some legal access to medically safe abortions. Thus, to challenge these defenses may be paramount to challenging legal access to abortion. Of course this need not be the case, if we can find other ways to argue for the constitutionality or moral necessity of some legal abortions. In searching, then, for other justificatory strategies, both to avoid individualist and absolutist liberal doctrines and to attempt abortion defenses that articulate the concerns women actually have about some abortions, we may want strategies that fit with our legal institutions as well.

To mobilize post-Enlightenment defenses of abortion, some theorists have begun to look at notions that our "enlightened" minds once dismissed as mere dogma and superstition—notions derived from traditions of religious worship. According to Elizabeth Mensch and Alan Freeman,

> The secular rights rationale of *Roe,* as adopted by feminists in the 1970s, was undeniably empowering in its affirmation of the capacity of women to take control of their own lives, to act as moral agents in the face of the conventional expectation that they passively accept preordained roles of dependency and self-abnegation. The language of rights, after all, is the language of membership in the moral community. Yet in its stark purity, the assertion of the unqualified right to individual autonomous choice as the foundation for moral and political thought ran counter to the religious traditions of most American women.[6]

Mensch and Freeman argue that the concerns many women have about abortion are not articulable in the secular, objectifying, and naturalist idioms constitutive of Enlightenment pictures of human rationality, but only in the ecclesiastical, subjective, supernaturalist idioms constitutive of pre-Enlightenment pictures of theistic faith.

Similarly, in her studies of pro-life and pro-choice women in Fargo, North Dakota, Faye Ginsburg discovered that the concerns and outlooks of both groups of women were often structured by commonly shared religious traditions.[7] And T. M. Scanlon summarizes well Ronald Dworkin's recent discussion of abortion as follows:

> we cannot account for the views of those on either side of the abortion debate if we suppose that individual rights and interests are the only moral values at stake. To explain what most people seem to believe we must recognize the existence of a further moral value . . . the intrinsic value or sacredness of human life.[8]

Dworkin argues that our notions about the sanctity of human life and what respect for it entail are essentially religious in character.[9] Yet it may be these notions that are insulted by abortions sought for trivial, weak, or misogynist reasons.[10]

Lawrence Tribe also has recently argued that casting the abortion debate in terms of a conflict of rights obscures the deeper values and concerns behind it.[11] This charge of obfuscation that Tribe and others have made against individual rights approaches to the abortion controversy has led to the formulation of what Nancy Davis refers to as the "iceberg hypothesis."[12] Initially pursued by Kristin Luker,[13] those who subscribe to the iceberg hypothesis see the struggle over access to abortion as indicative of deep cultural conflicts over a range of issues including, but not limited to, the personhood of the fetus. Nancy Davis summarizes and elaborates the iceberg hypothesis as follows:

> Abortion issues themselves are more perspicuously viewed as the tip of an iceberg which has many complex issues regarding female sexuality, procreation, the structure of the family, and (more generally) the meaning of life looming large and dark beneath the surface. Such issues are deeply archaeological—that is, they have many ideological, spiritual, and emotional layers—and so, when we argue about abortion, our disagreements express, and are in some important sense disputes about, many of these other issues.[14]

In short, on this view, disagreements about the meaning of abortion reflect disagreements not only about the meaning of fetal life but about the meaning of life itself and how it should be lived by women and others. Yet these larger philosophical disagreements implicit in disagreements over abortion are often overlooked by standard philosophical approaches to abortion.

For this reason, Davis argues that the iceberg hypothesis challenges standard philosophical approaches to abortion (and to ethics). Philosophers approach moral issues by reflectively resurrecting and reconstructing the logical presuppositions of opposing views, and then assessing these assumptions. Yet the philosopher's resurrections and reconstructions often fail to see what is culturally peculiar or idiosyncratic about the assumptions behind different views, and thus we often fail to expose further missing premises that might reveal their culturally idiosyncratic character. We often fail to expose what is culturally peculiar about the presuppositions we analyze because, as culturally shaped social actors ourselves, they may reflect our own cultural values. The iceberg hypothesis challenges us to take a more systematic approach to the archaeology of political and moral opinions. It challenges us to recover the moral understandings and descriptive vocabularies of multiple historical actors in the abortion dispute, and not just those of a few highly reflective philosophical natives. This approach requires, in short, not simply philosophical reflection and imagination, but social and historical analysis. Indeed, it is the latter that Luker, Ginsburg, Tribe, and Dworkin have set about to do.

The iceberg hypothesis calls for a pluralist and interpretive approach to ethics of the sort that has been developed by Charles Taylor, and of the sort that I have been elaborating and defending in this book. By taking this approach we do not treat our philosophical reflections as culturally detached pieces of wisdom (and thus we try to avoid ethno-centrism), and we gain the hope of overcoming the "inarticulacy" (to use Taylor's term) promoted by Enlightenment dogmas of rationality. In this chapter I will sketch out where such an approach to abortion might take us.

Women as Historical Actors

The iceberg hypothesis pushes us to look beyond questions of personhood and choice—insofar as they are conceived in terms of rights —as we reconstruct the beliefs that condition our and others' attitudes to abortion. For these questions, which have been the focus of our public and philosophical debates over abortion can obscure the deeper issues abortion raises for us. Indeed, by casting the abortion controversy as a debate between feminist liberals who support a woman's right to choose and conservative gender traditionalists who value fetal life, we obscure the deeper cultural principles behind each group's conferment of rights, and therefore behind their endorsement of liberal or conservative political agendas.

What is also obscured by this pre-iceberg characterization of the abortion debate is that, in American society, it is primarily a debate between women. According to Faye Ginsburg, while men have assumed positions of leadership in the pro-life movement, "Grassroots abortion activists on both sides of the issue are primarily white, middle-class, and female."[15] Similarly, Kristin Luker states:

> The abortion debate has become a debate among women, women with different values in the social world, different experiences of it, and different resources with which to cope with it. How the issue is framed, how people think about it, and, most importantly, where the passions come from are all related to the fact that the battlelines are increasingly drawn (and defended) by women.[16]

By noting the gender of the primary historic actors in this public controversy, Ginsburg and Luker both challenge the feminist assumption that the abortion controversy represents a power struggle between women and men—a struggle perhaps over the control of human fertility and sexual expression.[17] And by debunking this common assumption, we realize that whatever has polarized the debate over abortion, in the U.S., has polarized women. This realization should make some feminists less likely to desire a resolution of this debate by securing the complete victory of one side and the complete defeat of the other. Instead, we may want to seek a resolution through some process of depolarization.

That is, given this gendered picture of the parties in conflict, feminists will seek a final defeat of one side only if we can imagine that side as both politically immature and ultimately dominated by men. Of course, this is just what some feminists have managed to do, just as many anti-feminist women have managed to dismiss those of us who are pro-feminist by viewing our side as morally underdeveloped and as ultimately hostile to men. Ginsburg summarizes quite well the images we frequently conjure up of the "abortion other," and suggests an alternative to such conjurings. She states,

> Many feminists assume that anti-abortion activists are dupes of organized religion or conservative politicians, thus denying pro-life women the possibility of being active, rational members of society. On the other hand, some anti-abortion activists are convinced that pro-choice women are selfish and promiscuous, devoid of any moral concern. Each side, viewing the other as the personification of evil, renews itself through its vision of the opposition. A more fruitful approach recognizes women on both sides as social actors who respond to and reshape the ideological and material circumstances of their lives.[18]

In other words, a more promising approach recognizes that the opinions on each side are shaped by a relatively coherent set of values and particular life experiences. This approach requires that we do not uncritically privilege some women's voices as rational, competent, and autonomous, and discount others as irrational, passive, and dependent. By doing this we silence a subset of the female voices whose values, experiences, and passions (to echo Luker) have defined and shaped the debate over abortion.

Ginsburg's and Luker's reconceptualizations of the disputants in this controversy utilize an interpretive or hermeneutical critical framework. This framework instructs us to recover the inter-subjective meanings (to use Charles Taylor's term) constitutive of the contexts in which women make decisions about pregnancy, motherhood, sexuality, life and death. Moreover, this framework is an anti-reductionist or pluralist one in that it recognizes a diversity of sometimes incommensurable ideals that shape women's lives. In their work on abortion, Ginsburg and Luker[19] have both utilized this framework by talking to "pro-life" and "pro-choice" women.

Having both extensively interviewed "pro-life" and "pro-choice" women, Ginsburg and Luker each argue that the primary issue between women regarding abortion is the centrality and significance of biological motherhood in women's lives. According to Luker,

> women come to be pro-life and pro-choice activists as the end result of lives that center around different definitions of mother-

hood ... that motherhood is the most important and satisfying role open to a women, or that motherhood is only one of several roles, a burden when defined as the only role.[20]

According to Ginsburg, "pro-choice" activists tend to see abortion as a "safeguard" that insures a woman who takes on the roles or tasks of motherhood has consented to do so.[21] On this view, motherhood is not something one consents to merely by having sex, nor is it something to which she must consent in order to have sex. By contrast, for "pro-life" women, to treat motherhood as a role choice that a pregnant woman has, or that any woman has, is to devalue its importance in society. Ginsburg elaborates,

> Pro-life activists ... see abortion as a condensed symbol for the decline in the moral authority of motherhood and the attributes assigned to it in this culture. In Right-to-Life rhetoric, abortion epitomizes ... [the] devaluation of motherhood and caretaking; [the] loss of social guarantees that a woman with dependents will be supported ...[22]

Having placed conflicting beliefs about the optional nature of motherhood for women at the root of the abortion conflict, Ginsburg and Luker lead us to question why one set of women sees motherhood and thus abortion as a choice, and the other set sees neither as a choice. Ginsburg's and Luker's studies partly answer this question, but to answer this question more fully we need to consider cultural understandings of personhood as well as motherhood.

More specifically, Ginsburg's and Luker's studies give us some idea why these two groups of women take different sides on the optional nature of motherhood for women *as women,* but they do not explain why these groups take opposing sides on the optional nature of motherhood for *pregnant* women. To explain the former we need to appeal to different conceptions of what it means to be a woman. To explain the latter we need to appeal to different conceptions of what it means to be a woman carrying a fetus, (i.e., different conceptions of pregnancy and fetal life). I will briefly consider how Ginsburg's and Luker's studies explain different views on the optional nature of motherhood for women in terms of varying notions of femininity, and then consider how we might explain different views on the optional nature of motherhood for pregnant women in terms of varying notions of fetal life.

Motherhood and Gender

Both Ginsburg's and Luker's studies indicate that "pro-choice" women tend to see motherhood as one of many ways to be a woman, and as one among a number of ways that women can nurture or care for others. By balancing and coordinating different life possibilities, a woman can provide for herself and others, and contribute to her society materially, politically, artistically, spiritually, and so on. Consequently, "pro-choice" women see continuing an unwanted pregnancy not as a socially beneficial or altruistic sacrifice that a woman (or couple) can make, but as a decision that is likely to make it difficult for a woman to balance different life opportunities and to pursue economic and vocational security.

Moreover, in American society, when women enter motherhood unwillingly (and even willingly in many cases), they generally do not have the social resources to take on other roles, and sometimes not even the resources necessary to fulfill the role of mother adequately. Thus women who are mothers not only do not contribute much of what they are capable and desire, but such women generally increase their need to receive various forms of assistance from others (usually men). As income-dependants rather than income-generators, they render themselves more vulnerable to poverty and various forms of abuse by others (usually men).[23] Women as mothers must depend on help they receive from others because their children typically must depend upon them for the majority of their needs, and women receive little appreciation and material compensation from the U.S. government for meeting these needs.

By contrast, "pro-life" women see the nurturing of one's offspring and family as the primary way a woman contributes to society. Consequently, they view continuing an unwanted pregnancy as a worthy sacrifice a woman makes for the greater social good. Alternatively, the termination of an unwanted pregnancy is viewed by this group as a woman's avoidance of social responsibility—as her failure to meet the demands of a role assigned to her on the basis of her gender. Because all other roles are secondary, a woman's desire to avoid closing off other competing opportunities—e.g., for greater material security, professional accomplishment, and so on—cannot excuse her failure to rise to the demands of motherhood. Indeed, "pro-life" women hold that caring for human life cannot be traded off against material comfort or personal success. Women who fail to continue unwanted pregnancies make this trade-off, and thus demonstrate selfish and materialistic values.

Moreover, to legally sanction the practices that allow women to safely terminate their pregnancies is to sanction selfishness, materialism, and to socially devalue caring for others. It also diminishes social respect for those whose primary role is to provide nurturing through mothering and other noncommoditized forms of care-giving, (i.e., it diminishes social respect for women as women). In this way, legal abortion promotes the continued "loss of social guarantees that a woman with dependents will be supported," which compounds and intensifies the sacrifices women must make to continue their "unwanted" or unplanned pregnancies.[24]

To sum up then, one of the primary differences between "pro-choice" and "pro-life" women is that they see motherhood and the demands it imposes on women in very different terms. One group sees these demands as competing with a woman's other life opportunities, and as unreasonable, unfair, and sometimes unmanageable when imposed on a woman without her consent and without giving her needed social support. The other group sees the demands of motherhood as an essential part of a woman's social existence, and ones that a woman implicitly consents to take on when she gets married or has sex. Because she implicitly consents to meet these demands and because meeting them is the best way to be a woman, these demands are seen as reasonable and fair—and even manageable, if her heart is in the right place.

Having explored a larger piece of the abortion iceberg, we can now utilize the different understandings we have glimpsed of the relationship between motherhood and gender to explain why "pro-choice" advocates confer upon women a right of reproductive choice and why "pro-life" advocates confer upon fetuses a right to life. If we hold, with "pro-choice" women, that the demands of motherhood can unduly and unreasonably burden a woman and her capacity to balance different life options, then we are likely to hold that these demands should not be imposed on any woman without her consent—that is, reproduction should be a woman's choice rather than her unwilled destiny. Conversely, if we hold, with "pro-life" women, that the demands of motherhood are always reasonable and manageable for a sexually active and married (or marriageable) woman, then we are likely to hold that it is unreasonable and selfish of her not to respond to the needs of fetal humans who impose these demands, and not to value these lives.

At this point it might be tempting to try to resolve the controversy over abortion by bolstering one conception of motherhood and gender, and tearing apart the other. That is, our archeological undertakings need not lead us to greater respect and tolerance for the other, but may lead us back to our initial suspicion and contempt. We may, for example, try to represent the inter-subjective meanings that condition some women's attitudes to abortion as transculturally valid and "enlightened," and represent the inter-subjective meanings that condition other women's views as objectively invalid and "unenlightened." Yet, in doing this feminists run the risk of marginalizing diverse social voices and perspectives, in the way standard philosophical analyses do.[25]

Yet while we should not dismiss an entire system of beliefs and values wholesale, these systems are not incorrigible; that is, we need not commit ourselves to a simplistic relativism and evaluate each system of beliefs only in its own terms. Instead, by comparing these competing and in some ways incommensurable conceptions of motherhood and gender, we can see the distinct virtues and faults of each. We can see, that is, the ways that they each allow us to articulate our concerns and life experiences, and the ways that each distort some of our concerns and experiences. With "pro-life" women we might agree that caring for others is our most important social role—not just for women but for men as well.[26] But terminating a pregnancy does not necessarily mean we fail to live up to the demands of this role: instead, an abortion may make possible other opportunities for nurturing and caring. With "pro-choice" women we might agree that motherhood sometimes imposes unreasonable, unfair, and unmanageable burdens on women. But we can greatly lessen the extent to which it does this by committing more social resources to assist women and their children. By doing this we sanction the valuing of fetal human lives, as well as post-fetal human lives.

The "pro-life" view has the virtue for feminists that it allows us to articulate our admiration for care-giving work that occurs outside systems of capitalist production, e.g., for the work women do in their homes and communities. Feminists have often expressed discomfort with the social devaluation of the role of the homemaker, a historical phenomenon to which the feminist politics of entitlement has contributed. We make the distinction between working inside and outside the home, to underscore the idea that care-giving is work, but this does little to make it socially valued work. By stressing that a woman's or a man's greatest contribution to society may be the nurturing of others outside capitalist relations of production, the "pro-life" view redeems and valorizes the roles of homemaker and parent.

Moreover, the "pro-life" view makes it possible to articulate the concerns we have about some abortions. For perhaps by engaging in sexual activity we implicitly consent to face with dignity the outcome of this behavior. Thus we may question whether those who have abortions for trivial or misogynist reasons—e.g., because they do not like the sex of their fetus,[27] or because they want to enjoy uncontracepted intercourse without the ensuing demands of nurturance—have faced the undesired outcomes of their behavior with dignity.

Furthermore, the "pro-life" view is not as incoherent or inconsistent as some have charged. For example some argue that there is no way for "pro-lifers" to approve, without contradiction, abortions even in extreme cases like incest and rape. Yet if we take "pro-lifers" to hold that the demands of parenthood are reasonable and manageable for sexually active and married or marriageable people, then these demands may not be reasonably and compassionately imposed on all. Since rape and incest victims are not necessarily sexually active and married or marriageable, the demands of motherhood in these cases may be unreasonable and unmanageable ones. In short, these women, and these women only (for "pro-life" women), are not selfish or unreasonable not to value their fetuses.

I am less certain of the advantages the "pro-choice" view has for "pro-life" women, but that is only because I am not knowledgeable about the ways the "pro-life" view has proved inadequate for "pro-life" women. A friend of mine suggests that "pro-life" women may feel that fewer options exist for them than for other women they know, and they may experience deep conflicts with their gender role when they remain unmarried, childless, or when they are past child-bearing age. On these issues, the "pro-choice" view offers some distinct advantages.

The interpretive and pluralist ethics I am advocating does not require that "pro-choice" and "pro-life" women come to agree about certain things. We may see some advantages in each others' world views but that does not necessarily require that we give up our own. The ethics I am advocating does not aim to convince others to adopt one's own world view or opinions, but rather it aims to create the dialogue and mutual learning necessary for political compromise. The aim of an interpretive and pluralist ethics is to identify the clarity and distortion present in each view so that we can seek alternatives to the practices that are divisive and polarizing.

For example, rather than seek unconditional and absolute access to abortion, we should seek both conditional access to abortion and to minimize the need for abortion.[28] To create conditional access, or "windows" of access, to abortion we may want to rule out abortions of older fetuses. To do this we need to come up with coherent principles for defining these windows. In the next section where I discuss cross-cultural views of personhood, I will suggest some such principles. We may also want to adopt procedures that encourage women and couples to examine their reasons for an abortion,[29] though these procedures should not unduly burden people who are economically underprivileged. Since abortion is a medical procedure, perhaps the physicians performing them should discuss with their patients the moral and philosophical issues these procedures raise. Though physicians have been loath to do this with patients and would rather treat difficult questions of medical practice as routine medical procedure,[30] we need not submit to their professional distortions here.

To minimize the need for abortion we need both to minimize the number of unplanned pregnancies, and to maximize the conditions that make possible the continuation of some unplanned pregnancies. To accomplish the former we need to articulate the superiority of responsible sexual behavior on the part of men as well as women. This may involve articulating the moral concerns we have about non-procreative heterosexual intercourse between fertile individuals who do not practice contraception, but it may also involve creative social legislation. For example we may want to hold men more financially responsible for the pregnancies of their female sexual partners (even where paternity cannot be established) and, if the man is a minor, we may want to hold his parents financially responsible.[31]

Feminists are well aware of what is needed to maximize the conditions that would make some women welcome their unplanned pregnancies. The solutions we have proposed go on and on but our recommendations have not often been heeded. These include: state- and employer-subsidized child care, universal medical care, "wages for housework" (i.e., Social Security income, not welfare, for full-time and even part-time homemakers), flexible work hours and career ladders, and so on. That is, we need to reorganize American society in a way that reflects that we value children and the work of those who care for them. Perhaps "pro-choice" and "pro-life" women can work together to achieve this.

Four Authors in Search of a Resolution

According to Ginsburg,

> The procreation stories told by women on each side . . . offer two compelling yet incompatible interpretations for the place of women in America.
>
> By casting two interpretations of female lives against each other, the abortion debate masks their common roots in the problematic conditions faced by women living in a system in which wage labor and individual achievement are placed in conflict with reproduction, motherhood, and nurturance . . . In this sense, there is a tragic dimension to the polarization around the issue."[32]

As theorists begin to recognize this tragic dimension to the abortion controversy, some have begun to search for some sort of common ground between the parties to this dispute.[33] The hope is that, from this common ground, we can generate less divisive moral and legal approaches to abortion—that is, we may find a way to a compromise.

Elizabeth Mensch and Alan Freeman, two authors who entertain this hope, have attempted to find this ground in traditions of Christian theology that are more moderate than Roman Catholicism. Like

Ronald Dworkin, Mensch and Freeman find in these traditions the common notion that life is sacred, that it is a "gift from God."[34] They suggest that this essentially religious notion may be shared widely across the abortion divide, and thus may provide the common ground upon which less divisive polices can be fashioned—policies that would recognize the moral worth, though not personhood, of human fetuses.

Unlike Dworkin, Mensch and Freeman do not see the religious character and origins of the idea that life is sacred as rendering it unfit to guide public policy on abortion. That is, they do not fear that reflecting this idea in social policies and institutions will lead to the establishment of religion. Mensch and Freeman differ with Dworkin on this, because they endorse a post-Enlightenment approach to religion. This approach rejects the presumption "that theology be relegated to the status of irrational, supernatural, or backward."[35] According to Mensch and Freeman, "religion provides a counterforce to totalizing secular ideologies,"[36] and thus both have a legitimate role to play in public moral discourse. They conclude, in other words, that neither the secular ideologies of modern science, nor the religious ideologies of the premodern church, should be granted an ultimate claim to public authority in our postmodern society.[37]

Dworkin and Lawrence Tribe are two more authors in search of common ground upon which to reconcile the opposing sides in this controversy. Dworkin and Tribe find this common ground in a modified Enlightenment tradition of individual rights, instead of in moderate religion. But, while Dworkin's and Tribe's Enlightenment notions are modified to some degree by their acceptance of the iceberg hypothesis, neither appears to see how this hypothesis challenges their abstract defenses of liberal rights—how it challenges the cultural notions that form the basis for assignments of rights. And while both appear to recognize even the historical embeddedness of their liberal views, both appear to overestimate just how widely their particular liberal biases and philosophical intuitions are shared.[38] Thus, in searching for common ground, each attempts a resolution of the abortion dispute that completely vindicates the "pro-choice" side. For these reasons, I find the approach that Mensch and Freeman take to be theoretically more coherent, and to be more promising in terms of depolarizing the abortion debate.

Nevertheless, Mensch and Freeman also appear to overestimate just how widely their moderate Christian theology is shared. For example, they argue that "the starting point for a discussion about abortion ought to be the frank recognition that the issue is life or death. To abort a fetus is to kill, to prevent the realization of a human life."[39] On some secular conceptions of the fetus, a human fetus is no more a human life (or a potential human life) than is a human egg or sperm: in other words, that it is both living and human in origin does not make it more of a potential human being than any other piece of bodily tissue. From a biological science perspective, the notion of a potential human life has little meaning, since practically every body cell is a potential human life. And though I agree with Mensch and Freeman that such secular views of life should not have total authority, I would also contend that neither should religious ones.

Furthermore, it appears that in a number of societies around the world, not only is the personhood of the fetus in question, as it is in American society (and which Mensch and Freeman recognize), but its human origins, and thus its human-ness, are in question as well. That is, not all societies appear to believe that a fetus necessarily belongs to the same animal or metaphysical category as the woman carrying it.[40] Yet because Mensch and Freeman only consider American religious traditions, and not even a great variety of them, they fail to see the cultural peculiarities of their temperate Christian views about the beginnings of human life.

According to Lynn Morgan,

> The cross-cultural evidence reveals two culturally-constructed concepts used widely to divide the human life cycle continuum at its earliest stages: human-ness and personhood. In order to be granted status as a person, a fetus or neonate must first be recognized as a member of the human species. In some societies the decision to call a fetus "human" is not made until biological birth when the newborn's physical attributes can be assessed. Personhood, in contrast, is a socially-recognized moral status. Neonates may not be labeled as persons until social birth rites are performed, often several days or months after biological birth. Social birth gives the neonate a moral status and binds it securely to a social community. Biological and social birth are not recognized as separate events in Western societies, even though they structure the onset of personhood in many non-Western societies. The U.S. abortion debate thus replicates Western divisions of the life cycle, overlooking the fact that even the human developmental cycle is socially patterned.[41]

By taking for granted a particular cultural picture of the human life cycle, the abortion debate in the U.S. fails to appreciate the complex cultural factors that condition whether a being is recognized as having the moral status of a person and, thus, as having certain rights.[42] In short, Morgan concludes that "[i]n the United States, the abortion debate has been foreshortened by a culture-bound discourse on personhood."[43]

Below I shall consider some non-Western conceptions of the human life cycle, and then compare these with life cycle parsings that derive from Western religious and scientific traditions. I will then discuss the kind of compromises these different life cycle and fetal ideologies enable us to imagine on the issue of personhood, compromises that enable us to define windows of access to abortion where access hinges on some ideas about fetal development.

Life Cycle Stories

In analyzing the "pro-life" procreation stories she collected, Ginsburg notes that

> The right-to-life position rests, paradoxically, on a view of gender that is both essentialist and radically cultural: the category 'woman' is produced by but also disconnected from the female body ... female identity [is viewed] as an achievement gained through the acceptance of pregnancy and nurturance, rather than a biologically based ascription.[44]

Surprisingly, "pro-life" women seem to subscribe to the feminist idea that one is not born a "woman," rather one is made a "woman." Pro-life women seem not only to be both essentialists and social constructionists on the issue of gender, but their idea of gender appears to conflate the concepts of ascribed and achieved statuses. For pro-life women seem to treat the gender category "woman" both as an ascribed status—conferred automatically on the basis of body type (reflecting their biologically essentialist view of gender)—and as an achieved status—conferred only after someone assumes certain cultural or social roles.

The distinction between ascribed and achieved traits is an important one for understanding "pro-life" and "pro-choice" attitudes to personhood. Lynn Morgan claims that

> When viewed in cross-cultural perspective, the criteria for personhood are widely divergent: in one society personhood may be an ascribed status, conferred automatically when an infant is born alive or given a name; in another society the status may be achieved only through a very long, gradual process of socialization.[45]

In societies where personhood is achieved some period of time after biological birth, neonates and small children, as well as fetuses may not be recognized as persons. Some of the achievements necessary to acquire the status of person in different societies include linguistic fluency (and the manifestation of other culturally specific behaviors), readiness to handle particular productive chores, and merely reaching a particular age (which in many impoverished areas of the world is not a trivial achievement).[46]

The socially-constructed criteria for personhood in different societies are evident in a society's "social birth" rites and its "social death" rites: the things we do to mark the introduction and passing of a person. The former include naming rituals, "out-dooring" ceremonies, and the performance of some symbolically important bodily grooming such as hair-cutting, circumcision, or ear-piercing. The latter include mourning rituals and burial rites. Where the achievement of personhood, and thus social birth, occurs some time after biological birth (in some cases several days or months), neonates may be killed or allowed to die. In these cases their death will usually not be mourned and their bodies will not be buried.[47] According to Morgan, "an infant who dies before social birth has died before it was born."[48]

A neonate may be killed or neglected if it fails to satisfy one of the criteria for personhood. For example, a neonate that does not "exhibit the vigor, health, and affect of one destined to become a functioning member of the community" may be classified as a nonperson, and even possibly as a nonhuman animal, spirit, or ghost. If this sickly or deformed infant "does not die of its own accord, it may be neglected until it does die, or it may be killed."[49] To try to render what might seem culturally unfamiliar and grotesque more familiar and acceptable, Morgan emphasizes that such practices involve the death of an infant not deemed ready or qualified "to pass through the social birth canal . . . [and] be ceremoniously welcomed as a person into the community." Morgan also objects to using the term "infanticide" to describe these practices regarding neonates. Instead she suggest we use the term "post-partum abortion."[50] Like our practice of abortion, the postponement of social birth until well after biological birth, and the practice of killing neonates not ready or eligible for personhood, serves to regulate the investment parents make in their children, especially when reproduction is so risky.

Morgan argues that prior to the eruption of the contemporary abortion controversy in the U.S., "biological birth was the major moral dividing line along the life cycle continuum."[51] In other words, during earlier periods of our history, social birth coincided with biological birth. This meant that, at the moment of its separation from the mother's body (biological birth), the neonate in American society was automatically awarded the status of "person," and social birth rites, such as giving the infant a name, were automatically performed. Thus, in American society, then as now, the killing of any neonate would be considered unjustified murder (infanticide), though the neglect or killing of a fetus would not have been improper then.

The societal debate over abortion, the resulting Supreme Court decision in *Roe,* and possibly new fetal monitoring technology, has moved the social marker for personhood somewhere between biological birth and biological conception—at roughly "viability." Viability, of course, symbolizes not actual birth and separation from the maternal body, but the potential for biological birth, and thus the eligibility and readiness for social birth (personhood). That is, viability in this context means reaching a point of biological development capable of surviving separation from the maternal body, whereas biological birth means the actual occurrence of separation from the maternal body. By understanding the symbolic importance of biological birth and viability, we see that the cultural invention of a new life cycle stage "viability," and the concomitant separation of social and biological birth, is in many ways part of the same cultural logic. In short, we understand the dimensions of the societal change Morgan has observed.

Morgan suggests that biological events or states like biological birth and viability are "natural" social and moral dividing points for Westerners, because we tend to imbue biological events with great social significance. For example, in American society, some see the onset of menses as marking the onset of womanhood, and thus its cessation as threatening this status. Similarly, for some in American society, the beginning of a human life coincides precisely with the severing of the umbilical cord, the fertilization of the egg, or the implantation of the embryo in the womb. According to Morgan, "Many non-industrial societies, on the other hand, do not endow biological facts with the same degree of social importance."[52] In these societies, then, physiological events and states are less likely to become markers for the ascription of important moral categories.

As I argued above, Mensch and Freeman fail to notice the cultural peculiarities evident in our answers to the question "When does life begin?" In particular, they seem not to be aware of just how powerful biological events are for us, and how culturally distinctive this is. For example, after arguing that we ought to take advantage of the moral insights afforded by various religious traditions to resolve the conflict over abortion, Mensch and Freeman rightly recognize the notorious difficulties involved in using the biological notion of viability as the dividing line between persons and nonpersons, and thus as the line restricting access to abortion. Yet, rather than proposing a theological way of marking social birth, they suggest that we use the start of brain wave activity to mark the transition from nonperson to person.[53] Clearly the dominant religion in American society is neurobiology.

Nevertheless, there are religious ways of marking social birth: ensoulment is one such way. Indeed, people who believe in ensoulment believe that life is a gift from God, and thus a sacred gift—a notion

Mensch and Freeman suggest we make use of to guide our policies. The notion of ensoulment, like biological birth, represents another systematic way of dividing the human life cycle continuum for socially significant purposes. Some sects see ensoulment as coinciding with conception, but this is merely a biological reading of spiritual events. In other words, it is conceivable for ensoulment to take place at other points in the life cycle continuum, and perhaps theologians need to reconsider the doctrines which lead to particular biological interpretations.

Morgan acknowledges the variety of human possibilities for dividing the human life cycle continuum:

> Models of an individual life cycle, from the moment of conception to death and afterlife, are constructed differently from one society to the next. Societies divide the developmental cycle into segments, and mark transitions from one stage to the next by birthdays, marriage, parenthood, and religious rites of passage. Life cycle divisions are one way in which societies categorize their members.[54]

Morgan also emphasizes that though life cycle stages are socially constructed, they are constructed by groups of people in response to complex social, economic, and demographic factors. Thus they are not alterable by a few, albeit well-intentioned, social reformers, theologians and philosophers. In her words:

> The limits of personhood are not decided by individuals, but by the entire society acting on shared cultural beliefs and values. For this reason, personhood—the value placed on human life—is not a concept which will be altered by religious mandate, or by radical legislation by either the Right or the Left.[55]

This means that no individual can, even if she has good reasons, determine the best biological marker for personhood or ensoulment, or even human-ness. Yet we can look within our religious and secular traditions—particularly at the stories of human life they tell—to see if our contemporary biological readings of these significant social and spiritual transitions are the best ones.

Toward this end I would like to offer two life cycle stories that I learned growing up in the U.S. These are not event narratives, but rather distillations of the narrative principles that allow me to make sense of some events, or to make sense of how others make sense of some events. My hope is that by seeing the richness of each "meta-narrative" account, just as we saw the richness of "pro-life" and "pro-choice" accounts of motherhood, we may be able to create the understanding necessary for genuine compromise on the issue of restricted access to abortion.[56]

I will call one story "the fetal seedling account" and the other "the fetal gift account." A bumper sticker that I saw recently, which reads "It's a child not a choice," reminded me of these accounts. For, according to one story, a fetus and a child are quite dissimilar but, according to the other, they are essentially the same.

The fetal gift account holds that a human fetus is not merely the product of human or "natural" generation, but it is partly an artifact of divine or "supernatural" creation. What is most valuable about human beings, on this view, is that we alone, among all creations in the universe, were made to resemble a divine being who created us. Thus, unlike other divine creations, humans are equipped with an immaterial substance, spirit, or soul which is responsible for our ability to think, know and communicate eternal truths, and morally deliberate about issues such as abortion. This soul is present in the fetus from the moment the latter is biologically conceived, because a soul exists in all bodies that have human form, (i.e., which are genetically human). And because humans do not make the soul through biological (material) reproduction, the immaterial soul's presence in the body must come directly from its divine origins. In this way, the generation of a human fetus represents the divine production of new human life entrusted to human care—and as such is a divine gift.

As a gift from such a special source, it is an object with a special status—one that imposes weighty moral obligations. Moreover, given that the soul is responsible for the qualities we most value in a human being and the soul is present from the moment of conception, then the qualities we most value in a human being are present in the fetus, if only in some miniaturized or potential form. And, because the most valued qualities in a human being are seen as present in some form in a human fetus, a fetus is not much different from a child or an adult. Thus on the fetal gift view, the fetus is "a child not a choice": it is not the sort of thing whose continued existence should be a choice for another human being to make. Correspondingly, the pregnant women is a mother: motherhood is not "an option" for her.[57]

By contrast, the fetal seedling account holds that a human fetus is the result of the combination and germination of two seeds, an egg and a sperm. To grow into a mature human organism, this seedling needs abundant human care and attention. Moreover, it needs good soil, water, and a suitable climate. Indeed, the qualities we most value in the mature human organism are the result of proper and wise care and grooming, good nutrition, and a fortunate human environment. A human seedling deprived of these things may hardly be recognizable as human, such as the "wild child" in Truffaut's movie of the same name.

On this view, a human being is primarily the result of human labor rather than of supernatural conception. And the more human labor invested in it, the more likely it will possess the human qualities we value. This means, though, that the qualities we most admire in a human being are not present in the raw material, that is, the unnurtured seedling-fetus. Furthermore, since seedlings require abundant human attention and material resources in order to develop the human qualities we value, and since both are limited, we may need to thin out and pluck some seedlings to insure that others mature properly. However, plucking seeds that have managed to germinate is not a great loss (though it involves some loss), because the unnurtured fetus-seedling has few if any of the properties of the mature organism. Significantly, this is much less true of a semi-mature child or a mature human adult. Indeed, even with a small investment of labor we so anthropomorphize the raw material that it acquires considerable value for us. Therefore an older fetus, having been subjected to the human care that the continued pregnancy provides can have a much greater value than a younger fetus on this view. In short, while an older fetus may resemble a child, a young fetus is quite dissimilar to a child, and thus the elimination of the young fetus is a viable choice.

By taking an interpretive-pluralist-iceberg approach to abortion, we try to explain the conflict over abortion in the terms that groups of people use to explain it to themselves. Moreover we do not privilege one set of terms over others. Without privileging either the terms derived from traditions of religious worship or those derived from traditions of secular science, we can now explain the conflict over abortion as a conflict, in part, between those who accept a fetal seedling view of the human life cycle and those who accept a fetal gift view. In doing this, we better understand why some women are "pro-life" in all cases of abortion, and why some women are "pro-choice" regarding some abortions.

Those who adhere to the fetal seedling view are pro-choice regarding early abortions, not because they are anti-life generally or anti-fetal life, but because they do not regard immature fetal life as life that has been transformed into a human life. Therefore it is not life that must be preserved at virtually any cost. On other matters, however, many fetal seedling adherents are strongly "pro-life." For, as much as anyone, they value and want to protect human lives—lives that have been transformed and made human by other humans. By contrast, women and others who adhere to the fetal gift view are pro-life about abortion, not because they are anti-choice generally or against choices for women, but because no one should be given the choice to kill a child, which is how they view a human fetus. Yet on many other issues, fetal gift adherents are strongly "pro-choice." Indeed, fetal gift adherents who have liberal political leanings are more likely than anyone to value freedom from government interference in the economic choices of private businesses and individuals, in parents' choices regarding their children, and husbands' choices regarding their wives.

From these two accounts, we understand why, on the fetal gift view, anyone who injures or endangers the life of a fetus—of any age—is a potential murderer. For this person commits a grave moral offense against both the fetus's divine parent and the fetus itself. Potential murderers can include both the pregnant woman and her doctor. By contrast, on the fetal seedling view, a woman who injures, or threatens the continued existence of her young fetus, or a doctor who does so with her permission, neither commits an offense against anyone nor harms anything of precious value. The woman and her doctor do not even violate the parental rights of the male progenitor of the seedling, because the immature fetus has not been transformed into a human being either through a woman's or man's labor.

Moreover, from these two accounts, we see that fetal gift proponents treat "human-ness," or more exactly, "human being-ness" (the category of things which represent new or distinct human lives) as an ascribed status, one conferred upon the determination that something is the genetic offspring of humans. By contrast, fetal seedling proponents treat "human being-ness" as an achieved status, one conferred after some process of material and social maturation. Thus, for fetal seedling adherents, the conferment of "human being-ness" does not coincide with the onset of genetic reproduction, as it does for fetal gift adherents.

Rather, for fetal-seedling adherents, the achievement of "human being-ness" is likely to coincide with some socially meaningful maturation stage. This stage might be described in a neurological idiom, such as the stage marked by the onset of brain activity. Or it might be described in a phenomenological idiom such as "quickening," the stage when a pregnant woman can sense the fetus's movements or when the fetus communicates its motion to the maternal body. Whatever idiom is used will in some way be a function of how transition to the stage is monitored—with the maternal body itself, with a machine for registering brain waves, with a test for determining chromosomal composition, with a device for sonograph imaging, or perhaps with any procedure that allows for an assignment of the fetus's sex. But however the transition to this stage is marked, in contemporary American society, the achievement of "human being-ness" seems to occur some time before biological birth.

If having the status of a human being is the primary criterion for personhood in American society, then it may be useful to think about different life cycle stories and how each marks the introduction of a new and distinct human life. Those who see the transition to "human being-ness" as coinciding with the onset of genetic reproduction—the creation of a fertilized egg—may want to reexamine their theological traditions to see if this is the best biological reading of divine creation. Those who see the transition to "human being-ness" as coinciding with the onset of some stage of neurological, kinesthetic, or structural development may want to examine the ways their traditions of knowledge have rendered the everyday experiences of pregnancy meaningful. In the end, nevertheless, we are unlikely to agree on a single conceptual schema for dividing the human life cycle continuum. And, heeding Morgan's advice, we should not try to force agreement through religious or scientific mandates.

But the point of reflecting on our own and others' interpretive practices is not to secure agreement. The question really is, do we see enough richness in our and others' views to fashion a political compromise? More specifically, can we generate a political compromise on how our conceptions of fetal development should be used to restrict abortion? To imagine possible compromises, we need to see some good in each view.

The fetal gift view has the advantage in that it marks off human society as an especially valuable part of the world. While we may value other species, the fetal gift view gives us a coherent reason for valuing members of our own species more. Of course, some—such as those who oppose "speciesism" and hold some "enlightened" notion that all categories of things have equal worth—may not like this consequence. Yet without some way to make distinctions of value among things, we end up with the problem that care ethicists have—of having no principles to make responsible decisions about who and what to value. The fetal gift view teaches us that there is something divine, something sacred, about all human beings.

The fetal seedling view has the advantage in that it does not arbitrarily invest the onset of genetic reproduction with singular importance. This view recognizes that, while being a human being has something to do with having the form of a human being, an entity does not necessarily have that form at the onset of genetic reproduction. That is, this account seems to recognize that the acquisition of the special status of "human being-ness" needs to be coordinated with how pregnancy is experienced and monitored by other human beings, rather than some arbitrary moment in a reproductive continuum.

By resurrecting the good in each account, we may want to accept with the fetal gift adherents that human beings are sacred, but hold with the fetal seedling adherents that being recognized as a human being is an achieved status. If we do this, then we can define our window of access to abortion in terms of the achievement of the special status of "human being-ness." Now, of course, the difficulty lies in determining what stage of pregnancy marks this achievement. I propose that we consider quickening as the stage that symbolically represents this achievement, in part because the monitoring required to judge its onset occurs outside of the bureaucratic institutional structure of modern medicine. Also the onset of this stage does not fluctuate with changes in machine monitoring devices. In saying this, I do not mean to reflect sentiments that are anti-machine or anti-technology, but rather qualitative judgments that regard the maternal body as the superior device for monitoring important stages of pregnancy. Furthermore, the notion of "quickening" neither privileges the notions of modern science nor those of Christianity. Finally, in the everyday experiences of pregnancy that many women in American society share, quickening marks the beginning of the maternal monitoring of one's offspring that continues for life.[58]

To accept this political compromise does not require that fetal gift and fetal seedling adherents give up their distinct views of the human life cycle continuum. That is, it does not require that we legislate a particular view of human life stages. It merely requires we see enough validity in the views of others to respect the need for compromise. This particular compromise reflects our willingness to make some abortions accessible to fetal seedling adherents while at the same time acknowledging that, for fetal gift adherents, this constitutes the failure of society to adequately protect children. Yet, by compromising, we acknowledge the cultural diversity in American society regarding the meaning of pregnancy and its termination.

Morgan ends her article on abortion with the following reflections:

> How can the range of cultural variability discussed here affect the U.S. abortion policy debates? In spite of the relativist stance presented here, I will not argue that Americans should weigh the merits of post-partum abortion—that would be ignoring a fundamental U.S. cultural reality which gave us the term "infanticide". Nonetheless Americans have felt forced to construct convoluted philosophical justifications for their positions on these issues, even when contorted logic theoretically could be avoided by admitting the existence and relevance of cultural variation.[59]

My aim in this chapter has not only been to pierce through some of the contorted logic that the abortion debate in American society has produced, but also to imagine the new policy options that the appreciation of cultural variation affords. In doing this I hope to steer feminists and others to a more promising path for defusing the abortion debate and other conflicts as well.

4

Feminism and Sexuality

Toward a Radically Cultural and Historical Politics of Sexuality

The interpretive and pluralist ethics that I have been elaborating opens feminist moral debates to diverse cultural voices, including those of women who may not identify themselves as feminists, but whose lives are affected by the policies we advocate. This post-Enlightenment approach allows us to see that our reasons for dismissing these voices are as ideological as the voices we are dismissing. Faye Ginsburg's study of "pro-life" and "pro-choice" women is a pioneering feminist work in this regard, for it is one of the first to genuinely utilize this idea.[1] By adopting this approach, she is able to show that what is at stake in our societal controversy over abortion is neither the validity of a set of eternal moral truths that some women possess, nor the inherent virtue or lack of virtue in particular actions that some women take. What is at stake are continued commitments to historically shaped ideals and lifeways that different groups of women have inherited. It is by uncovering these ideals that we can develop the contours of sustainable political compromises on the practice of abortion. For by making this compromise on abortion, we allow the incommensurable voices of women to be heard together and to determine the shape of our political compromises; we do not treat one voice as objective and one as ideological.

Ginsburg's work on abortion provides a general model for future feminist critical examinations of our own accounts of female sexual liberation and equality. One set of issues that is currently provoking some feminist activists to rethink existing codifications of feminist sexual politics pertains to the moral status of minority sexual orientations. In the U.S. and elsewhere, there exist minority sexual orientations that tolerate playful sexual violence, cross-generational sex, sex devoid of all personal attachment (e.g., bathhouse sex), and mercenary sex, such as prostitution ("pay per sex act") or pornography ("pay per graphic view mass media sexuality"). These sexual customs or "tastes" have drawn considerable feminist attention and moral criticism. Yet some of this criticism has been advanced without much social analysis of the behaviors criticized. More specifically, the criticisms often ignore that these sexual customs are widely regarded as gendered and classed in ways that contribute to and perpetuate the stigmatization of social minorities such as gays and lesbians, women of color, and working-class women. Given the cultural associations that exist between particular sexual customs and particular sexualized, raced, classed, and gendered social groups, feminist moral analyses of these diverse sexualities run the danger of contributing to existing societal hostilities toward marginalized social groups. This danger is one that any program for a feminist sexual politics needs to consider.

Gayle Rubin has argued that feminist criticisms of the practices of particular erotic minorities generally assume an essentialist picture of human sexuality—a picture of human sexuality framed in terms of various biological or psychological universals. This picture, though, ignores much recent scholarship on human sexuality, especially recent writing on gay and lesbian history. Historians writing on the gay and lesbian past have significantly advanced our understanding of how our own sexual categories and concepts have been shaped by historical and cultural forces, and thus their work seriously challenges essentialist models of sexuality.[2] Rubin argues that such work can be beneficial for feminist theory, for conceiving sexuality as a human rather than naturally given product ultimately leads to a more fruitful and liberatory feminist sexual politics. According to Rubin,

> Once sex is understood in terms of social analysis and historical understanding, a more realistic politics of sex becomes possible. One may then think of sexual politics in terms of such phenomena as populations, neighborhoods, settlement patterns, migration, urban conflict, epidemiology, and police technology. These are more fruitful categories of thought than the more traditional ones of sin, disease, neurosis, pathology, decadence, pollution, or the decline and fall of empires.[3]

Rubin contends that moral and political analyses of sexual behavior that remain tied to ahistorical models of human sexuality can uncritically perpetuate social norms that serve to oppress erotic dissidents. Rubin especially singles out the feminist anti-pornography movement here for critical feminist self-examination. According to Rubin, the anti-porn rhetoric and

> anti-S/M discourse developed in the women's movement . . . easily
> become a vehicle for a moral witch hunt. It provides a ready-made
> defenseless target population.[4]

Rubin argues that a moral or sexual witch hunt against particular sexual nonconformists is not only unlikely to help women, it can serve reactionary political purposes. And not surprisingly, Rubin notes, "Feminist rhetoric has a distressing tendency to reappear in reactionary contexts."[5]

In this chapter I will argue that an interpretive and pluralist approach to diverse sexualities can provide the kind of social contextualization needed to eliminate the reactionary and repressive aspects of our feminist accounts of sexual politics. For rather than pathologize, medicalize, biologize, or psychologize human sexuality, interpretive accounts try to understand sexual practices in the terms that those who participate in them understand them. These are not the terms, though, of an allegedly value-neutral socio-scientific discourse that Rubin's passage above seems to favor—the statistical terms of epidemiological or migration studies, or the terms of urban sociology or population dynamics—though these may be important too. For the terms of these scientific discourses allow for only "thin" and not "thick" descriptions of human behavior, to use Geertz's and Ryle's terminology.

Rubin appears to prefer thinner descriptions of social analysis, for she is suspicious that accounts that seek the meanings of sexual behavior have political motives similar to accounts that seek their physiological causes. According to Rubin, interpretive accounts often lead to

> an accusation that sexual dissidents have not paid close enough
> attention to the meaning, sources, or historical construction of their
> sexuality. This emphasis on meaning appears to function in much
> the same way that the question of etiology has functioned in discus-
> sions of homosexuality. That is, homosexuality, sadomasochism,
> prostitution, or boy-love are taken to be mysterious and problem-
> atic in some way that more respectable sexualities are not.[6]

Rubin argues that when we search for the cause or meaning of some sexual behavior, we are typically in search of some way to gain control of behavior that our accounts problematize. In short, she claims that etiological and interpretive accounts generally have unliberatory aims and effects.

But the thin or thinner descriptions of human sexual behavior that Rubin prefers do not show how our sexual concepts and categories themselves are products of historical and cultural forces. For these thinner descriptions do not pay attention to other people's constructions of their behavior, and to our constructions of their constructions, to echo Geertz. Thus they do not contribute to the project of showing how sexuality and our discourses about it are socially produced—a project that Rubin thinks has so powerfully undermined biologically essentialist approaches to sexuality.

Nevertheless, Rubin's criticism of interpretive accounts of sexuality contains an important caution: such accounts need to problematize their own problematization of particular sexual customs. In other words, they need to try to see how their selection of behaviors for interpretive analysis itself reflects social and cultural forces. For we can not and should not claim that our interpretive accounts stand outside these forces. Yet to heed Rubin's warning and show more critical awareness of the forces that motivate our accounts of sexuality, we need not give up the project of interpretation. Instead, we should develop interpretive accounts of more "respectable sexualities"—such as heterosexuality, middle-class marital sexuality, or male sexuality—as well as more stigmatized ones. For like some sexual dissidents, most sexual conformists have not paid enough attention to the social and cultural origins of their sexuality. Moreover, if we fail to show the cultural origins of socially mainstream sexualities, and focus our accounts exclusively on socially marginal sexualities, then we will contribute to the further marginalization of sexual minorities, as Rubin fears.

At the risk of appearing to contribute to the social marginalization of others, in this chapter and the next two, I will try to develop an interpretive account of sexual prostitution, one of Rubin's less respectable sexualities. For though prostitution is not fully respectable, some forms of it reflect or imitate mainstream sexualities in ways that are of concern to feminists. And one reason for this is that, while prostitutes are marginal figures in many societies, their clients are usually not. It is the client's sexuality and its social origins that I would like to focus on. The issue of prostitution especially interests me because societal controversies over mercenary sex have been especially polarizing for feminists, which has not been so true of other sexual issues, such as the general controversy over abortion.[7] Thus prostitution creates conflicts between women who espouse similar political values. As feminists, we should have some interest in trying to resolve these conflicts. Surprisingly though, prostitution has received far less attention from feminists than the issue of pornography, which has been equally polarizing, as Rubin's discussion of it demonstrates. Thus I am interested in exploring prostitution, not so much to make up for this lack, but because the sides in this debate, due to lack of attention, may be less concretized. In sum, unlike pornography and abortion, prostitution may provide an issue where existing and entrenched polarizing discourses can be more readily defused.

Prostitution and Progressive Public Policy

The degree to which feminists are divided on the issue of prostitution is substantial. Feminist theorists and activists disagree about the social origins and effects of prostitution and, consequently, about its social meaning and moral status. More specifically, some see prostitution as a profound symbol for the degradation and domination of women, whereas others see prostitution as merely unconventional and sometimes demeaning work that nonetheless women should be allowed to choose.[8] On the former view, the prostitute is the quintessential victim of patriarchy and, on the latter, she is merely a working woman who, like numerous other women, is engaged in marginal, sexist, and low-status work.

There is a surprising twist, though, in feminist debates over prostitution that is absent from debates over pornography or abortion, and which may account for its lack of attention from feminists. Those who hold opposing moral views on pornography or abortion typically hold opposing views on whether and to what degree the government should regulate these customs, though as some have pointed out this need not be the case.[9] Yet feminists who hold vastly divergent views on the morality and meaning of prostitution do not typically hold opposing views about the government's regulation and prohibition of prostitution. More specifically, while feminists disagree over what prostitution symbolizes, feminists on both sides of this debate for the most part agree that the legal and political instruments available to control prostitution are problematic. In general, feminists who entertain the hope of eliminating sex commerce, and those who do not, all favor removing existing legal prohibitions against it.

Feminists generally agree on policy questions regarding prostitution because laws that prohibit or regulate prostitution generally place the burden of responsibility for prostitution on women. Thus their enforcement usually enhances rather than reduces the oppressive aspects of prostitution for women. Though the laws regulating or criminalizing prostitution could conceivably be reformed to redistribute blame, many feminists believe that solutions to prostitution should not involve punitive state power, but a redistribution of social and economic opportunities.[10] For the criminal prohibition or regulation of prostitution does little to change the conditions of women's lives that lead them to prostitution. In addition, prostitution, unlike abortion and pornography, does not appear to involve significant harm to innocent third parties, though it may be a social nuisance.

Without denying the nuisance factor, most feminists also oppose less punitive systems of social regulation that have been designed to minimize the potential public annoyances created by prostitution. Feminists who oppose prostitution on moral grounds, and who oppose socially regulated prostitution, claim that social regulation institutionalizes inequality.[11] Those who see prostitution as legitimate but stigmatizing work tend to oppose nonpunitive legal systems of social regulation, because such systems are primarily used not to protect the prostitute, but to limit her rights.[12] Thus, though these systems are not generally punitive toward the clients of prostitutes, they are punitive in more subtle ways toward prostitutes.

In accepting neither the legal prohibition nor the social regulation of prostitution, feminists implicitly give support to a policy of complete decriminalization. This policy has been explicitly endorsed by some mainstream feminist political organizations and some less conventional feminist organizations, such as prostitute advocate groups.[13] While the policy of decriminalization tolerates some regulation of sex commerce, the regulations usually proposed are limited to the minimum necessary to prevent business fraud or coercion. Thus, those who support decriminalization are ultimately proposing the sort of minimal regulation on industry that even Milton Friedman would approve. Feminists who support decriminalization typically hold that the state should not treat commerce in sex as a special sort of industry requiring a special regulatory apparatus to protect consumers, workers, or state and community interests.

These liberal to libertarian feminist demands for decriminalized prostitution are motivated by concerns similar to those underlying calls for decriminalized gambling. Liberals argue that while we may disagree about the harmfulness of gambling or prostitution to those who engage in it, we agree that they are only an annoyance to everyone else. They are, so to speak, "victimless crimes." Moreover, liberals contend that, while using punitive or regulatory state power may abate the annoyances gambling and prostitution create for others, the use of such power can intensify the self-harms inflicted from gambling and prostitution, or create imbalances in their distribution.

Nevertheless, the policy of decriminalization has some significant pitfalls for feminists. For, as we have seen in regard to numerous industries, decriminalization with minimal regulation can lead to the creation of large-scale, nongovernmental, profit-oriented enterprises that have a power of their own to inflict harm on and manipulate human beings. Because of this danger, as Roger Matthews has argued, "decriminalization is not as radical as it might first appear."[14] Acknowledging the general ineffectiveness of, and pernicious practices created by, liberal regulationism in Britain, Matthews contends nevertheless that

> decriminalization is unlikely to reduce the overall level of exploita-
> tion of prostitutes but rather to increase it. For as Elizabeth Wilson
> has pointed out 'wholesale decriminalization would simply mean a
> free for all for men' . . . and would undoubtedly encourage large
> financial and business interests pursuing the vast profits potentially
> available through the extensive commercialization of prostitution.[15]

In this passage Matthews argues that a policy of decriminalization—
meaning the absence of any special regulatory apparatus—would create a laissez-faire climate for capitalist sex commerce. In such a
climate there would be few legal guidelines to curtail how profits are
drawn from this trade. Since access to the bodies and sexual services
of women would be the primary "merchandise" traded, such a climate
would leave women vulnerable to extreme capitalist exploitation.

Given the dangers inherent in decriminalization, especially for
female laborers, Matthews argues that we need to develop a policy of
socialist or "radical regulationism" that differs from the traditional
liberal and conservative policies that have been tried.[16] Such regulationism would differ from previous ones, Matthews states, in that

> it would not necessarily be preoccupied with the public and visible
> aspects of female prostitution, nor with the elevation of expediency
> over justice, nor with denying that the mobilization of legal sanc-
> tions is based on moral concerns. And in opposition to the brand
> of regulationism currently being developed by the New Right it is
> not based exclusively upon traditional religious moralities which
> object to prostitution on the grounds that it is 'dirty', that it is a
> nuisance which interferes with the 'normal' processes of reproduc-
> tion . . . Left regulationism would also, unlike other variations, see
> prostitution as a social and historical, and therefore, transformable
> product, rather than a 'natural' or trans-historical entity.[17]

In short, such regulationism would not be concerned with making
prostitution safe for men and society at the expense of some women.
It would also not essentialize the women who work as prostitutes or
the activity in which they are engaged, and thus it avoids one of the
problems that Rubin notes in some radical and feminist critiques of
prostitution.

Unfortunately, Matthews ends his discussion, "[w]ithout entering
into the specific details of legislation."[18] Yet he does offer us some
general principles to guide future legislation regarding prostitution.
They are:

> a) a clear commitment to general deterrence; b) the reduction of
> annoyance, harassment and disturbance; c) protection from coer-

cion and exploitation; and d) the reduction of the commercializa-tion of prostitution.[19]

Let me very briefly summarize the main direction in which each of these principles is intended to take us. To achieve deterrence—the aim of Matthews's first principle—Matthews argues that we need to be aware of the social values that generate the demand for prostitution as well as the supply. More specifically, he states

> The critical role of legislation of this type is to question and poten-tially undermine the widely-held male expectation that women and/or young men ought to be purchasable to service their sexual desires and fantasies.[20]

Legislation premised on Matthews's second principle—containing a potential public nuisance—should, according to Matthews, aim at the offender's offense rather than at her or his person or character. It should also respect all disputants equally, including the prostitute, her business partners and clients, and non-participating third parties. Matthews claims that legislation premised on his third principle—pun-ishing coercion or exploitation—should neither assume the complete passivity nor the complete autonomy of the prostitute. Rather, it might treat the prostitute in relation to her business and non-business part-ners somewhat like the law treats a wife in relation to her husband. But in doing this, our legal institutions need to find more complex ways of distinguishing genuinely abusive and exploitative partners from more benign ones. Finally, to reduce the commercialization of prostitution—the aim of Matthews's fourth principle—Matthews states that we need to reconsider laws that give legitimacy to "the brothel" as the primary site for prostitution, because brothel systems organize prostitutional labor and commerce in ways that lead to the isolation and disempowerment of the prostitute.

In summarizing the potential outcomes of these recommendations, Matthews states:

> The combined effect of concentration and restructuring these four areas of legislation would be ultimately to reduce the level of exploitation and coercion directed towards women—particularly those who are most vulnerable—and ultimately reduce the inci-dence and profitability of prostitution.[21]

Also Matthews's proposals, if realized, would reduce the harassment some women face not only from their partners but also from our legal institutions. For these reasons, Matthews's proposals and defense of them indicate that women are better off under a policy of regulationism rather than decriminalization when, and only when, the regulations imposed are informed by a progressive politics.

Because of the dangers inherent in laissez-faire prostitution that Matthews has well described, I support his call for radical regulationism, instead of the liberal and libertarian feminist calls for decriminalization. I also believe his work goes a long way toward defining the basic goals and form of this new kind of regulatory apparatus. In the hope of promoting the kinds of legal restructuring that Matthews has outlined, in this chapter and the following two, I will explore some issues that might afford us a more specific picture of what radical, socialist and also feminist regulationism might look like.

In particular, regarding Matthews's first guideline, I will explore the social origins of the widely held male expectation that the sexual services of women and others should be commoditized for their benefit. Identifying these origins may help us understand better how to deter prostitution in the U.S. and elsewhere. But I will also question whether this cultural expectation guides all forms of prostitution, and whether it is the only significant cultural assumption guiding prostitution wherever it occurs. An answer to these questions will tell us whether we should always seek to deter prostitution in any social context, as Matthews's principle seems to suggest.

Unfortunately, in proposing this legal guideline, Matthews does not appear to be treating prostitution as a transformable, historical product, but as a "natural," trans-historical phenomenon that always needs to be suppressed. That is, he appears to be treating prostitution in the essentialist ways that he rejects and Rubin criticizes. In this way, Matthews's call for an interpretive analysis of the demand for prostitution does indeed have the potentially repressive and reactionary motives that Rubin fears. To genuinely treat prostitution as a transformable, historical product, we need to explore how commerce in sex is and has been transformed by different historical and cultural settings, and then examine whether in all such settings it is something we would want to deter. It is only by questioning the appropriateness of deterrence that we call into question our own socially and historically shaped motives in theorizing about prostitution, as Rubin rightly recommends we should. In short, before we utilize social analysis to develop legal avenues for deterring prostitution, as Matthews proposes, we need to utilize social analysis to determine whether it is something that we should always seek to control. This question will be the primary concern of the following chapter.

Matthews's second guideline is less problematic and more fully worked out. To apply it we need to insure, as Matthew indicates, that the prostitute's civil rights and liberties are respected. And respecting her rights means that any charges against her should be subject to strict standards of proof, which means that police testimony should not be sufficient to establish that a crime has occurred. The application of this guideline will require changes in specific legal statutes, but rather than address the needed changes, I will defer to better-trained legal specialists.

In regard to Matthews's third principle, I support his suggestion that the law treat the prostitute's relationship with her associates (pimps, husbands, and boyfriends) as a "private" matter, so long as we recognize how the private sphere is structured by constraints on the public one—that is, that the division between them is actually quite blurred. However, Matthews's analogy between the prostitute and the wife here is a helpful one. Just as the state may need to intervene to protect wives and children from the criminal behaviors of their husbands, the state should intervene to protect the prostitute from the criminal behaviors of her partners. Here again, I will leave the specific details of carrying out this proposal to others better equipped to do it.

Matthews's fourth guideline is somewhat more problematic than the previous two, for, like the first guideline, it is not so fully fleshed out. Here Matthews tells us that we should rethink the regulated brothel system as the accepted means for containing large-scale business interests that might otherwise gain control of this industry. But he does not offer us another regulatory model for controlling how profits are to made through sex commerce. Because of his silence on this, I will attempt to enter some specific details of an alternative regulatory system in a subsequent chapter. The system I will propose will attempt to address the concerns that Matthews and others have raised about brothel systems. For the system I will propose is motivated by the concerns of feminist activists and prostitute activists, and will involve their continued collaboration.

Are Good Girls to Bad Girls as Feminists are to Nonfeminists?

Both Ginsburg and Luker argue, as we saw, that the abortion debate in American society is better represented as a conflict between women rather than one between women and men. While the dispute over sex for pay in American society has involved numerous social reformers, it too is best represented as a conflict between women, many of whom, but not all, see themselves as feminists. Most recently, the dispute over prostitution has heated up between numerous feminist political leaders and numerous feminist civil rights advocates for prostitutes, many of whom are prostitutes or former prostitutes.[22] To gain voice in this debate, the latter group has had to cast off the common stereotypes applied to them—of brainwashed, irrational, and helpless, fallen women—stereotypes that the former group has promoted. Likewise, the former group has had to contend with a derogatory image of itself promoted by the latter group. For prostitute advocates often regard feminist leaders as prudish, bourgeois, and hypocritical women, who maintain a punitive sexual politics that only serves to reinforce an anti-feminist social division of women into good girls and bad girls, and even feminists and nonfeminists.

Though feminist leaders and prostitute advocates do not necessarily vilify each other as abortion opponents do, they each see the other as fundamentally misguided, and thus in somewhat patronizing terms. Following Ginsburg, I maintain that a more fruitful approach to prostitution should recognize the intellectual coherence and independence of the views of both feminist leaders and prostitute advocates regarding prostitution. Such an approach will not view prostitute advocates as necessarily unreflective and uncritical about the sexist and patriarchal values of contemporary, capitalist societies. Nor will it view feminist leaders as necessarily naive about human sexuality or oblivious to their class biases. Instead, this approach will explore the ideological and cultural differences that may exist between these two groups, and seek to frame a compromise based on this understanding.

To explore these differences, we need to have a better idea of the cultural and social identities of the sides in this debate. Significantly, the division between women on the issue of prostitution does not divide neatly into feminist political leaders and feminist prostitute advocates, just as it does not divide into women who see themselves as feminists and those who do not. For some prostitute advocates, many of whom are former prostitutes, oppose prostitution, and some feminist spokespersons seem to want to tolerate it. How then shall we describe the opposing sides in this debate?

Steven Seidman's distinction between sexual romanticists and sexual libertarians may be helpful here. As with the issue of adultery, his distinction provides a useful and accurate characterization of some of the beliefs and values that divide women over the issue of sex for pay in American society. Sexual romanticists are likely to see commercial sexuality as evidence of the violent and dehumanizing character of social relations—as society's corruption of some natural and more pure sexuality. These are the feminists who see prostitution as evidence of the dehumanization and devaluation of women.[23] Alternatively, sexual libertarians are likely to see commercial sexuality as one of many legitimate forms of sexual expression—one that may carry some risks, but risks we have a right to assume. These are the feminists who subsume prostitution under the category of work, and treat the occupation as just one more pink collar ghetto. The sexual romanticist/libertarian dichotomy cuts across the feminist/prostitute spokesperson dichotomy. For the romanticist camp includes radical, Marxist, and socialist feminist leaders, as well as the prostitute advocates who formed the organization WHISPER (Women Hurt in Systems of Prostitution Engaged in Revolt).[24] The libertarian camp includes liberal feminist intellectuals, as well as the prostitute advocates who formed the group COYOTE (Call Off Your Old Tired Ethics), among others.[25]

Barbara Meil Hobson notes some of the odd, crisscrossing divisions between women on the issue of prostitution, and she also notes that no large and organized feminist campaign to reform or abolish existing prostitution laws has developed (unlike the legal reform movements regarding pornography and rape).[26] She then speculatively attributes the latter state of affairs to the former. If she is right about the causes of the striking feminist inertia on the practical political questions of prostitution, then we need to depolarize this issue so that our policy proposals might lead to the formation of a broad feminist coalition. Certainly the existing punitive legal prohibitions in the U.S., and sexist liberal regulationism that exists in Europe and elsewhere should be pretty intolerable to all feminists, "good girls" and "bad girls" alike.

In subsequent chapters I will attempt to elaborate and justify some policy proposals that I hope will begin the coalition-building required to secure the needed reform of our current prostitutions laws. My proposals and their justification will be drawn from some interpretive analyses I will offer regarding the social origins of the demand for prostitution in the U.S. and elsewhere. But before I sketch out these interpretations, I will examine existing feminist accounts of the origins of prostitution and try to expose their weaknesses.

Feminist Origin Stories[27]

In preparing the groundwork for the moral and political analysis of prostitution, feminist theorists have tried to develop a single account of the origins and social evolution of prostitution—that is, a general account of how prostitution arises in any society. Presumably if the social forces that give rise to prostitution are morally problematic, then so too is the resulting social practice itself. Alternatively, if prostitution has morally unproblematic origins, then its moral character needs to be reevaluated accordingly.

Two origin stories have predominated in the feminist literature regarding prostitution. One has been offered by sexual romanticist, socialist feminists who argue that prostitution is caused by capitalism and patriarchy. The other has been offered by sexual libertarian, but basically liberal, feminists who argue that prostitution is caused by a "natural" human desire for unlimited sexual gratification.[28] Yet these social evolutionary tales, and the moral analyses they support, suffer from a lack of cultural and historical contextualization.

Christine Overall offers a relatively recent version of the socialist feminist origin story.[29] According to Overall, "sex work is an inherently unequal practice defined by the intersection of capitalism and patriarchy."[30] One obstacle that socialist feminist accounts of prostitution need to negotiate is that numerous forms of labor can be traced to the rise of patriarchal capitalist societies and the social inequalities that evolve in them. Thus, we must either object to all of these labor forms or show that prostitution is more morally objectionable than other apparently similar kinds of work. Overall faces this obstacle, and attempts to meet it by offering a new way to configure the contrast between prostitution and other occupations that appear to derive from the economic and social inequalities of capitalist patriarchy.[31]

She begins by identifying occupations other than prostitution that reflect, and thus may be produced by, the gendered division of labor maintained by patriarchal capitalism. She does this by considering low-status work where women are usually placed in subordinate roles vis-à-vis men: for example, housework, clerical work, nursing, and child care. Overall then compares prostitution with these other jobs and finds that

> sex work differs in a crucial way from other forms of women's labor . . . While cooking, nursing, and child care need not necessarily be commoditized, sex work is by definition the commoditization of sex. What is essential to prostitution is not sexual activity itself but the buying of sexual activity.[32]

Presumably, cooking, nursing, and child care, even when conceived as work, can be performed in ongoing social relationships where they are exchanged in kind, on a reciprocal basis. That is, these kinds of work can exist independently of capitalist and patriarchal social relations. Yet sex, when conceived as work, according to Overall, cannot be exchanged on a nonmonetary or noncommoditized basis. For when sex is exchanged on a nonmonetary or noncommoditized basis, Overall claims it is not "sex work" but "a sexual event or relationship that does not involve service for the sake of material gain."[33] By contrast, when cooking, nursing, and child care are exchanged on a nonmonetary or noncommoditized basis they are still work—they do not become a "cooking event" or "cooking relationship," or a "nursing event" and so on. Thus, unlike "housework" or "child work," to treat sex as work is to treat it as a commodity, i.e., something that is exchanged outside ongoing social relationships in order to maximize material gain.

For Overall, then, sex work cannot exist independently of capitalist and patriarchal social relations for it essentially involves the commoditization of sex or, more specifically, the commoditization of the sexuality of gendered and classed individuals. According to Overall, "Prostitution is a classist, ageist, racist, and sexist industry, in which the disadvantaged sell services to those who are more privileged."[34] In sex work, the sex buyer is always more socially privileged by class, age, race, or gender than the sex seller, according to Overall. For this reason she claims that prostitution is not "reversible": it has no "value independent of the conditions of sexual and economic inequality under which it is performed."[35] That is, sex *qua* work has value only when it is performed by socially defined inferiors for their socially defined superiors. It has no value or purpose when it is performed by men for women, whites for blacks, middle class people for working-class people, adults for children, or even women for women, men for men, etc.

By contrast, Overall argues that other forms of nurturing and domestic work, which currently place women in subordinate roles vis-à-vis men, are "reversible":

> That is, there is nothing in the nature of the work itself, insofar as we can separate it from its working conditions, that would prevent it from being performed by men for men, by women for women, or, most significantly, by men for women. Moreover, the labor of office workers, sales clerks, cooks, cleaners, and child care workers has a value independent of the conditions of sexual and economic inequality under which it is done, and much of it would still be socially necessary in a postcapitalist, postpatriarchal world.[36]

But sex work would be socially unnecessary "in a postcapitalist, postpatriarchal world," for it has little or no value when it is not part of a commoditized transaction between a member of a socially privileged class and a member of a socially underprivileged class.

While Overall's analysis of prostitution isolates many disturbing features of sex work in American society, it fails as an account of sex work in many other societies, even other patriarchal capitalist ones. Yet Overall intends her analysis to apply to all patriarchal capitalist societies. In this regard, there is a fundamental contradiction in her account. For on the one hand, she claims to be looking at prostitution only within patriarchal capitalist contexts and to be isolating the attributes it has in those contexts—attributes that are likely to be contextually contingent. On the other hand, because she sees prostitution as caused by the transcultural forces of capitalism and patriarchy, she treats many aspects of prostitution within these contexts as essential attributes—applying to all contexts—rather than as contextually contingent attributes.

Moreover, because Overall sees capitalism and patriarchy as social systems that together create the necessary conditions for sex work, she sees all patriarchal capitalist contexts as essentially alike with respect to sex work. Yet by considering sex work in a range of patriarchal capitalist societies (especially nonindustrial, non-Western ones), we see that the social contexts that shape its meaning are interestingly distinct.

For example, Overall rightly points out that much sex work in patriarchal capitalist societies involves customers privileged by gender, race, class, and age (e.g., adult, bourgeois and/or First World, white males) and prostitutes socially disadvantaged by all of the same factors (adolescent, working-class and/or Third World, women of color). However, her analysis oversimplifies the dynamics of social privilege as it pertains to the reversibility of sex work across patriarchal capitalist contexts. For Overall overlooks the existence of patriarchal and capitalist postcolonial contexts where sex work involves customers who are disadvantaged by gender but socially privileged by race and class (First World, bourgeois white women) and prostitutes who are privileged by gender but disadvantaged by race and class (Third World, proletarian men of color).[37] If prostitution were an "inherently unequal practice defined by the intersection of capitalism and patriarchy," then this case would be impossible.

Similarly, Overall ignores patriarchal capitalist colonial contexts where sex work involves primarily men and women of the same economic, race, and age classes: e.g., customers who belong to an indigenous, dislocated, and impoverished colonial adult male labor force and prostitutes who belong to the same indigenous and impoverished, colonized adult population.[38] In the latter case, the economically disadvantaged are selling sexual services to the economically disadvantaged, which would be impossible if prostitution were inherently classist (in an economic sense). Moreover, in some instances in these contexts, the economically more advantaged are selling sexual services to the economically more disadvantaged. For example, in describing prostitution in colonial Nairobi, Luise White states,

> prostitutes were not proletarians. Malaya prostitutes were petty-bourgeois women who actively controlled profit-generating enterprises—the sale of sexuality, the sale of domestic skills, the rental of rooms, or all three—for which they provided the labor.[39]

Like small-scale capitalists, these prostitutes charged more for their wares than it cost to produce them. By contrast, their customers were proletarian men, whose only source of income was the exchange of their labor for wages.

One basic error in Overall's account, then, is that while commerce in sex in most industrial Western societies may be sexist, racist, classist, and ageist, it is not inherently or essentially sexist, racist, classist, and ageist in all cultural contexts. Indeed, without examining prostitution in a greater variety of cultural contexts than Overall has done, she has no grounds to claim it is inherently or essentially anything. Though Overall attempts to avoid essentialism by specifying the contextual parameters of her account, she treats these parameters as the universal causes of prostitution and not as principles for assessing its social meaning. Unfortunately, such causal accounts have an internal logic that begets "insights" into the essence or nature of an activity—one presumably given to it through and in the act of genesis. Furthermore, if capitalism and patriarchy are the causes of prostitution, then Overall's analysis implies that sex commerce should not occur in social contexts where capitalism and patriarchy are absent, and thus her analysis applies beyond the parameters she has specified.

Another error in Overall's account pertains to her claim that sex work differs from other kinds of work in that to treat sex as work is to treat it as a commodity. Overall's claim assumes that sex cannot be constituted as work when it is exchanged on a noncommoditized basis, whereas cooking, for example, can be constituted as work even when it is exchanged on a personal basis. However, when services other than sex are exchanged on a noncommoditized basis then, like sex, they may cease to be culturally regarded as "services" or work. For example, though cooking in the context of a noncommoditized exchange may not be treated as an "event" or a "relationship," it may be conceived as a recreation, an entertainment, or an "interest" rather than "work." Conversely, though sexual activity in the context of an ongoing social relationship may in most circumstances be culturally constituted as a social event or recreation, in some cases it may be culturally constituted as a service or as work without being commoditized. For example, White claims that in colonial Nairobi, "customers [of prostitutes] occasionally became boyfriends or even husbands."[40] Presumably in such cases sexual activity occurs in the context of ongoing social relationships whose purpose is not primarily individual material gain, and yet at the same time it is culturally constituted as "work" or a "service" from which each individual profits.

Therefore, the cultural constitution of sex as work, and thus prostitution as an occupation, need not depend on capitalist forms of exchange, as Overall's account implies.[41] As White states,

> prostitution is a capitalist social relationship not because capital-
> ism causes prostitution by commoditizing sexual relations but
> because wage labor is a unique feature of capitalism: capitalism
> commoditized labor.[42]

In part, this means that capitalism shapes sex work into commoditized forms of labor and exchange rather than causing sex to be constituted as a category of labor. Whether sexual activity is work in one
context and a social event or recreation in another is not a function of
universal forces that distort or preserve the essence of sexual activity.
Instead it is a function of culturally specific principles that shape the
social contexts in which sexual activity takes place.

In addition, Overall fails to distinguish a monetary exchange from
a commoditized exchange. Yet an exchange can be a monetary one
without necessarily being a commoditized one, as for example when
money is exchanged as gift between family members or friends. When
a prostitute's client becomes a boyfriend or a husband, then sexual
activity may still occur as part of a monetary exchange in this context
but not as a commoditized exchange. Similarly, when a wife and husband participate in a system of exchange in which the wife receives
money and her sexual activity is culturally construed as a service to
her husband, the wife's receipt of money is not part of a commodity
exchange but a monetary gift exchange. This is a gift rather than a
commodity exchange because the wife's services are not traded impersonally with just any buyer to maximize profit.[43] Whether the wife in
this context is a "sex worker" or a "prostitute" I will leave to the
reader's cultural imagination, but her labor is neither commoditized
nor dependent upon capitalist social relations.

In seeking, like Overall, to improve the socialist feminist account of
prostitution, we should develop a socially contextualized and comparative account. This account should not seek the universal causes of sex
work, and it should not presuppose the universal meaning of sex.
Instead, our account should seek to understand how the nature and
meaning of particular sexual behaviors vary in relation to different cultural contexts. It should also acknowledge the fiction of treating prostitution as an isolable phenomenon possessing a single transcultural
meaning. Moreover our account should recognize that while the meaning of sex work in American society is determined by sexist, classist,
and racist ideologies, in other contexts its meaning may be determined
by dominant social ideologies that are not sexist, classist, and racist at
all, or at least not in the same way as ours. Furthermore, it should not
dismiss the possibility of sex work occurring in a "postcapitalist, postpatriarchal world" (or a prepatriarchal, precapitalist world), even

though the social definition, justification, and significance of this labor form would be quite different from outwardly similar labor forms in the U.S. The upshot is that, with a socially contextualized and comparative account of prostitution and sex, a socialist feminist need not treat sex work as a special, and more egregious, case of capitalist exploitation—despite our own cultural sensibilities.

Overall speculates that because the topic of prostitution is so divisive for feminists, feminists have written little on it (compared with, for example, the issues of pornography or rape).[44] Yet, while feminist moral and political theorists have given sexual commerce less attention than the topics of sexual representation and sexual assault, a number of feminist historians have recently completed some richly detailed histories of sexual commerce and the various laws enacted to control it.[45] Thus the potential divisiveness of this issue has not stalled all feminist investigations of prostitution. Moreover, because of these new histories of prostitution, a socially contextualized and comparative moral analysis of prostitution is now feasible. Finally, while Overall has rightly attended to the voices of prostitute women in some industrialized societies in formulating her analysis, by utilizing these new histories we can open the debate on prostitution to prostitute women from other kinds of societies as well. I will consider some of this recent historical work on prostitution in the next chapter. Yet, before turning to this, I will summarize another powerful "totalizing" feminist origin myth regarding prostitution, one told by liberal and libertarian feminists. This account also reveals the need for comparative studies of prostitution.

Liberal and libertarian feminists argue that prostitution originates in the pre- or amoral realm of nature: i.e., in our presumed "natural" and unlimited need for sexual gratification—usually of the heterosexual variety. Liberals also assume that the economy in which the satisfaction of sexual need occurs mirrors our more general economic situation: though needs are unlimited, the resources for satisfying them are scarce.[46] Since liberals construct heterosexual intercourse as a natural, and therefore normal, human need, though access to it is limited, liberals believe that one must find ways to satisfy this need under both comfortable and impoverished circumstances. On this view, prostitution represents merely a commercialized form of sexual need satisfaction that occurs under the inevitable condition of scarcity in our sexual economy.[47] Moreover, though liberals recognize that the services and products which are commercially available are often inferior to those that are "homemade" or "handmade," they assume that it is better to alleviate a need with an inferior product than to leave it unsatisfied. Thus Janet Richards, the "sceptical feminist," comments,

> What, then, have we got against the prostitute? It is said that people who go in for sex without love are missing a lot. That may be true, but it provides not the slightest argument for never having it without love. You might just as well say that because the pleasantest way to eat was with friends at dinner parties, no one should eat in any other circumstances.[48]

In short, just as we cannot go without eating when we are without the kind of company that renders our meals pleasant, it does not seem rational to liberals to go without sex when we are without the kind of company that renders it loving, unique, or possibly magical.

Lars Ericsson also employs an analogy between sex and food in his comment,

> We must liberate ourselves from those mental fossils which prevent us from looking upon sex and sexuality with the same naturalness as upon our cravings for food and drink. And, contrary to popular belief, we may have something to learn from prostitution in this respect, namely, that coition resembles nourishment in that if it cannot be obtained in any other way it can always be bought. And bought meals are not always the worst.[49]

Ericsson's remark shows that, in rationalizing the use of commercial, and thus impersonally exchanged, products and services, liberals tend to fetishize the qualities of commercial, as well as noncommercial, ones. For example, David Richards states,

> some patrons are able to achieve with prostitutes the natural and fulfilling expression of sexual tastes and fantasies that they cannot indulge in their marriages or central personal relationships. It is a species of dogmatism to assert that these people do not in this way more rationally advance their ends; to the contrary, the use of prostitutes is all *too* rational. Of course, in using prostitutes, a person does not cultivate the higher capacities of sensitivity, taste, and testing that the romantic love tradition celebrates.[50]

In short, liberal and libertarian feminists see commerce in sex as the inevitable expression of a natural and unlimited human appetite for (heterosexual) sex in an economy of sexual scarcity, and thus they see it as rational and potentially beneficial to human beings.

Moreover, in this view, though the resources for meeting our sexual appetites are generally scarce, they can become even more scarce when sexual activity is socially repressed as a result, in part, of rigid and sexist gender roles.[51] The social repression of sexual activity both increases the demand for commercially mobilized sexual resources, while it demeans their use. And in a sexually repressive society, women—who predominantly provide the resources for alleviating sexual needs—will find their sexual services to be commodities in great demand. Yet in a situation where sexual expression is repressed, women who exploit the market for their sexual services will be degraded and demeaned. What is responsible for the degradation of women in these circumstances, according to liberal feminists, are unenlightened attitudes or "mental fossils" (to echo Ericsson) that distort our view of sexuality and gender. According to Janet Richards,

> there is quite enough degradation in the *surrounding circumstances* to account for women's being degraded, without having to resort to the idea that there is something bad about unsanctioned or commercially available sex . . .
> It seems to be sex alone which has the ability to degrade unless it is purified by the proper sanctions; if no longer of marriage, then at least of love.[52]

Richards argues that the attitudes to sex that are reflected in its ability to degrade derive from the rationally unjustifiable and often patriarchal dogmas of religion, which feminists ought to reject. Thus Richards suggests that feminists should strive to eliminate gender-based sexual repression rather than sexual commerce. According to Richards,

> In fact it seems in keeping with some feminist ideas to think that when in the liberated future a man wants sex and his woman doesn't, she will pack him off to a prostitute to pay for the pleasure he was hoping to get free from her.[53]

The truly liberated woman and feminist, in the liberal view, is liberated from the constraints of the repressive social customs that are ultimately responsible for the degradation of commercial sexual activity. Thus the truly liberated and rational feminist is one that can regard prostitutional sex "as an ordinary business transaction," as Alison Jaggar states in her depiction of this liberal mentality.[54] Moreover, from this liberal perspective, the women who participate in these business transactions are pursuing their own rational self-interest for, as Richards's comment observes, they get paid for what other women give away for free—or almost free.

Ericsson echoes Richards's vision of the future feminist society. He claims that because of the irrational, biological character of the impulse for sex, prostitution will exist until all persons are granted sexual access upon demand to all other persons. Since we are unlikely to create, or want to live in, a society where anyone can have sex on demand from anyone else, we should reconcile ourselves to the existence of commercial sex.[55] And if our future society is a feminist one—where there is both limited private sexual access and social equality between women and men—Ericsson predicts that

> the degree of female frustration that exists today . . . will no longer be tolerated, rationalized, or sublimated, but channeled into a demand for inter alia, mercenary sex.[56]

Thus while Janet Richards is ready to pack men off to prostitutes in the future liberated feminist society, Lars Ericsson hopes to send women off to commercial sex providers.

Unfortunately, the liberal and libertarian feminist origin myth for prostitution relies upon ignoring cultural and historical diversity with regard to sexual norms, and especially cultural diversity regarding perceptions of human sexual needs. Moreover, this origin story ignores diversity within our own society, by treating sexual behaviors and attitudes more characteristic of men as the norm for women as well. If the assumptions behind this account of prostitution were true, then we could not explain societies like the Grand Valley Dani, where healthy married adults go without sex for many years and do not seem particularly concerned about it.[57] In short, the liberal theoretical tool that hypothesizes a state of nature, where individual needs and appetites are free of cultural and social intervention, is of dubious worth when analyzing social institutions. For the analytic separation of a human (social) world from a natural (individual) world represents a murky distinction at best. There is always a tendency for such theories to see the "natural" as what is culturally familiar, and the "unnatural" as what is culturally foreign. At least it is incumbent upon theorists who presume to know what is "natural" to indicate the culturally neutral sources of this knowledge.

Though the assumption that sexual desires are unlimited while the resources for satisfying them are scarce is quite questionable, it is one that is implicit in the dominant political and sexual discourses of American society. By contrast, the belief that capitalism and patriarchy are dehumanizing forms of social organization does not frame these discourses. Since the former belief represents a cultural principle that defines prostitution and rationalizes its existence for members of American society, when I examine prostitution in this context, I will consider how it shapes its meaning. Before I turn to this, however, I will look at some studies of similar behavioral forms elsewhere. These studies will help to illuminate how the prostitute and her work are constructed in other social contexts and, by contrast, in the U.S. as well. Moreover, by constructing a comparative account of prostitution, we will be better able to assess its desirability.

5

Comparing Prostitutions

Totalizing and Particularizing Narratives about Sex Work

A number of feminist accounts of prostitution begin with the question reflected in the title of Christine Overall's recent paper: What's wrong with it?[1] Perhaps our accounts of prostitution would serve less the reactionary ends Gayle Rubin has noted, if we began them with a question Alison Jaggar raises: What is it?[2] For this question recognizes that defining prostitution requires a defense of particular analytical tools, and that mounting this defense is not a trivial task. As Jaggar states,

> the disagreement on what constitutes prostitution is merely a surface manifestation of a disagreement over the fundamental categories to be used in describing social activities and over what are the important features of social life which need to be picked out.[3]

Before we can define prostitution then, we need to resolve numerous questions regarding how best to analyze social phenomena: as Jaggar states, we need to have "a comprehensive social philosophy."[4]

I have argued that the framework of a critical but nonethnocentric comprehensive social philosophy should be an interpretive one. To accept this framework is to accept the idea that understanding human practices requires that they be "thickly" described, in Geertz's sense: that is, that they are seen in relation to the categories that organize social relations in the societies where these activities occur. In this way, interpretive accounts of human practices and institutions do not treat them as the inevitable expressions of transcultural forces, but as artifacts created and transformed in different historical and cultural settings.

To treat prostitution as an historically transformed and transformable product, we should not attempt to provide a single, unitary, evolutionary description of it, as many previous socialist and liberal feminist accounts do. Instead we need to interpret behavioral forms that, though they occur in different social contexts, are interestingly similar. Though our interpretations may show that these comparable behavioral forms reflect incommensurable beliefs and values, by comparing them with one another we appreciate the distinctive virtues and disadvantages of each.

In this chapter I will attempt such a comparative analysis of prostitution by evaluating and comparing monetary exchanges involving sexual behavior in four quite different social contexts. By doing this, I hope to uncover some of the inter-subjective meanings constitutive of these transactions in their respective contexts. To construct this comparative account of prostitution, I have relied entirely on the ethnographic and historical accounts of other scholars. Nevertheless, to derive my interpretations, I often have had to read against the grain of their reports, especially when the descriptive tools employed appear to be in conflict with the data being reported. This is somewhat problematic since I am rereading these texts without first-hand knowledge of the data. However, the challenges of rereading need not become serious obstacles to projects of the sort I am undertaking, if we do not loose sight of the primary goal of interpretation. This goal is not to provide true, distortion-free readings, but readings that critically inform our judgments and practices. Any serious distortions that I introduce will, I hope, be corrected by others who have more familiarity with the historical and ethnographic sources I discuss.

Sex Commerce in Ancient Babylon

Women have participated in relatively impersonal, nonmarital sexual activities where some type of material recompense is expected in a variety of historical and cultural contexts. The Greek historian, Herodotus, provides an account of such activity among the ancient Babylonians:

> Every woman born in the country must once in her life go and sit down in the precinct of Venus [Mylitta], and there consort with a stranger ... A woman who has once taken her seat is not allowed to return home till one of the strangers throws a silver coin into her lap, and takes her with him beyond the holy ground ... The silver coin may be of any size ... The woman goes with the first man who throws her money, and rejects no one.[5]

According to Gerda Lerner, the impersonal sexual transactions described by Herodotus were part of a religious ritual whose basis "was the belief that fertility of the land and of people depended on the celebration of the sexual power of the fertility goddess."[6] These celebrations appear to have involved actual and symbolic sexual acts between strangers, usually resulting in a donation to the temple by the male temple patrons and participants in these acts.

Emma Goldman offers a similar explanation of these sexual transactions by attributing to the ancient Babylonians a belief that "the generative activity of human beings possessed a mysterious and sacred influence in promoting the fertility of Nature."[7] Adding more contextualization, Lerner maintains that the ancient Babylonians were a "people who regarded fertility as sacred and essential to their own survival."[8] Thus, according to Lerner,

> What seems to have happened was that sexual activity for and in behalf of the god or goddesses was considered beneficial to the people and sacred.[9]

While women's service to the temple through these activities took a variety of forms, there was a class of women "who were prostitutes attached to the temple."[10]

In order to determine the meaning of these women's occupation to their contemporaries, Lerner analyzes *The Epic of Gilgamesh*. According to Lerner,

> The temple harlot is an accepted part of society; her role is honorable—in fact, it is she who is chosen to civilize the wild man [Enkidu, in the poem]. The assumption here is that sexuality is civilizing, pleasing to the gods. The harlot does "a woman's task"; thus she is not set off from other women because of her occupation. She possesses a kind of wisdom, which tames the wild man. He follows her lead into the city of civilization.[11]

In a social context where impersonal, materially remunerated sexual transactions are conceived and rationalized in terms of the beneficial promotion of nature's fecundity, an occupation in which one performs such transactions will have a significantly different meaning from an outwardly similar occupation in American society. Though we need not accept the moral conclusions of people in a different social context, we cannot ignore the context-specific meanings of this occupation in drawing our own moral conclusions about it.

Though Lerner acknowledges that ancient and modern forms of sex commerce are premised on different cultural assumptions, she nevertheless imports a number of modern assumptions about sex commerce into her analysis of the ancient variety. For example, Lerner first accuses modern scholars of generating confusion by classifying both religiously motivated and commercially motivated impersonal sexual activities as "prostitution."[12] Instead, Lerner argues for maintaining a distinction between "cultic sexual service" (or "sacral sexual activity") and "prostitution" (or "commercial sexual activity")—a distinction which relies upon whether the women involved passed on the material rewards they earned to the temple or kept part (or all) of it for themselves. According to Lerner,

> What earlier was a purely religious cultic function may have become corrupted at a time when commercial prostitution already flourished in the temple precincts. Sexual intercourse performed for strangers in the temple to honor the fertility and sexual power of the goddess may have, customarily, been rewarded by a donation to the temple. Worshipers regularly brought offerings of food, oil, wine, and precious goods to the temple to honor the deities and in the hope of thus advancing their own cause. It is conceivable that this practice corrupted some of the temple servants, tempting them to keep all or some of these gifts for their own profit.[13]

But, curiously, there is no evidence in Lerner's own account, nor that of other scholars she cites, that the distinction between cultic and commercial sex was significant to the contemporaries of these practices; that is, that these terms defined different social institutions informed by different beliefs. While I agree with Lerner that the label "prostitution" may obscure important differences between historically and culturally distinct cases of sex commerce, importing distinctions that may make sense in our culture into another may similarly obscure important historical and cultural distinctions.

Though Lerner's distinction finds little support in her data, it does serve her theoretical aims. For Lerner emphasizes the distinction between cultic and commercial sexual activity in order to raise doubts about what she alleges is "the most widespread and accepted explanation of the origin of prostitution: namely, that it derives from 'temple prostitution.'"[14] Lerner's distinction allows her to argue that modern forms of prostitution derived not from ancient "temple prostitution" conceived as sacral sexual service to the temple, but from ancient "temple prostitution" conceived as a more commercially oriented sexual activity. And, regarding the latter, Lerner states: "It is likely that commercial prostitution derived directly from the enslavement of women and the consolidation and formation of classes."[15] Thus Lerner derives modern forms of prostitution from ancient gender oppression and classism, rather than from ancient fertility worship. She thereby solves a problem for socialist feminist accounts of prostitution, which see it as the social precipitate of gender and class domination, though she does not necessarily enhance our understanding of the social origins of ancient prostitution.

Though I agree with Lerner that previous scholarly accounts of the causes of prostitution are intellectually suspect (those that see our modern practice of commercial prostitution as the causal descendent of the ancient Babylonian religious sexual practice), Lerner's own causal account is equally suspect. For it uncritically reflects Lerner's modern and possibly Eurocentric perspective. Not only is this perspective uncritically reflected in her distinction between two varieties of impersonal, materially compensated sexual activity, but it is reflected in other assumptions behind her causal account. These assumptions are worth examining, so that we may determine what her case study reveals about prostitution, and what it does not.

Lerner's account involves the dual claim that the distinction between cultic and commercial prostitution is and was significant, and that our modern commercial practice of prostitution derives from an ancient commercial practice. Moreover, she argues that the ancient commercial practice depended upon the emergence of institutionalized social inequalities—slavery through military conquest and the division of society into propertied and nonpropertied classes. Commercial prostitution particularly depended upon the division of society into economic classes, according to Lerner, not only because the formation and reproduction of these classes made women available for prostitution, but it also created the need for prostitution. For with class formation, upper-class women were seen as sexual and reproductive capital, and thus men's sexual access to upper-class women became limited. According to Lerner,

> As the sexual regulation of women of the propertied class became more firmly entrenched, the virginity of respectable daughters became a financial asset for the family. Thus, commercial prostitution came to be seen as a social necessity for meeting the sexual needs of men.[16]

Lerner's primary piece of evidence for the Babylonians' interest in the sexual regulation of women is a Middle Assyrian law which requires the veiling of certain women and forbids the veiling of others. According to Lerner the law distinguishes types of women

> based on their sexual activities. Domestic women, sexually serving one man and under his protection, are here designated as "re-

spectable" by being veiled; women not under one man's protection and sexual control are designated as "public women," hence
unveiled.[17]

Lerner here suggests that the veiling law distinguished between sexually controlled or monogamous (respectable) women from sexually
promiscuous (nonrespectable or public) women, and it discouraged
men (presumably bourgeois men) from associating with either type
indiscriminately.

However, contrary to Lerner's explanation of this law, it does not
seem to be a woman's sexual activities per se that distinguish one
woman from another, but only perhaps her presumed sexual activities
at a particular point in her life. For, according to Lerner, concubines
and temple prostitutes were to be veiled, like wives, if they were in a
marital or marriage-like relationship with a man. Indeed, this latter
factor, and not their "sexual activities" (current or past), seems to be
the more salient distinguishing criterion reflected in this law. In other
words, the law seems to distinguish women in terms of their marital
or filial status—a status which may correlate with a particular style of
sexual activity while that status is recognized—and not in terms of
"their sexual activities," if those are taken to include their sexual history, and their virginal and nonvirginal status. In short, the moral
weight that Lerner assumes the law gives to a woman's sexual practice seems to reflect Lerner's own cultural biases.

Similarly, Lerner notes that the law groups unmarried religious
prostitutes together with unmarried commercial prostitutes, many of
the latter being the daughters of slaves. Lerner appears puzzled that
the law did not morally distinguish these two groups of women, and
that it erased the difference in their class origins. Lerner attempts to
explain this "peculiar" feature of the law by claiming that this grouping constituted

> a distinct declassing of the former [religious prostitutes]. The
> sacral nature of sexual temple service is no longer the decisive fac-
> tor; more and more the temple prostitute is regarded the same way
> as the commercial prostitute.[18]

Yet why does this grouping not suggest the enhanced social status of
the commercial prostitute, or that the commercial prostitute was
regarded like the religious prostitute? Perhaps it suggests that the distinction Lerner makes between them, and upon which her causal
account depends, is not coherent. Moreover, to assume that the equa-
tion of these two groups of women would "declass" the "higher"
group, is to assume that the Babylonians held the commercial prosti-

tutes in low esteem, which contradicts Lerner's analysis of *The Epic of Gilgamesh*.

Furthermore, Lerner makes the questionable claim that, with the legally enforced sexual regulation of women, "commercial prostitution came to be seen as a social necessity for meeting the sexual needs of men."[19] Her claim assumes that the Babylonians had the same conception of men's sexual needs as we do in our culture. Yet, again, Lerner's data does not support this claim, nor the claim that the Babylonians saw men's sexual needs as different from women's. Lerner's claim in this instance is an example of how feminist scholars can inadvertently reproduce the sexist principles of contemporary Western industrialized societies by treating these principles as ahistorical universals.

I am not arguing that prostitution did not have something to do with slavery and class inequalities in ancient Babylon. These social facts may have determined which women entered prostitution and which did not. In addition, like the religious beliefs that supported sex commerce, social conventions and beliefs pertaining to slavery and class divisions may have contributed to the social meaning of sex commerce in ancient Babylon, a point which Lerner does not address. Furthermore, I am not claiming that an interest in female virginity and its economic worth does not have something to do with prostitution in industrialized capitalist societies. What I oppose in Lerner's treatment of Babylonian prostitution is her attempt to use it to generate an account of the social origins of sex commerce in all social contexts, including our contemporary world. I am particularly puzzled that while she recognizes that sex commerce has multiple culturally specific meanings, she nevertheless assumes that it has a single transcultural cause. Moreover, to make her historically contextualized account of impersonal, remunerated sex compatible with her larger ahistorical theoretical project, Lerner seems to have carried into her interpretation of Babylonian prostitution assumptions that are not supported by her historical evidence. This renders her historical reading of Babylonian prostitution, as well as her ahistorical one, implausible.

Lerner's account of Babylonian prostitution has competing aims: on the one hand, she wants to show that similar forms of gender oppression, such as prostitution, have existed in all societies, including non-capitalist ones, and on the other, she wants to buttress the feminist moral argument which derives prostitution from the dehumanizing forces of capitalism and patriarchy. Yet what she shows us is that Babylonian prostitution may have been organized by very different cultural principles than roughly similar work in contemporary Western industrialized societies. More specifically, rather than reveal the presumed common commercial aspects of sex work in ancient Babylon, Lerner's analysis draws our attention to the noncommercial aspects of the sex work of the temple prostitute. More precisely, the temple prostitute's services were not part of a commoditized exchange (though there was presumably a monetary dimension to these exchanges). The prostitute's relationship with her patron existed, not primarily to allow each to pursue his or her individual gain (though each may have received some material benefits), but rather to facilitate a form of community service. In short, temple prostitution was not a profit-oriented, commodity exchange.

Lerner's descriptions of Babylonian prostitution show how monetary sexual transactions can be shaped by social forces other than capitalism. And by isolating the culturally specific forces that shaped sex work in this context, we may render visible some of the culturally specific forces that determine the meaning of sex work in American society. For example, we uncover our own cultural convictions that human sexual activity has little influence over nonhuman fertility, and that it is not necessarily civilizing. It is cultural principles like these that are relevant to our social and moral analysis of contemporary forms of prostitution, and not some alleged universal cause.

Colonial Kenyan Prostitution

In her book *The Comforts of Home: Prostitution in Colonial Nairobi,* Luise White examines sex commerce in Kenya from the early to mid-twentieth century. According to White,

> women, in the absence of formal employment opportunities, earned the money with which to acquire property through prostitution ... There were no pimps at any time in Kenya's history, so that prostitutes were able to retain control over their earnings— when they so desired—and have intimate and stable relations with the laboring men who were their customers ...
>
> Not all Nairobi prostitutes acquired urban property. Some subsidized their families' farms, others bought livestock ... women saw prostitution as a reliable means of capital accumulation, not as a despicable fate or a temporary strategy ... The work of prostitutes was family labor. Prostitutes' patterns of reinvestment reproduced families: either with themselves as heads of household, as in the case of women who bought property for themselves, or for their families of origin, as daughters' revenues restored the shattered fortunes of agriculturalists.[20]

White describes prostitution as the creative and dynamic response of the urban and rural poor to the social and economic disruption caused by the British colonial state. This state created a large wage labor force in Nairobi that consisted primarily of male migrants from the Kenyan countryside. Since the wages were low, these men were not able to set up households in their places of employment that might serve to reproduce their labor power. According to White

> Migrant laborers were removed from their own homes, in jobs that provided neither food nor someone to cook it, let alone a context in which meals might be truly replenishing. The only way a laborer could obtain that was to establish a family presence where he worked—a cost that was impossible. Prostitution divided and commercialized such services—a working man could buy, for a bit of his wage, a piece of the totality he could not possess while working.[21]

Thus commoditized sexual and domestic labor allowed migrant proletarian men to provide and reproduce their labor power under the labor conditions imposed by colonial rule.

White emphasizes that the subsistence needs that these men had, and which were partly met by the commercialization of sex and domesticity, were not the "natural" needs of men under such circumstances, but needs that were culturally shaped. According to White,

> The needs that are met by sexual relations—their frequency, duration, and nature—and the allocation of food and shelter within sexual relationships are determined by wider ideologies, not biological absolutes. In Nairobi wartime prostitution, men sought the kinds of relationships that they believed they needed, the relationships that most closely approximated the contexts in which they wanted to receive intimate relationships, including food and shelter. Their labor power was reproduced and maintained by the degree to which they were satisfied with the arrangements they had thus authorized.[22]

In short, the subsistence needs of these workers were shaped in a wider social context, and then addressed and transformed again through commercial relationships that these men pursued.

Prostitution not only served proletarian male subsistence needs, it served the petty-bourgeois aspirations of women and the peasant interests of their rural families as well. For, according to White, the social forces that drew peasant sons away from their parents to the cities for waged work—a depression in agricultural and peasant production—impoverished peasant families and communities. Since the waged work created by colonial interests was unavailable to the daughters of peasants, these daughters attempted to find alternative avenues for raising income for themselves and their families. Many found or created these alternative avenues by providing, on a commercial basis, domestic services to the migrant male laborers in the cities. In this way, prostitution was shaped by the culturally shaped needs and aspirations of both men and women. In White's words,

> Women's concerns about how to reproduce a household, in the long run or for a few minutes, determined how prostitution was conducted in Nairobi ... [P]oor men could purchase fleeting domesticity while skilled and self-employed men could afford night-long imitations of married life. Men nevertheless determined what these relationships would consist of. Bathwater, bread, cleanliness, respect ... not only did these reproduce labor power but they did so in a gendered vision of service that working men could purchase.[23]

In sum, prostitution in this context was organized by multiple cultural assumptions and contextually shaped needs—the gendered assumptions and subsistence needs of a male proletarian work force, and the familial needs and petty-bourgeois interests of peasant daughters.

Here we have prostitution in a capitalist and patriarchal context, and yet there is no reason to distinguish sex work from other kinds of commercial domestic work that women perform, contra Overall. For neither the sex, nor the cooking and cleaning, are part of a transaction that is inherently unequal, that is, one that takes place only between a social inferior and her social superior. Thus, this work does not reflect a large discrepancy in social power between the transacting parties. In other words, commoditized sexual labor here is not the expression of class or social privilege, but the expression of the context-specific needs of men transformed in the colonial context from peasant sons to wage laborers, and the context-specific needs of women transformed in the colonial context from peasant daughters to petty-bourgeois entrepreneurs.

In this context, sex commerce took the place of marriage among the working classes of Kenyan society, though, as White states, it was "illegal marriage"—marriage not officially sanctioned.[24] It was also polyandrous "marriage"—also not officially sanctioned, at least by the colonial regime. Certainly, prostitution was not a "safety valve" created and maintained by the ruling classes to preserve bourgeois marriage, and to protect upper-class women from the excesses of male sexuality at the expense of lower-class women. Instead prostitution was created and maintained by former peasants, and it took the place of marriage for some of them in this colonial society.

Ironically, the common analogy that some Marxist theorists draw between prostitution and bourgeois marriage has a high degree of validity in this context, though not for the reasons they allege.[25] For the analogy holds not because bourgeois marriage often has crass material motives, but because prostitution can serve legitimate social interests. Moreover, in this context, a corresponding analogy holds between the prostitute and the conventional wife, though also not for the reasons conventional Marxists and some feminists think.[26] Again, this analogy holds not because the bourgeois wife is merely a prostitute, but because the prostitute in this context is merely a wife. She is perhaps a part-time wife, or a wife in an illegal polygamous marriage, but a "wife" nonetheless. Indeed, White informs us that in colonial Kenya it was not uncommon for prostitutes to be recruited by their clients to be their full-time, legal wives, and thus some prostitutes eventually entered legal, monogamous marriage.[27]

That prostitutes were considered marriageable by numerous men suggests that in colonial Nairobi prostitution was not an especially socially degrading form of work. At least, any claim that prostitution was degrading to women in this society would have to be based on something other than the social reality that defined prostitution in this context. But if we avoid importing dubious psychological or biological universals into this context, we can see that the commercialization of sex here did not create a distinct, especially harsh and socially stigmatizing form of labor exploitation.

Having seen the "unusual" features of prostitution in the context she studied, White claims that her sources challenge and "contradict prevailing notions about the place of prostitution, and the exploitation of prostitutes, in capitalist societies."[28] White's sources and her interpretation of them especially challenge socialist feminist accounts of prostitution, such as Overall's and Lerner's. For just as prostitution does not appear to be a function of the social inequalities between the prostitute and her client in this patriarchal and capitalist context (as Overall's analysis suggests), it does not appear to derive from bourgeois interests in regulating women's sexuality (as Lerner's analysis of it would lead us to expect). According to White,

> Prostitutes and respectable women are not discrete categories, but both serve the needs of male migrants who go from migrancy to settlement to migration again.[29]

Men went to prostitutes in colonial Nairobi, not because the ruling classes had restricted sexual activity with their social peers ("respectable women") in order to secure and strengthen the social capital they had invested in their daughters and sisters; men went to prostitutes in colonial Nairobi because the ruling classes had so restricted the economic activities of proletarian men that their culturally shaped desires for domestic comforts were frustrated and redirected. In this context, if the ruling and nonruling classes distinguished prostitutes from women with greater social capital ("respectable women"), it would have been primarily on the basis of a woman's place in the racist and nationalist colonial hierarchy, and not for the purpose of regulating her sexual activity. Indeed, as White impressively demonstrates and argues, when socialist feminists conceive the prostitute primarily in terms of her sexual activity or promiscuity, rather than on the basis of her place in a network of relations of production, they reflect bourgeois Western thinking.[30]

To show more critical awareness of our Western bourgeois biases, White urges Western and feminist scholars to reconceptualize prostitution in terms of its different labor forms, and in terms of the systems of labor of which it is a part. She also encourages us to eschew the European and American nineteenth-century social reformist categories for analyzing prostitution—those that treat prostitution as evidence of some societal disease, pollution of nature, or corruption of morals. For White maintains that these medical, ecological, and theological images of prostitution derive from nineteenth-century reformists' fears and prejudices about the sexual and work habits of the laboring classes. When invoked in contemporary feminist scholarship for the purpose of understanding "what's wrong with prostitution," these images, and the categories of analysis used to derive them, distort the everyday experiences and realities of some who participate in prostitution. According to White, these descriptive categories

> have naturalized prostitutes in the language of biological processes, explaining women's labor in an idiom of inevitability, corruption, and decay.[31]

In this way, these images have served to mask the active role some women have taken in particular historical processes; that is, they have served to obscure the contributions of some women to transformations in the relations and modes of production.

By contrast, because White's study of prostitution emphasizes the different labor forms that prostitution encompassed in colonial Kenya, White's work serves to render visible how women's labor has shaped history, and how women "as social actors . . . respond to and reshape the ideological and material circumstances of their lives," to repeat Ginsburg's words. For example, White distinguishes three forms of prostitution practiced in Nairobi in the early to mid-twentieth century: the *watembezi, malaya,* and *wazi-wazi* forms. She distinguishes these forms in terms of where the work was performed, how customers were solicited, the services customers could get and how they were provided, the social characteristics of the prostitutes and clients, whether the prostitutes worked with associates or alone, the pace at which the work was performed and its profitability, and how profits from the work were reinvested. She analyzes these labor forms in terms of the labor discipline they imposed, the workers' strategies of capital accumulation, and the ways the work and workers were embedded in historically shaped systems of kinship, labor, ethnic, and class relations. And the details White provides in order to individuate and evaluate *watembezi, malaya,* and *wazi-wazi* prostitution reflect the ways women actively responded to and reshaped the circumstances of their lives.

Moreover, White's descriptions and analyses of these forms of prostitution are especially noteworthy for the relationships they reveal between specific labor conditions, the social aspirations of workers, the codes of conduct that existed between service providers and the clientele served, and the workers' sense of kinship obligation. Indeed White uncovers some surprising relationships that defy previous stereotypes of different types of prostitutes, their motives, and their social relationships. For example, White notes,

> It is of great importance that we understand that work performed one way in one place can have the opposite meaning in another place, and that the most aggressive prostitution, conducted from windows and stoops, was performed by the most dutiful of daughters. The women who walked the streets were also working for their families. It was the women who waited decorously and discreetly in their rooms, peaceful and isolated, deferential and polite, who were in fact entirely out for themselves, eager to disinherit fathers and brothers and to establish themselves as independent heads of households.[32]

In general, White's case study of prostitution shows that commercial sex work performed in colonial Nairobi has different social meanings and consequences than commercial sex work performed in the contemporary U.S. The similar class backgrounds of the worker and customer, the role of sex work in serving the subsistence needs of clients and the class aspirations or familial needs of sex workers, and the workers' significant degree of control over their work and earnings, are features of prostitution in the former context that distinguish it from prostitution in the latter. These features are highly relevant to any moral analysis of prostitution in contemporary America or colonial Nairobi, and suggest a need for different moral analyses of each.

Prostitution in West Nepal

Just as many dutiful daughters of Kenya's rural poor engaged in urban sex commerce to support their natal families, virtually all the daughters of the Nepali untouchable Badi caste engage in prostitution to support their parents. According to Tom Cox,

> Prostitution in Badi society is very much a family affair. Badi girls generally prostitute themselves right in their parent's home. When a client arrives, he will sometimes sit, and, over a glass of *rakshi* (homemade liquor), talk with the Badi girl and her parents. After awhile he will then take the girl to some other room in the house and have sex with her. There are times when a Badi mother and father will see a man looking for a girl, and offer him the services of their own daughter.[33]

In the above passage, Cox is describing contemporary Badi society. In previous centuries, Badi families made their living from a combination of singing, dancing, storytelling, and prostitution, according to Cox. But by the middle of this century, the demand for the nonsexual aspects of Badi entertainment seems to have disappeared, due to a number of social, political, and economic changes in Nepali society. Thus, the families have come to rely increasingly on the sex commerce of their female members.

Though Badi men secure some food by fishing, and some income by selling drums and pipes, most of their family income comes from the prostitution of their sisters or daughters.[34] Cox states:

> Badi girls, from early childhood on, know, and generally accept the fact, that a life of prostitution awaits them. Their parents, and other Badi, tell them that prostitution is, and always has been, the work of women in the Badi caste, and that to aspire to any other profession would be unrealistic. Badi girls see all the young women around them, and often their own mothers and sisters, prostitute themselves on a daily basis. Indeed, they virtually never see any Badi women engaging in any profession but prostitution.[35]

In sum, Badi girls are socialized into prostitution by their own families and communities.

Because of the dependence of Badi families on the income of female children from prostitution, Badi sons do not marry Badi girls but women from other castes. The daughters of these unions usually become prostitutes too. According to Cox, "Badi parents, in an effort to maintain their income from prostitution, often try to prevent their daughters from getting married."[36] Yet, though parents discourage their daughters from marrying, some do marry. Cox describes some cases where Badi prostitutes have married their clients with whom they have had children.

While the Badi are a low caste in Nepal, the male clients of Badi prostitutes come from both high and low castes, and include foreign men from India and Kathmandu.[37] Though orthodox Hindu law heavily restricts intimate relations between members of high and low castes, these laws are frequently violated, according to Cox. Thus some Badi sexual transactions may violate caste taboos in the way, perhaps, that some prostitutional transactions in American society violate racial taboos. Cox, however, does not discuss the impact of these violations on the social taboos themselves.

Cox claims that because prostitution is the sexual and occupational norm for women in Badi society,

> Badi girls . . . are not usually emotionally traumatized by prostitution. They are no less (or more) happy than the rest of us. They accept prostitution as their fate, the only way of life open to them.[38]

Moreover, he compares the psychological effects of prostitution on Badi women with its effect on prostitute girls in the Philippines and Thailand. He then speculates,

> that what is so emotionally traumatic for some prostitutes—in the Philippines, Thailand and elsewhere—is not the physical act of prostitution, but the stigma that society places on it. There is no stigma on prostitution in Badi society. On the contrary, it is the norm. It is precisely because Badi prostitutes receive emotional support from other members of their community, that they are not traumatized, as some prostitutes in other societies are.[39]

Though there may be no stigma on prostitution in Badi society, prostitution appears to be a stigmatized activity in Nepali society as a whole.[40] Cox mentions that "The Nepali government has always considered Badi to be an embarrassment to the country,"[41] and that the government has given some Badi families land to farm and a school for their children in order to discourage their sex commerce. Moreover, while Badi prostitutes do not have any low or special status within their own caste, they do have a low status within Nepali society. However, it is unclear from Cox's study whether this is due to their low caste status or their stigmatized occupation, or what the connection is between these. He does state that Badi girls who attend private or public school "are often severely harassed by students from other castes," and one was turned away from a school out of a concern that she might "corrupt the other students."[42] This suggests that their low status within Nepali society stems from their work and not merely their caste. Thus, while Badi prostitutes may receive emotional support from their own communities, they appear to receive little support and acceptance outside them.

It seems reasonable to conclude from this initial study that sex commerce has a different social meaning within Badi society than within the larger Nepali society.[43] Though Cox does not draw this conclusion, his account seems to suggest it. If the meanings of prostitution vary widely in different Nepali contexts, then Badi women may live with conflicting definitions of and social responses to themselves and their work. That is, prostitution may place Badi women in a double-bind: by performing this work they live up to their ideals of family responsibility, filial respect, and productivity, while at the same time they violate larger social norms of gender, sexuality, and spiritual purity. A moral analysis of prostitution in Nepal, therefore, should take account of the conflictual aspects of prostitution, and how they are managed. And certainly the relationship between prostitution and the inequities of the caste system would need to be explored.

The Prostitute in Medieval Occitania

From the middle of the fourteenth century to the middle of the fifteenth, many medieval cities in what is now southern France established and maintained public houses of prostitution. According to Jacques Rossiaud, "the *prostibulum publicum* held a central place in civic imagination, standing at the core of the city between the cathedral and the City Hall."[44] These urban institutions were frequented primarily by young unmarried men who, Rossiaud claims, "were given permission to use the services of the public prostitutes from about sixteen to eighteen years of age."[45] According to Leah Otis, these institutions, in some cases, generated profits for municipal governments but, in other cases, public brothels were subsidized by their host cities.[46]

Significantly, during this period, the women who worked in these public brothels were not socially marginal. The prostitute was an active participant in public life, and she enjoyed many of the rights and privileges of ordinary workers. Rossiaud claims that prostitutes participated in public ceremonies, and the rape of a prostitute "was treated like the rape of any woman of the lower echelons of society and was subject to the same sentences."[47] Otis states that prostitutes testified and accused "in criminal cases without any objection being made to the propriety of this procedure."[48] Moreover, Rossiaud states:

Prostitutes resident in the city could be on good terms with "respectable" people, and they joined in all the rites of living in society. Their children lacked neither godfathers nor godmothers. The clients of the brothels were normal men who had not yet settled down in marriage.[49]

Furthermore, prostitutes were legally free and socially eligible for marriage. Rossiaud states that "marriage represented the end of a life of prostitution for public prostitutes, but it was also an ordinary civil status for many 'common prostitutes.'"[50] Citing the work of Rossiaud and others, Leah Otis claims that

> There were apparently no practical limits to the legal capacity of the prostitute in southern France in the fifteenth century. J. Rossiaud has found several marriage contracts of prostitutes from this period in which their profession is clearly stated. Several wills of prostitutes have also been preserved, indicating that they were free to dispose of their possessions as they wished. Last, as we have seen, there were apparently no limits on the capacity of the prostitute to conclude contracts; municipal brothels were farmed out to prostitutes as well as to men. From the end of the fourteenth century to the sixteenth century, prostitutes would seem to have enjoyed the same legal capacity as honest women.[51]

In the medieval urban centers Otis and Rossiaud describe, the prostitute was not an outlawed, criminal figure eking out a living in the underground worlds of her society.

Rossiaud attributes the rise of the city brothel to the desire of both secular and church authorities to contain the sexual predatoriness and violence of young men. In this era it was evidently common for there to be bands of young men whose activities included the abduction and gang raping of other men's wives and daughters.[52] These sexually aggressive and confrontational behaviors Rossiaud attributes to marriage customs that allowed more mature men to choose their wives

> from an age group in which they competed with younger men . . . This siphoning off of young wives was considerable enough to be clearly felt by the young in sixteenth-century cities, as it had been in the fifteenth century.[53]

In other words, the marriage and social customs of the period, which valorized young women as wives, positioned older and younger men as competitors. This competition created, according to Rossiaud, a certain amount of social tension between penniless and wifeless young men and more fortunate men who had both . . . This rivalry may have contributed to age-based solidarities and collective behavior patterns unique to young men.[54]

The tension and rivalry may have been eased, Rossiaud suggests, by promoting prostitution as an alternative for wifeless young men. In other words, prostitution in this context was socially functional.

Moreover, because the sexual appetites of unmarried young men were seen as natural in medieval theological and secular discourses, and the suppression of these appetites as individually and socially harmful, both religious and secular authorities saw prostitution as an inevitable outlet for these appetites and one morally preferable to homosexuality, rape, or masturbation. Thus the municipal brothel represented a desire to appease these sexual appetites in a way that both was consistent with the dominant social ideologies and was socially practical.[55] In Rossiaud's words,

> In all fifteenth-century France from Burgundy to Provence, prosti-
> tution, official or tolerated by all the powers that be, thus appears
> as the natural result of demographic structures, of a certain social
> order and a specific moral code. It exercised a mediating function,
> and the bordello . . . was considered an institution for harmony
> between age classes and social groups. All the young and many of
> the less young went to fornicate freely in the brothels. Prostitution,
> municipally sponsored or not, tempered the aggressive nature of
> adolescents, though it failed to eliminate it. All the city's youth,
> from burghers' sons to kitchen boys . . . had raped a poor girl at
> least once during their young years without being rejected by the
> city . . . Male adolescence was a dangerous and turbulent time, a
> period of resentments and frustrations, but it was also a time for
> adventure, night-time mascarades, and free sex.[56]

In sum, Rossiaud sees the municipal brothel as the "natural result," that is the functionally rational resolution of particular social problems—problems created irrationally by historically specific forces but solved by functional necessity.

Otis rejects Rossiaud's functional explanation of the city-sponsored brothel. She argues that the policy of institutionalizing prostitution cannot be explained simply by marital patterns and demographic factors that created a need for prostitutes. For this need could have been met merely by municipal policies of passive toleration toward informal or private forms of prostitution. Under such conditions, a market in prostitution would have thrived as well as it did under public sponsorship.[57]

Instead, to find evidence of the motivation for institutionalization, Otis looks not to what is "functionally rational" but to the rationales provided by the municipal authorities themselves. In their rationales for creating and regulating public brothels, Otis finds that their primary concern was not only, or even, to avoid the danger of unsatisfied male sexual need, but to avoid the danger that unconfined prostitution would pose for the temptation and corruption of nonprostitute women. According to Otis,

> the theme that pervades the documents is the effect that contact with prostitutes might have on honest women ... Languedocian police regulations insist on the strict segregation of dishonest from honest women for this reason.[58]

Thus prostitutes were seen not only as a civic necessity but as a civic liability, for they could have a bad influence on "honest" women.

Though this partly explains why public brothels were thought to be functional, it does not explain, as Otis recognizes, the paternalistic attitudes of the municipal authorities toward nonprostitute and presumably adult women. Otis delves into medieval ideologies about gender in order to explain these attitudes. She states:

> The dominant medieval concept of female nature was that women were the more carnal sex, ruled by passion rather than reason. The municipal authorities feared that honest women, once having witnessed the material as well as the pleasurable rewards of sin, would abandon the connubial bed for the street. "One diseased ewe," warned the authorities of Lacaune in 1337, "infects the whole flock." In case of contagion, the best remedy was quarantine. Authorized red-light districts were the guarantee of female virtue, not only against those who threatened, but also against that which tempted.[59]

In sum, the institutionalization of prostitution, and hence its confinement, was seen as necessary to protect people who might be "honest," but whose natures rendered them subject to carnal and irrational impulses.[60] While the prostitute could abate the danger created by the unsatisfied lust of unmarried men, she created the danger of encouraging sexual promiscuity in married and marriageable women. In Otis's words,

> Sexual desire was natural, prostitution was inevitable, but the need to limit prostitution by defining its perimeters, sealing it off from the mainstream of society, reflected a need to protect society from itself, as it were, by relegating incitement to a limited place.

> Prostitutes in Languedoc were not so much the heroines of hetero-
> sexuality or the guardians of honest women's besieged virtue as
> they were the sometimes mistrusted pawns in the effort to hedge
> off sexual and social disorder.[61]

Otis argues that her account better explains the ambivalent attitudes of medieval society toward the prostitute. For though she was
an accepted part of it in many ways, she was subject to laws govern-
ing her dress, her place of residence, and her work, which marked her
from other women and limited her freedom. On Otis's account, the
prostitute was valued because her existence presumably reduced the
threat of rape to nonprostitute women, and it may have been seen as
reducing the supposed threat of homosexuality. But she was also mis-
trusted because her existence was believed to create a significant
threat of moral corruption to nonprostitute women. It is the general
mistrust the prostitute engendered, and not the general appreciation
of her social function, that led to the institutionalization of prostitution, according to Otis.

By focussing on how particular institutions are historically and
culturally constructed, rather than on their presumed universal functional properties, Otis illuminates the institutionalization of prostitution in medieval Occitania. Particularly notable is Otis's discussion
of the relationship between dominant ideologies about gender and
sexuality, on the one hand, and the social organization and control
of prostitution, on the other. Though these ideologies did not lead to
the extreme marginalization of the prostitute, they did circumscribe
her rights and activities, which any moral analysis of prostitution
would need to take into account. Moreover, we might look at the
relationship between cultural assumptions about sexual desire (in
men and women) and the oppression of women generally in society,
in analyzing institutions that epitomize and perpetuate these assumptions. If the relationship is a positive one, we may need to broaden
our comparative knowledge of human sexual desire in order to
decenter some of these assumptions. And finally, though there are
many ways in which sex commerce in these medieval cities differs
from sex commerce in contemporary American cities, Otis's focus on
gender and sexual desire in the former context raises questions that
may help us understand the significance of this activity and its social
control in the latter context as well. In the next chapter I will attempt
to uncover some cultural assumptions about gender and sexuality
that motivate and reshape the commercial trade in sex in the U.S.
and elsewhere.

Conclusion

By this comparative and contextual study of prostitution, I hope to have shown that there is no single thing as "prostitution" that can be evaluated apart from a cultural framework. Instead there are many particular prostitutions that have varying social origins and social consequences. Thus there is no need for a unifying origin myth to illuminate the moral status of prostitution.

I also hope to have shown that it is not therefore obvious that we should always seek to deter or control prostitution, as Matthews suggests. Perhaps prostitution predicated on fertility worship or prostitution that functions as informal polyandry serving valuable social interests may be left alone. For these prostitutions, which occurred but no longer exist in ancient Babylon and colonial Kenya, do not appear to constitute degrading and undesirable forms of human sexuality. I am less comfortable with the prostitution that took place in Occitania and the prostitution now occurring in West Nepal, primarily because they may be implicated in the pernicious naturalized social hierarchies of gender and caste, respectively. Insofar as the commercialization of sex in these contexts reinforces these hierarchies, we should seek to minimize and reshape it through creative social policies that serve to challenge and denaturalize these social hierarchies. In the next chapter I will consider some policies that may potentially serve this goal in our own society.

6

Exotic Erotica and Erotic Exotica: Sex Commerce in Some Contemporary Urban Centers

---

What's In a Term?

Although the commercialization of behaviors having sexual meaning may go a long way back, prostitution is probably not one of the "oldest professions," for this claim implies that erotic activity was one of the first forms of human activity to be commercialized. It also implies that, in the earliest human societies, there were occasions when some people's (men's?) participation in erotic activities with others (women?) was facilitated through an exchange of goods. Yet we have little evidence that in early human societies sexual access to bodies of women, children, or men was exchanged commercially. Thus, this small piece of cultural wisdom seems to represent the projection of our modern values back into the past.[1]

In this chapter, my discussion of prostitution is not about some human practice whose beginning coincided with the beginning of human history, as our current mythology has it. Instead, my discussion will pertain to a practice whose origins are more usefully traced to cultural sources in our own society. More specifically, in my discussion of prostitution, I will consider, interpret, and evaluate sex commerce as it predominantly occurs in numerous contemporary American cities and some urban centers in other parts of the world sufficiently like ours in the relevant ways. My analysis will also encompass some urban centers in societies that are quite different from ours, but which participate in a global system of sex commerce with us.

Moreover, in discussing prostitution, I am not particularly concerned to illuminate the general moral concept or category "to prostitute oneself." In the English-speaking world, the term "prostitution" has a kind of double, layered meaning. It designates both sexual activity that is commercially oriented, and the act of debasing oneself for a material reward. The term "prostitute" correspondingly signifies both a commercial sex provider and someone who debases herself for material gain. These significations are dynamically linked, in that exchanging sex for pay is regarded by some English speakers as the paradigmatic form of personal debasement. Thus we often fail to separate these two meanings. Yet the paradigmatic association we make between these two significations is not logically necessary but culturally contingent, even though our dual use of the term "prostitution" obscures this.

As I have been using this term in this book, I have meant to emphasize the more morally neutral meaning of this term; but my intentions here are probably not sufficient to accomplish this. Because words do not mean whatever we say they mean, many civil rights advocates for prostitutes prefer to replace the term "prostitution" with the more neutral term "sex work," and the term "prostitute" with the more neutral term "sex worker." I have not limited myself to this new terminology in this book because I am not sure to what extent the somewhat commercialized and sexualized religious activities in, for example, ancient Babylon were socially constituted as "work." That is, I am not sure that all societies make the distinction that we do between work and leisure. I do not think we can even be sure to what extent the activities Herodotus describes were conceived and constituted as "sex," and thus the fusing of these two possibly modern notions in the term "sex work" may distort these activities as much as the term "prostitution."

Yet to continue to use the term "prostitution," especially in reference to contemporary practices and institutions, involves a problematic ethnographic choice between competing representations of a particular activity. On an interpretive approach, our descriptive labels should emphasize those aspects of the activity that are most salient to members of the society in which the activity occurs; and they should emphasize these aspects in a way that can reintroduce or refamiliarize the activity to those for whom the translation is made. Lynn Morgan's choice of the term "post-partum abortion," for example, over the term "infanticide" for describing the reproductive practices of others accomplishes this well. In choosing between alternate descriptions of commercialized sexual activity in American society and many contemporary international urban centers, the interpretive approach instructs us, then, to consider whether the nineteenth-century reformist and theological concept of self-debasement continues to capture our contemporary image of prostitution, or whether the possibly Protestant concept of self-disciplined industriousness captures it better.

In some ways, commercialized sexual exchanges in the U.S. and elsewhere resemble what people do for "work." First, the people who mobilize the social resources for such exchanges are generally attempting to make a livelihood. Second, as White's research suggests, the people who exchange sex for material rewards often have the same attitudes to and aspirations regarding these activities as people have toward other "jobs." Third, as White's research also suggests, making a livelihood from commercialized sexual exchanges often requires the same forms of labor discipline as other activities that afford us livelihoods. Fourth, in attempting to make a livelihood from commercial sexual activities, a person significantly affects her future economic and social opportunities. In other words, commercial sexual activities condition one's class identity and status in the same way as other livelihoods. Fifth, one's class position and kinship network often condition one's entrance into the commercial trade in sex, just as these factors condition entrance into other occupations. And sixth, commercial exchanges of sex are supported by social structures containing both hierarchies of social power and codes of conduct that govern all exchanges of goods. In short, commerce in sex is maintained through social structures similar to ones in more socially legitimate industries and businesses.

Yet for many members of our contemporary society, including some who participate in commercialized exchanges of sex, these activities epitomize the very absence of the moral and personal discipline required for productive work and human industry. To some, these activities just symbolize personal debasement, physical and spiritual defilement, and moral corruption. For many of these people, commercial sexual activities are perceived as a threat to social cohesion and to common standards of human decency. Sex commerce represents the valuing of material wealth over human beings: it blurs the line between things that are purchasable and things that are not (such as other humans, babies, body parts, etc.). In sum, the commercialization of human sexuality stands for the encroachment of materialistic values into realms of our lives that should be guided by nonmaterialistic ideals.[2]

The term "prostitution" captures the features of commercialized sexual activity that are most prominent to people who are concerned about the encroachment of materialistic norms, while the term "sex work" captures features more prominent to those who recognize the analogous natures of commercially oriented sex and other commercially oriented activities. Therefore, when we employ one of these terms for ethnographic description, we emphasize a particular subcultural perspective on prostitution. And, depending on which perspective we choose to emphasize, we either contribute to the delegitimization of sex commerce, or we participate in its legitimization.

It would be nice—for ethnographic purposes—to have a term that captures both sets of features or one that was more neutral between them. Perhaps the term some prostitutes use, when they talk about entering "the life," does this to some degree, for it emphasizes that prostitution is a way of life, but one somehow different from the ordinary. One set of terms that I have been using repeatedly in this book, and which are relatively neutral includes "sex commerce," "commercialized sexual activity," "commercial trade in sex," and other variations on this theme. Commerce and trade are perhaps less dignifying than "work," which can be both materially and spiritually rewarding. The categories "commerce" and "trade" emphasize concern with the practical, and thus not spiritually elevating, mundane and sometimes messy affairs of the world. And following the logic of this terminology, the prostitute might become a commercial sexual resource, provider, or trader.

Perhaps better intermediate terms would be "sex lending," "sex trafficking," or even "sex sharking," as they carry some of the pejorative connotations of illicitness while placing the activities they describe in the realm of business or trade. On this view, the prostitute represents tabooed cultural merchandise or capital to be illicitly dealt or loaned out and returned with higher than normal rates of interest. Perhaps, she and her pimp are "sex sharks," a phrase that suggests both the illicit and business nature of their enterprise. These terms not only better capture our ambivalent and conflicting cultural attitudes to sex commerce, but their relative uncommonness may give them the advantage of reintroducing prostitution to us in ways that emphasize its cultural meaning.

Because of these advantages, I will experiment with these terms in this chapter. But because new language only serves the role of denaturalizing colloquially more familiar expressions when it is used interchangeably with them, I will continue to employ the more familar expressions as well.

Should Feminists Seek to Deter Sex Trading in Our Society?[3]

While many political and moral analyses of prostitution begin with the question, "What's wrong with it?" many social analyses of sex work begin with the question, "Why would a woman want to do it?"

These analyses seek the deeper psychological or sociological determinants behind a woman's apparently voluntary participation in a socially stigmatized activity. Because in American society we associate commercialized sexual activity with sexual deviance, and we treat commercial sex providers as sexual deviants,[4] the widespread participation of women in sex commerce is a mystery to us that needs to be explored.

My analysis of the traffic in sex will not focus on this question. For such questions are usually raised in the hope of predicting who is likely to become the sexual deviants among us, and thus preventing or controlling these potential outcomes—a hope which, as Gayle Rubin suggests,[5] is itself problematic. Moreover, though such questions may illuminate to some degree why some women become sex sharks and others do not, they do not explain why there is a demand for sex sharking. And by attempting to illuminate the origins of women's vulnerability to sex sharking, rather than the origins of the demand for the merchandise loaned, such questions suggest, as Carole Pateman notes, that prostitution is "a problem about the women who are prostitutes, ... [rather than] a problem about the men who demand to buy them."[6]

Pateman's comment might suggest that a better approach to prostitution would problematize, instead or additionally, the men who seek prostitutes, and then seek the causes of their sexual deviance.[7] Yet such an approach seems equally to lack some self-awareness of its own problematic assumptions and motives. Rather than take this approach, though, our interpretive model of social analysis directs us to render the actions of the commercial sex provider and her client intelligible by seeking the categories and terms in which they perceive and experience their activities, and in which those around them do as well. In other words, an interpretive approach to prostitution inquires, not after the psychological or sociological causes of sexual deviance, but after the inter-subjective meanings constitutive of commercialized sexual practices and the contexts in which they occur. Thus my analysis will begin with questions concerning the cultural principles that serve to organize this activity and condition our understanding of it.

For example, my analysis will raise questions such as the following. Do contemporary Americans, like the ancient Babylonians, see sexual desire and activity as civilizing forces, and as forces which promote natural abundance? Or do they see sexual desire and activity in terms of uncontrollable, disruptive urges that threaten civilization and require neutralization? Does commercialized sexual activity serve the subsistence needs and economic aspirations of certain social classes in American society, as it did in colonial Kenya? Or does it serve a bourgeois class interest in regulating women's sexuality for the purpose of controlling marital and reproductive resources? Is commercialized sexual activity tied to a social caste hierarchy; and does it conform to some of the social ideals of the caste that provides the human resources for it, while violating some of the social ideals of other castes that are eligible to exploit these resources, as it is in West Nepal? Or is commercialized sexual activity in American society not conditioned by class and ethnic differences and hierarchies? And finally, has sex commerce been institutionalized in the U.S. in ways that reflect social hierarchies based on gender, as was done in medieval Occitania? Or, are American commercial sex practices unrelated to gender stereotypes and the gendering of human sexuality?

My analysis, of course, will not answer all of these questions, though I do hope to address some of them. First, I will attempt to uncover some American cultural convictions about sexual desire, sexual activity, gender difference, and personal identity that are constitutive of both American prostitutional practices and the contexts where commercialized sex exchanges are negotiated. Uncovering these principles will help us understand how acts of prostitution are read in American society, and thus some of their wider and narrower social consequences. Second, I will attempt to uncover some of the cultural principles that especially condition the behavior and choices of the male clients of female prostitutes. Here I will especially focus on racialized gender stereotypes as a factor implicit in the consumption preferences of this male clientele. By attempting to render the customer's behavior intelligible in terms of cultural norms rather than personal idiosyncrasies, I hope to show that prostitution is not a marginal, deviant social practice but one whose social origins are nearer to the center or mainstream of American society. This would, of course, have significant implications for how we respond to prostitution in the U.S.

From my analysis I will argue that commerce in sex in American society, and in some societies we dominate economically, is organized and reproduced by particular cultural beliefs about sexuality, race, and gender—beliefs that cross-cultural perspectives should lead us to view as contingent. These beliefs not only serve to perpetuate the commercial trade in sex but they serve to perpetuate the marginalization of people of color and women in the U.S. and elsewhere. Thus, I conclude from my analysis that feminists and others should want to deter prostitution in American society and many other contemporary urban contexts. I will end my discussion by proposing a regulatory apparatus that would seek to deter prostitution by subverting some of the principles that have shaped it. This regulatory device also aims to protect women in nonpaternalistic ways from extreme capitalist exploitation.

Social Constructions of Reality

Some anthropologists have studied two relatively distinct communities in New Guinea—the Sambia and the Etoro—where people commonly assume that male children, at a certain age, need to be removed from the feminine environment created by their mother's care and placed in an entirely masculine environment. People also commonly believe that, in order for boys to develop the qualities of men, they need to ingest male fluid or semen, much as we believe that young infants need their mother's milk or some equivalent to be properly nurtured. Moreover, just as we act on our belief about nurturance by breast-feeding infants, the Etoro and Sambia act on their belief by "penis-feeding" young male children—a practice where boys "fellate" their older male relatives, often uncles.[8]

From our cultural perspective, the Etoro's and Sambia's practice involves behaviors that are highly stigmatized: for we are inclined to see this as a practice that involves the adult sexual exploitation of children, and incestuous and homosexual sex. Precisely because of this, an anthropologist might introduce a translation like "penis-feeding," so that the Etoro's and Sambia's custom can be re-presented in ways that call attention to its radically different meaning and purpose in Etoro and Sambia society. This particular translation emphasizes that these behaviors seem to be culturally subsumed under things having to do with child-rearing rather than eroticism, or that the world in which "penis-feeding" occurs is not one where nurturance and eroticism are opposed. Certainly, the Etoro and Sambia organize the world differently than we do, and thus part of rendering their "exotic" practice intelligible involves understanding how they socially construct reality. In this way, our knowledge and understanding of human beings is created not by our ability to assume some godlike perspective, or by our ability to assume some scientifically neutral perspective, but from our ability to assume multiple and distinct human perspectives.

It is often difficult to see the ways members of our own society construct reality, because the customs that might make these constructions visible to us usually appear to be quite normal. That is, customs in our own society generally appear to be the normal and inevitable expression of the biological or political forces that we take for granted. For example, as we have seen, liberals tend to see prostitution as the normal and inevitable expression of certain physiological universals. And socialists tend to see prostitution as the inevitable expression of political interests that divide societies into classes—something which both religious prostitution and prostitution within a single social class challenge. While socialists locate the origin of prostitution in human history rather than human biology, their history obscures how sex commerce has been shaped by women's labor and creativity, and other social forces as well. In short, both liberals and socialists treat sex commerce as a normal and unexotic custom—one that reveals only what we already think we know about ourselves, and thus one that has ceased to be mysterious.

Though it is difficult to see the idiosyncratic features of our own customs, we need to treat sex lending as alien and exotic in order to understand the cultural principles that produce it. One way to gain some cultural distance from our own social practices is to study the comparable practices of others. For example, in the last chapter, I tried to do this by examining comparable customs involving sex commerce in radically different societies. I also tried to note the "unusual" features of these practices. Having done this, I will now try to determine whether commercialized sexual activities in American society are "unusual" in some of the same or similar ways—that is, whether they are shaped by some of the same kinds of principles. According to Geertz,

> Theoretical ideas are not created wholly anew in each study . . . they are adopted from other, related studies, and, refined in the process, applied to new interpretive problems.[9]

In short, by cross-cultural comparison we find the terms to theorize about our own customs.[10]

There are four principles, at least, that shape commercial sexual transactions and condition our attitudes to them. I have derived these principles from stories I have heard and read about prostitution both as a native and a researcher. As a female native I have also learned about prostitution by being made aware of the exchange value of my own sexuality. As a researcher, the social texts I have studied are mostly those by other native analysts, some of whom are writers who have lived "the life."

These four principles are then: first, people in the U.S. generally believe that human beings (especially males) naturally possess, but socially repress, powerful, emotionally destabilizing sexual appetites. Second, members of American society generally believe that men are naturally better suited than women to assume authority and leadership in directing sexual activities. Third, in American society, people assume that sexual contact with men, in most contexts, is damaging and polluting to women. And fourth, people in the U.S. believe that our sexual habits divide us into persons of different type—for example, as heterosexuals, harlots, virgins, perverts, etc. I will discuss each of these four principles, and then consider how together they contribute to the meaning and consequences of sex commerce in American society.

The universal possession of a potent sex drive.—In describing the nature of sexual attraction, Schopenhauer states:

> The sexual impulse in all its degrees and nuances plays not only on the stage and in novels, but also in the real world, where, next to the love of life, it shows itself the strongest and most powerful of motives, constantly lays claim to half the powers and thoughts of the younger portion of mankind, is the ultimate goal of almost all human effort, exerts an adverse influence on the most important events, interrupts the most serious occupations every hour, sometimes embarrasses for a while even the greatest minds, does not hesitate to intrude with its trash, interfering with the negotiations of statesmen and the investigations of men of learning, knows how to slip its love letters and locks of hair even into ministerial portfolios and philosophical manuscripts, and no less devises daily the most entangled and the worst actions, destroys the most valuable relationships, breaks the firmest bonds, demands the sacrifice sometimes of life or health, sometimes of wealth, rank, and happiness, nay robs those who are otherwise honest of all conscience, makes those who have hitherto been faithful, traitors; accordingly to the whole, appears as a malevolent demon that strives to pervert, confuse, and overthrow everything.[11]

Freud, of course, used the term "libido" to refer to this powerful natural force—a force that manifests itself, he believed, as early as infancy. Like Schopenhauer, Freud believed that libidinal drives and impulses have a considerable influence over a person's mental development, character, and behavior.

Schopenhauer's description of the human sexual instinct is notable for its emphasis on the wicked, disruptive, intrusive, unmanageable, destructive, and devilish character of this instinct. Unlike the ancient Babylonians, our nineteenth-century European intellectual ancestors certainly did not view sexuality as a civilizing force in human society, nor as an activity that promotes nature's fecundity. Compare, though, Schopenhauer's description of our so-called sex drive with Karl Heider's description of the Grand Valley Dani of New Guinea:

> Especially striking is their five year post-partum sexual abstinence, which is uniformly observed and is not a subject of great concern or stress. This low level of sexuality appears to be a purely cultural phenomenon, not caused by any biological factors.[12]

Evidently, sexual desire is not experienced by the Dani as an overwhelming force or need—as a "malevolent demon" that possesses them. In this society, adults characteristically forego or neglect sexual activity for periods as long as three to five years following the birth of a child. Having searched without success for signs of repression and sublimation in Dani activities and customs, Heider concludes that the Dani's degree of interest in, and need or desire for, erotic activities is quite low. Having also searched for genetic, medical, and ecological explanations of the Dani's relatively low degree of libidinal energy, Heider concludes that the Dani's sexual instincts have been culturally shaped.

The moral of Heider's anthropological account is that our own sexual instincts, and our perceptions of them as well, have also been culturally shaped. Yet, while the Dani do not seem to be controlled by powerful libidinal urges and impulses, we need not conclude from this that we are not. For cultural forces have a powerful influence over our lives—sometimes more than the natural material that these forces shape. However, from the Dani's libidinal peace, we can conclude that one of our rationalizations for commerce in sex reflects, as Heider says, a purely cultural phenomenon.

The "natural" dominance of men.—One readily apparent feature of the commercial sex industry in the U.S. is that it caters almost exclusively to a male clientele. Even the relatively small number of male prostitutes at work serve a predominantly male consumer group. That women are absent as consumers in this market appears to reflect some kind of incompatibility between their social identities as women and their social role as consumers of commercial sexual products.

The role of a consumer of any product carries with it a certain social authority and power—expressed perhaps by the aphorism "the customer is always right." This authority or power often places the vendor of a commercial service in a socially subordinate position: this person's role is merely to please the consumer. When women are consumers of, for example, home furnishing and cleaning products, or clothing and cosmetic products, they do not overstep the boundaries of their socially defined authority. When women buy cars or building tools their interactions with male vendor subordinates can be socially awkward, and indeed in these situations the vendor may assume greater authority. Often a male vendor of a male-identified product will prefer to deal with a woman's male associates, even when she is the primary buyer.

Women as consumers of commercial sexual services overstep their socially defined power and authority in numerous ways. First, women are not supposed to have extensive knowledge about sexual matters, even about their own sexual needs and tastes. In assuming the role of a sex consumer, she implies that she possesses authority and knowledge that, as a woman, she is not supposed to have. By contrast, the male vendor who might cater to the woman sex consumer would be expected to have considerable knowledge of sexual matters, including knowledge of what women want and need sexually. Thus, to please her, the vendor would have to assume authority over his buyer in a way that vendors of a commercial product generally do not. Indeed, in the relatively few situations where women provide men with income in return for sexual favors, the male sex vendor is "gigolo" not a prostitute—that is, he has a specially marked social role that is less subordinating than the role of a mere sex seller. In short, the role of the sex client is incompatible with a woman's socially defined gender role and, likewise, the sex provider role is incompatible with a man's gender role.

Second, women as sex consumers not only assume some authority and knowledge of sexual matters, they assume a certain amount of social power—that is, a right to lead a particular kind of social transaction. The role of sex consumer is an especially awkward role for women, since the transaction they assume the right to lead is a sexual one—an activity where women are socialized to follow their partners, not to lead. Similarly, the subordinate role of the sex provider is an awkward one for men, for in this role men are required follow and take directions in sex from their female sex partners.

What these reflections show is that if we hope to move toward a society where sex partners have roughly comparable authority and control in a sexual encounter, then the buyer/seller relationship is not a good structure to impose on potential sex partners. That is, we do not move toward a more sexually egalitarian society by merely challenging the incompatibility between a woman's gender role and the sexually authoritative and dominating role of sex consumer, or by challenging the incompatibility between a man's gender role and the self-effacing, subordinating role of the sex provider. We move toward a more sexually egalitarian society by abolishing the roles of sex provider and sex consumer. This is not to say that there are not other kinds of social relationships that may serve as models for monetary sexual relationships: for example, the roles of artist and patron, therapist and client, or teacher and pupil. If commercial sexual activities were organized in terms of these roles, and if women and men could both assume the roles of sex artists, therapists, or teachers, as well as the roles of sex patrons, clients, and pupils, this might challenge some of the pernicious assumptions about gender constitutive of both commercial and noncommercial sexual relationships.

The idea that men are naturally better suited than women to assume dominant sexual roles may be part of a more general belief that men are naturally inclined to assume dominant roles in all social activities and practices. This general idea often remains unchallenged even in some feminist social evolutionary narratives. For example, some socialist feminists argue that men's dominant role in reproduction allowed them to assume a dominant role in production. But this argument does not explain how men came to have a dominant role in reproduction, and suggests that their dominance in the reproductive sphere is somehow natural.

Gayle Rubin has attempted to explain men's dominance in reproduction in terms of how human societies were created. Developing an idea from Claude Lévi-Strauss, she argues that the organization of people into social groups may have started when men began to exchange their sisters and daughters as gifts for the sisters and daughters of other men. This gift exchange between men, according to Rubin, affirmed

> a social link between the partners of the exchange . . . confer[ing] upon its participants a special relationship of trust, solidarity, and mutual aid.[13]

And, as a result of these gift transactions, certain people became "kin." However, since women were not partners to the exchange but, rather, the objects traded, they were denied the social rights and privileges created by these acts of giving. Rubin states:

> the relations of such a system are such that women are in no position to realize the benefits of their own circulation. As long as the relations specify that men exchange women, it is men who are the beneficiaries of the product of such exchanges—social organization.[14]

Thus Rubin suggests that Lévi-Strauss's writings on kinship should encourage feminists to look for the origin of male dominance not in the principles of capitalist exchange, but in more basic principles of social organization. These principles would allow us to explain the contemporary "traffic in women" for sex in terms of an original "traffic in women" for wives, rather than explain it in terms of capitalist economic relations or in terms of human biological processes.

Nevertheless Rubin recognizes that "the exchange of women" is a problematic notion, for if we take a marital gift exchange in which men assume dominant positions to be necessary for the creation of society, then nothing less than the abolition of society will end the oppression of women. I am not sure Rubin recognizes just how problematic this concept is, though she admits it does not well describe the marriage customs in all societies. But does it describe them in any? It certainly leaves unexplained how men came to assume dominant positions in some early marital exchanges. That is, it only raises the question of how women—rather than men or opposite sex pairs—became the objects of these affinal exchanges that led to the formation of some cultures. It is even unclear that women began in society in such subordinate positions, and feminists who assume this may be reproducing our own cultural ideologies. Lévi-Strauss himself admits that it is not logically necessary that these original exchanges be patrilineal ones:

> It may have been noted that we have assumed what might be called . . . a paternal perspective. That is, we have regarded the woman married by a member of the group as acquired, and the sister provided in exchange as lost. The situation might be altogether different in a system with matrilineal descent and matrilocal residence . . . The essential thing is that every right acquired entails a concomitant obligation, and that every renunciation calls for a compensation . . . Even supposing a very hypothetical marriage system in which the man and not the woman were exchanged . . . the total structure would remain unchanged.[15]

In short, affinal exchanges need not involve exchanges of women to create social relations, although that they involve exchanges of women is, for Lévi-Strauss, empirically accurate and biologically motivated.

Rubin also treats as empirically accurate the idea that the earliest society-creating exchanges were socially subordinating marital gift exchanges of women, but she sees the original dominance of men in these exchanges as socially, and not biologically, conditioned. She argues that to understand their origins, we need to look at how gender and sex are produced.[16] Unfortunately, Rubin does not appear to recognize that a social evolutionary account of this would have to start before the beginning of society—that is, before the creation of the marital practices that led to creation of kinship bonds and other forms of social organization. In other words, because she is looking for the origins of some custom that gave rise to society, these origins would have to be presocial in some sense. Rubin is not deterred by this, and she looks for these presocial origins in the rise of "socially" mandated heterosexuality, for, as she states, "gender is a product of the social relations of sexuality."[17] She argues that the incest taboo that created marital exchanges between men seems to have presupposed a taboo on homosexual relations. In short, male sexual and gender dominance comes about as a result of the social (or presocial) dominance of heterosexuality.

Rubin's account here merely forces the question of how the taboo on homosexuality came about. Moreover, since the creation of this taboo presumably preceded the creation of society, we need to ask in what way were the relations of sexuality that Rubin mentions "social" relations? For it would seem that once we place the origins of a social phenomenon at a time prior to the formation of human cultures, the phenomenon in question cannot be conceived as culturally determined. Despite these theoretical tensions in Rubin's account, Rubin may be right that heterosexuality and the oppression of women are connected in some ways. But in rendering heterosexual domination more fundamental and original than gender dominance, Rubin only leaves us with the task of explaining the original dominance of heterosexuality. However, we need not render one type of oppression as more basic and original than another, and then attempt to explain the first. Instead, we should take Rubin's expanded origin story to show that neither the contemporary phenomenon of male dominance nor the contemporary phenomenon of heterosexual dominance can be explained by a single social or biological evolutionary tale. Though both types of social dominance have historical and cultural roots, these roots probably do not account for the existence of practices that oppress women, lesbians, and gays in all other societies where they are or have been oppressed.

A culturally produced belief in the natural, sexual, and fundamental dominance of men is inscribed in many American societal institutions, but it is especially evident in the commercial sex industry, which is oriented primarily toward men as buyers of sexual merchandise. Whatever regulatory apparatus we develop, it needs to subvert the buyer/seller model of commercialized sexual exchanges, while at the same time subverting the belief that women are unsuited to direct sexual activities. Moreover, a belief in the natural superiority of heterosexuality may also be inscribed in our commercial sex industry, though there is some segment of this industry that caters to the sexual orientations of gay men. Our regulatory apparatus should also aim to undermine heterosexism, not only because it may be implicated in the oppression of women, but primarily because it is implicated in the oppression of lesbians and gay men.

Sexual contact pollutes women.—In American society, women in their premarital sexual prime who are chaste, and even perhaps virginal, are regarded as having greater social worth and status. Indeed, for women, sexual experience can be a source of social embarrassment, and allegations of sexual conduct are often used to "put a woman down," assault her integrity, and establish for her a socially damaging reputation. By contrast, sexual virginity and inexperience in men are a source of social embarrassment—even in relatively young men, as the recent Disney movie *Hocus Pocus* demonstrates. In this film, a young man's virginal status inadvertently enables him to initiate a causal sequence that wreaks supernatural havoc on a contemporary American town.

Mary McIntosh notes:

> Men who do not feel impulses towards sex for its own sake or who do not care for erotic fantasies are despised. Women for whom sex is not subordinated to a relationship are treated much more harshly. In adolescence they are hounded by police and social workers for being in "moral danger" or "sexually delinquent." In some age groups the behavior most likely to get you in trouble with the police is "sexual delinquency" . . . behaviour which is often acceptable for boys or for older people. In adulthood promiscuous women can attract the attention of psychiatrists and become labeled as "nymphomaniacs."[18]

Some sex workers see laws criminalizing prostitution as part of the pattern that McIntosh identifies here—one that involves the social enforcement of repressive norms of feminine sexuality. In other words, some sex workers claim that criminalizing prostitution contributes to the stigmatization and suppression of all active and autonomous expressions of female sexual desire.[19] McIntosh, however, sees prostitution itself as a cultural institution that is produced by, and reproduces, repressive norms of feminine sexuality. For McIntosh claims that American, and perhaps even global, commercial sex practices reflect and reinforce the myth that women have weak, easily repressible sex drives, whereas men have sexual urges that go beyond what can be managed by noncommercial sexual relationships. In short, for McIntosh, the circulation of a myth that attributes to women libidinal levels unequal to those of men is what appears repressive. Because she believes this to be the dominant sexual myth about women in American society, she overlooks the possibility that the suppression of prostitution could reflect fears about sexual wantonness in women.

Paradoxically, commercial sexual activities in American society and their criminalization probably both serve to enforce and reinforce repressive norms of feminine sexuality. For the commercial sex industry perpetuates myths about gender-differentiated sexual needs, and its suppression contributes to the stigmatization of women who do not conform to our notions of feminine sexual and emotional need. More specifically, the commercial sex industry and its suppression may not so much deprive women of libidos as enforce the idea that women must subordinate their libidinal and even economic impulses to other things. Moreover, even if the myth that women have lower levels of libidinal energy were a dominant social myth, it would not explain by itself how sex commerce is socially produced. For in a society where people believed that a woman's sexual appetite was equivalent to a man's, but that it was inappropriate for her to pursue its gratification through promiscuous and commercial sex, we might have a commercial sex industry much like the one we have.

I have suggested that in the U.S. we seem to regard a woman's active pursuit of sexual gratification as somehow grotesque because such pursuits involve her assumption of sexual authority and leadership, and this illicit assumption of social power on her part distorts and deforms aspects of her identity as a woman. In other words, a woman's pursuit of sexual or economic gain is perceived as grotesque not because she is not supposed to desire pleasure and wealth, but because she is supposed to desire them primarily as means to something else. Later in this chapter, when I consider racialized and sexualized perceptions of women, I will argue that myths about women's carnal natures are raced, and thus what McIntosh identifies as a myth about women may only be a myth about white women. And when we consider racial as well as gender myths, it may be more apparent that American society's simultaneous promotion and policing of women's commercial and noncommercial sexual activities reflects not only a belief in some women's relative frigidity, but a belief in some women's relative lack of self-control.

Moreover, women are socially hounded for and harmed by sexual activity, not because it is seen as expressing an unfeminine appetite for sex, but because we imagine that women—perhaps as feminine beings—are more vulnerable to physical, psychological, moral, and emotional harm from sex. More specifically, we seem to believe that a woman's individual constitution is tied directly to her sexual practices—that her moral innocence and purity are tied to her sexual innocence and purity. This ideology is reflected in social hierarchies that exist between prostitute and nonprostitute women, and among sex traders themselves. And it is evident in our numerous cultural images of the ravished, fallen female. Many feminist-prostitute civil rights advocates understandably want to debunk this culturally distorted image of the sexually active woman.

The cultural image of the sexually damaged woman is evident in the common vulgarisms we employ to describe sexual encounters. As Robert Baker has pointed out, women can be "fucked," "screwed," "banged," "had," and so forth, while men (coarsely conceived as "pricks" and "dicks") are the agents who do the "fucking," "screwing," and so on.[20] The metaphors for sex contained in this language are revealing. Women are "had" sexually, suggesting that they can be used up; women are "screwed," suggesting that they can be twisted on their threads; and women are "banged," suggesting that, in intercourse, they are bumped and bruised. Even some feminists have succumbed to the power of these metaphors. According to Andrea Dworkin, "The thrusting is persistent invasion. She is opened up, split down the center. She is occupied—physically, internally, in her privacy."[21] Dworkin invokes images of bodily mutilation, military aggression, and imperialist domination in her characterization of heterosexual copulation, and thereby expands the usual set of cultural metaphors. For Dworkin, women's bodies are penetrated, entered, invaded, and colonized by men in heterosexual sexual activities. Though aware of the nonliteralness of this language, Dworkin appears to believe that these metaphors are motivated by natural features of the world. However, it is equally natural to imagine that, in acts of heterosexual intercourse, men's bodies are enveloped, enclosed, swallowed, squeezed, and consumed by women's bodies. That one set of metaphors seems more natural to us than another is a purely cultural phenomenon.[22]

Ann Garry also notes the connection we make between sex and harm to women in our culture. She states that

> Because in our culture we connect sex with harm that men do to women, and because we think of the female role in sex as that of harmed object, we can see that to treat a woman as a sex object is automatically to treat her as less than fully human.[23]

Garry's comment indicates that, because we imagine women to be harmed by sex—even if they are "really" not—to represent women commercially as potential sex partners carries a specific social meaning. In representing women as sexually purchasable, we convey that harming women is permissible, which of course dehumanizes women.

The women who are most dehumanized by commercial sex are the sex providers themselves. For, even though sex with male sex consumers really does not use women up, pollute, or contaminate them, sex workers who, by virtue of their job, have a great deal of sexual contact with different men will be regarded as used up, polluted, or contaminated.[24] Indeed, the sex worker's social injuries from her job are compounded: she is socially harmed both by frequent sexual contact with men and by treating herself and her sexuality as a commodity. Seen then by others as commercial equipment for "screwing" and "penetration," sex workers have a less than fully human status—that of diseased pets or spoiled merchandise.

This status may explain why prostitutes are not usually sought for wives in the U.S., and why the families of women who have been recruited voluntarily for commercial or noncommercial sexual activities with men often seek justice for the harm that has been done to their female members, unlike families in West Nepal. Though the social attitudes reflected in these behaviors may not be commendable, it does little good to disregard, as liberals do, the "mental fossils" that shape these attitudes. For women who perform sex work will still be perceived as harmed, and will experience themselves as harmed,[25] whether some of us are liberated or not. A better response to sex commerce in this context would be to shape social policies that challenge our cultural associations between sex and female harm—something that decriminalized prostitution is unlikely to accomplish alone.

The reification of sexual practice.—Carole Pateman argues that

> The services of the prostitute are related in a more intimate manner to her body than those of other professionals. Sexual services, that is to say, sex and sexuality, are constitutive of the body in a way in which the counseling skills of the social worker are not . . . Sexuality and the body are, further, integrally connected to conceptions of femininity and masculinity, and all these are constitutive of our individuality, our sense of self-identity.[26]

Pateman appears to overlook, though, how the work of a dancer, athlete, model, or actor is intimately related to his or her body. Basically, the only thing that distinguishes their use of their bodies from the prostitute's is sex. Nevertheless, there is an interesting point buried in these remarks, and that is that one's sexual practices give a person a particularly meaningful self-identity, or rather social identity.

In American society, we distinguish people not only by their gender and race, but also by their sexual habits. Thus we mark people in terms of the kind of persons with whom they have sex, e.g., heterosexuals, homosexuals, and bisexuals. We mark women in terms of the number of partners with whom they have sex, e.g., virgins, harlots, sluts, and whores. And we mark men and some women in terms of the unusualness of their sexual activities and our attitudes toward them, e.g., queers, perverts, fetishists, exhibitionists, voyeurs, rapists, and so on. We do this to some degree with other activities, and the social relationships we form as a result of them, as well. We mark people by their occupations and recreations; by their unusual eating habits (vegetarians); by their marital status or their unusual marital practices (bigamists, polygamists); and by the cities, states, countries, and continents where they reside. When we identify someone in one of these ways, we often think we have learned something important about them.

Yet often these identifications are hollow, and obscure the complexities of people's lives. For example, many "blacks" and "whites" have mixed ancestry, many "lesbians" have slept with men, many "straights" have been confused about their sexual identities at some point in their lives, and many "women" competently fill male social roles. Despite the obfuscations they engender, we not only fit others into particular social identities, but we also fit ourselves into these available social place-holders. In the next few paragraphs, I will relate a personal incident that may indicate how strained this process can sometimes be.

When I was six years old, my mother sent me to school with a plate of hamantaschen to share with my first grade class in our regular "show and tell." She also told me a story that I could repeat to the class—the telling part of my "show and tell." What I told the class (according to my teacher and my mother) was something like the following: "We eat hamantaschen to celebrate the time when Queen Esther saved the jewels." Evidently, my teacher tried to correct what she perhaps perceived as verbal slippage on my part, insisting that I must have meant "Jews" instead of "jewels"; but I stuck to my version of the story. For, as I remember this childhood episode, it made little sense to me that one would or even could save Jews. Jews had something to do with our Jewish relatives in New York, and why would they need to be saved? I also remember that my teacher seemed somewhat delighted about Jews, at least she seemed delighted to discover one in her class, and thus she began her own "show and tell" about them. Pointing at me she said something like: "She is Jewish, and Mark and Debbie and Chris and . . . that is, we are all Christians." Thus began my consciousness of being a Jew.

My parents are Jewish atheists and they moved away from their Jewish family to California when I was four. We did not regularly belong to, much less attend, a synagogue. Up until this humiliating first grade event, my awareness of my marked identity consisted, I suppose, of knowing that we sometimes celebrated different holidays from our neighbors. For example, I probably knew we did not "celebrate" Christmas, but my mother hung up stockings for us and we watched all the Christmas shows on T.V. For Hanukkah (the holiday we "celebrated"), my mother sometimes bought a Christmas tree, spraypainted white, and hung dreidels on it—and some blue and silver decorations—and called it a "Hanukkah bush." We then put eight presents per child under it and lit candles. Moreover we often celebrated our Hanukkah with our Californian (Christian) friends, and they celebrated their Christmas with us. The only other Jewish holiday we "observed" was Passover. It too usually involved inviting some of my parents' Christian friends over and telling them about what "we" did on Passover. For us the ritual did not so much involve remembering that some of our ancestors were slaves, rather it involved presenting ourselves as Jews to our contemporaries. And our contemporaries then obliged us by including us in their Easter festivities—which for children, in a town where it was pretty difficult to find matzoh, kosher wine, or even lamb shanks, were a lot more interesting. Indeed, it was mostly on these holidays that our identities as Jews and Christians were fussed over; the rest of the time they were ignored.

As I grew up, of course, I learned that being a Jew meant having a different religion. But my mother taught me that people who were religious were superstitious and ignorant, and this attitude kept us, at least, from making a religion out of being Jewish. When asked the question "What are you?" or "What religion are you?" I knew eventually that I was supposed to answer "Jewish." I would often follow such answers with "but I'm not religious." Even with this admission, it was clear that my marked identity remained. Yet in what did my distinct identity consist?

As I grew older, revealing that I was Jewish to other Jewish people often led to socially awkward results. In one of my first teaching jobs, the chairman of my department was a man for whom it was very important to be a Jew. During my first few weeks on campus he would pop into my office and say something in Hebrew or Yiddish, to which I would respond with something vague, such as "great" or "sure." Then I would call my mother on the phone and try to reconstruct for her what he had said. To my surprise she was usually able to translate ("He was wishing you a good sabbath"). But in early September he came into my office to ask if I had some place to spend the holidays. What holidays? I couldn't think of any coming up, so I asked him. He was a bit shocked and said "Yom Kippur, of course." I actually knew what Yom Kippur was (I had only forgotten when it occurred), and said something like "Oh, I only celebrate the fun holidays." That ended his treating me as a fellow Jew.

I am now married to a Jew, and in many ways it seems like an inter-ethnic marriage. When we visit his relatives he has to instruct me in advance on what not to do or say ("Don't kiss Uncle Robert—he's Orthodox, and don't show the picture of Hannah at the Easter Egg hunt to Aunt Evelyn"). And coming to know "real Jews" has left me more confused about whether I can be one or not.[27] Certainly I can affirm a Jewish identity and say that I now know what I was all along. While 95 percent of the enculturation process that might have taught me what I am was missing in my life, nevertheless I have finally discovered my true self. Thus in one fell swoop of affirmation I might resolve the tensions brought on by my "unorthodox" upbringing. And to affirm my Jewishness now, of course, might even reflect ethnic pride. I also know that by affirming it, some people would feel closer to me, though some would feel more distant. But claiming this identity also means that I would have to disown the Christian traditions I grew up with, and it imposes on me the burden of overcoming my ignorance about "my people," "my race," and "my religion." In short, it imposes on me the burden of becoming more socially pure—that is, more purely of some type.

I believe that the relationship I have to my Jewish identity is similar to the relationships many others have to their identities as "women," "blacks," "lesbians," "prostitutes," and so on. And though the ambivalence I describe may be more characteristic of how we experience our socially marked identities, if we were to pay more attention to our unmarked identities, it might characterize how we sometimes experience them too.

Yet, even though these pure, reifying identities mask hybrid lives, these identities structure the contexts of our social negotiations. By assuming them, some people feel closer to us and some people feel more distant. And by assuming them, we gain certain social advantages and certain social burdens. Moreover, when we do not conform to the identities we are socially assigned, we create new and more awkward social identities, for example, in the way that my own holiday customs and gaps of social knowledge mark me as a problematic and queer Jew, especially to Jews. In American society, the sexual customs of the sex provider earn her a meaningful social identity—one that creates large social distances between her and others, one that imposes numerous social burdens and few social advantages, and one that is incompatible with her socially defined gender role in ways that render her a problematic and queer kind of woman.

According to Sander Gilman,

> The prostitute is little more than a Jew herself. Both are on the margins of "polite" society. And . . . such sexuality in a woman leads to corruption and physical decay.[28]

Just as the Jew "becomes a surrogate for all marginal males" the prostitute is the symbol of all marginal women. Like the Jew, she "is a source of corruption, if not for the individual, then for the collective."[29] And like the Jew, she represents disease, physiological anomaly, and most of all the venality of capitalism and sexuality, "For both Jew and prostitute have but one interest, the conversion of sex into money or money into sex."[30] In sum, like the Jew, the notorious personal traits of the prostitute, whether real or imaginary, are the locus of difference in women.[31]

Moreover, as I have tried to show, Jewishness is both a status ascribed on the basis of ancestry or "race" and achieved through the performance of particular "sacred" or social rituals. Similarly, I will try to show below that "whorishness" is a status sometimes ascribed on the basis of ancestry or "race," just as it is achieved through the performance of particular "sexual" or social rituals. And once this status is achieved, it is not "reversible," to use Christine Overall's term. Thus, there is a way in which prostitution is not "reversible," but not in the way Overall imagined.

The principles I have identified in this section suggest that the commercial sex industry in the U.S. is produced by, and reproduces, the following cultural myths: the myth of a powerful human sex urge, the myth of male sexual and social dominance, the myth of female pollution through sexual contact, and the myth of the existence of a category of women we variously call "harlots," "whores," "prostitutes," and "sluts." Though as individuals we may repudiate some or all of these myths, they render our actions meaningful. Of course we can imagine, and find examples of, societies where commerce in sex is based on other social myths: myths regarding the civilizing influences of sexuality, myths regarding the desirability of commercial polyandry, and myths regarding the sexual artistry, therapy, or wisdom of some women. But American society is incongruent in many ways with the ones that contain these myths, though it may be worth imagining how we can move in their direction. Merely criminalizing commercial exchanges of sex, or decriminalizing them, however, will do little to challenge these myths.

Sexual Otherness and Prostitution

Cornel West recently states that, "most social scientists who examine race relations do so with little or no reference to how sexual perceptions influence racial matters."[32] Likewise, many social scientists who examine gender and sexual relations do so with little or no reference to how racial perceptions influence sexual matters. For example, few social scientists have explored how racial stereotypes and beliefs condition commercial sex practices. Making a similar observation, Patricia Hill Collins states that in the "flood of scholarly and popular writing about Black heterosexual relationships" by black feminists, little attention has been paid to the connection between race and women's participation in commercial sexual activities. According to Collins,

> Theoretical work explaining patterns of Black women's inclusion in the burgeoning international pornography industry has been . . . neglected. Perhaps the most curious omission has been the virtual silence of the Black feminist community concerning the participa-

tion of far too many Black women in prostitution. Ironically, while the image of African-American women as prostitutes has been aggressively challenged, the reality of African-American women who work as prostitutes remains unexplored.[33]

The pattern of omission in black feminist thought that Collins describes is repeated in feminist thought—in general—about gender and sexuality. That is, while most feminist researchers have paid attention to the prostitute's and customer's gender, few researchers have explored how race and gender together condition one's participation in prostitution. Few have explored, for example, why it is that a disproportionate number of prostitutes are women of color though their clients are largely white men.

More generally, when we look at sex commerce cross-culturally and historically, one thing that stands out but stands unexplained is that a large percentage of sex customers seek (or sought) sex workers whose racial, ethnic, national, or class identities are (or were) different from

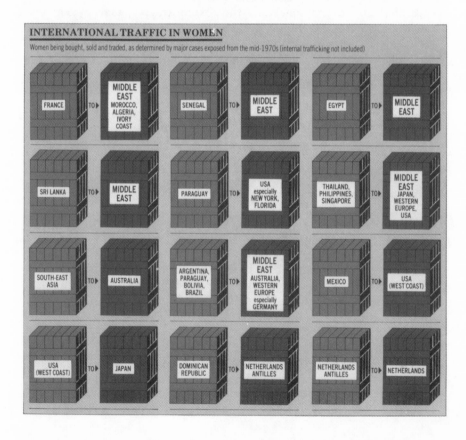

INTERNATIONAL TRAFFIC IN WOMEN

Women being bought, sold and traded, as determined by major cases exposed from the mid-1970s (internal trafficking not included)

FROM	TO
FRANCE	MIDDLE EAST MOROCCO, ALGERIA, IVORY COAST
SENEGAL	MIDDLE EAST
EGYPT	MIDDLE EAST
SRI LANKA	MIDDLE EAST
PARAGUAY	USA especially NEW YORK, FLORIDA
THAILAND, PHILIPPINES, SINGAPORE	MIDDLE EAST JAPAN, WESTERN EUROPE, USA
SOUTH-EAST ASIA	AUSTRALIA
ARGENTINA, PARAGUAY, BOLIVIA, BRAZIL	MIDDLE EAST AUSTRALIA, WESTERN EUROPE especially GERMANY
MEXICO	USA (WEST COAST)
USA (WEST COAST)	JAPAN
DOMINICAN REPUBLIC	NETHERLANDS ANTILLES
NETHERLANDS ANTILLES	NETHERLANDS

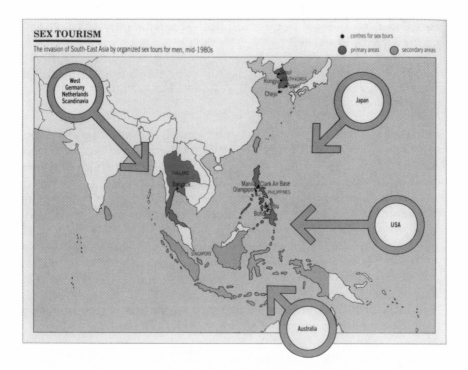

SEX TOURISM

The invasion of South-East Asia by organized sex tours for men, mid-1980s

● centres for sex tours

● primary areas   ● secondary areas

West
Germany
Netherlands
Scandinavia

Seoul
Kongju   SOUTH KOREA
         Pusan
Cheju

Japan

THAILAND
Bangkok

Manila   Clark Air Base
Olangapo
         PHILIPPINES
         Cebu
Bohol

USA

SINGAPORE

Australia

their own.[34] For example, Jacques Rossiaud claims that, in the medieval Italian cities, the prostitutes in the public houses were "overwhelmingly of foreign origin. They came from Flanders, from the Rhine valley, or from northern France."[35] Similarly, many Asian cities today (such as Bangkok, Seoul, Manila, and Taipei) are considered centers for "sex tourism," and they are visited predominantly by North American and European men, and Asian foreign nationals who seek the paid sexual services of local women.[36] And, in Japanese hostess bars today, evidently, white American and European women are popular with Japanese men. The *Los Angeles Times* describes these foreign women as "blond geishas," in a way that emphasizes one of the more culturally salient features of their ethnic-racial-national difference.[37]

In one of the few case studies that involves female clients ("jeans") and male prostitutes, the clients are predominantly white North American women (from Canada and the U.S.) and the prostitutes are men of color from the Caribbean (Barbados).[38] In West Nepal, as I described in chapter 5, the women of one particular social caste (Badi) perform the work of prostitutes, while their customers are men of other castes, ranging from the highest social castes to social castes regarded as more equal to the Badi. In the contemporary U.S., according to Richard Symanski,

> Black prostitutes have always been popular in red-light districts, their clientele being mainly white. Racism has not greatly dampened the demand.[39]

Indeed, according to Symanski, "until recently, prostitution has been the major source of interracial sex."[40] American women of Asian descent, American Indian descent, Mexican and Latin American descent, as well as Jewish descent, and women perceived as biracial have been popular with white Christian male customers in different regions of the U.S. at different historical moments. Symanski states that

> Surveys have long shown that the percentage of blacks and other minorities in prostitution is higher than whites in proportion to relative representation in the total population.[41]

And Licia Brussa claims "that thirty to sixty percent of prostitutes in the Netherlands are women from South America, Southeast Asia, and Africa."[42]

Does the current popularity of interracial and international prostitution suggest that racist and xenophobic hostilities are subsiding? Given that this "current rage" does not appear to represent a significant departure from the past, any optimism about subsiding hostilities may be unfounded. Yet if we do not assume that racism and xenophobia have diminished, then we might wonder how inter-ethnic "sex tourism" manages to be compatible with the ongoing existence of racial and national hatreds and fears—especially when such sentiments create barriers to intermarriage and, in general, to greater social cohesion in most areas of our lives. How does sex trading overcome these hostile sentiments? Or, if it does not, does interracial prostitution reflect an interracial rape mentality more than one of interracial respect?

Commenting on the increased sexual interaction between black and white Americans, Cornel West states,

> I view this as neither cause for celebration nor reason for lament. Anytime two human beings find genuine pleasure, joy, and love, the stars smile and the universe is enriched. Yet as long as that pleasure, joy, and love is still predicated on myths of black sexuality, the more fundamental challenge of humane interaction remains unmet. Instead, what we have is white access to black bodies on an equal basis—but not yet the demythologizing of black sexuality.[43]

Perhaps, what we have with contemporary "sex tourism" is white male access to female bodies of color on an equal, or greater than equal, basis with men of color—but not yet the demythologizing of the sexuality of women of color.

In this section and the next, I will explore some globally distributed and familiar myths regarding the sexuality of women of color. I will suggest that myths of this sort may very well condition the demand for much commercial sex; that is, they may condition the consumer behavior and choices of today's client. But before I turn to this, I will consider again Rossiaud's study of medieval prostitution and one other study, as they raise questions that may help us understand the various ways in which racial perceptions can influence sexual matters.

Rossiaud is one of the few social scientists who addresses and attempts to explain the ethnic composition of the prostitute labor force in his case analysis of prostitution. As a first step, he attributes the presence of foreign prostitutes in the medieval Italian brothels to particular cultural beliefs about the sexuality of foreign women, and to some men's tastes for such women, as well as the foreign prostitute's possibly destitute condition. He states that

> a large proportion of the women came from northern lands (Artois, Picardy, Flanders, lower Rhine valley). These regions had been through sorely trying times, but it is also probable that the high proportion of northern women was due to Mediterranean men's tastes for women physically different from the women they dealt with every day. Their reputation may also have entered into the picture, and several travellers, Pero Tafur or Hieronymus Munzer, for example, speak of the sensuality of Flemish women.[44]

Rossiaud's explanation in this passage may raise more questions than it answers. For example, do all men have tastes for women they perceive as physically exotic, that is, women who are regarded as somehow physically different than the women they usually have contact with? If so, this might explain the current popularity of "blond geishas" with Japanese men. Moreover, where do these tastes come from: are they derivable from some psychological or physiological norms regarding men's constitutions, or are these tastes socially and culturally shaped?

Similarly, is the perceived sensuality of the northern women of whom Rossiaud speaks derivable from some personal aspect of these women—e.g., their behavior or physical appearance? Or is it derivable from some tendency to associate what is exotic—i.e., culturally different or unusual—with what is erotic? Unfortunately Rossiaud fails to address, much less answer, some of these issues. In short, while he

attributes the preponderance of foreign women in the medieval brothels to both a preexisting taste for sexual "others" on the part of Italian
men and their belief in this "other's" sexual desirability, he does not
attempt to explain these extraordinary tastes and beliefs.

Rossiaud's failure to problematize the customer's tastes and beliefs
is a far too common problem in social science thought on prostitution.
Most researchers appear to regard the customer's motivations as normal, natural, and ordinary, though they typically regard the prostitute's motivations as psychologically, socially, or sexually deviant. For
this reason, there has been very little attempt to explain the social origins of the customer's motivations, while a great deal of research has
sought the social origins of the prostitute's seemingly unnatural behavior. Not surprisingly, one of the few interesting attempts to explain the
social origins of the customer's motivations pertains to a case study
where the customer is a woman. This study, by Cecilia Karch and
G. H. S. Dann, involves white North American female customers and
black Barbadian male sex providers.[45] The authors also examine the
social origins of their prostitute-informants' motivations, who in this
case are men.[46] But often when the customer or even prostitute is a
man, we generally assume that what he wants is sex; and when the
customer or prostitute is a woman, we take for granted that she must
want something else. Though I am not inclined to believe that the typical female prostitute or customer is after mere sex, I am no more
inclined to believe that the motivations of the male customer or prostitute derive from mere ordinary sexual desires. For why should we
assume, as Rossiaud appears to, that the desire for physically exotic
women is a mere ordinary, and unmysterious, male sexual desire?

Karch and Dann rightly do not assume that their female clients and
male sex providers are after mere sex. In probing the mystery of their
client-informants' sexual and economic behaviors, Karch and Dann
attribute these behaviors to racialized sexual fantasies that they possess
regarding men of African descent. According to Karch and Dann, "The
myth of black sexual prowess heightens the desire to overcome culture
taboo."[47] As Karch and Dann suggest, in our cultural imaginations,
men of African descent are seen as hypersexual and hypermasculine in
some ways. For example, African men are imaged as having larger gen-
itals than other men, and as having greater physical strength and sta-
mina than other men. Such images do not so much prompt social actors
to disregard taboos, but to construct sexual encounters in particular
ways—as exciting, desirable, more intensely erotic, and so on.

Moreover, in probing the mystery of their prostitute-informants'
behavior, Karch and Dann rightly attend to the "sociohistorical significance" of these behaviors. They state:

Formerly hotels in Barbados were clubs which practiced racial discrimination. Even today in some quarters a "de facto" color bar is perpetuated and there is little mixing between races or intermarriage among members of the local population. The mere presence of the beachboy on tourist premises thus represents a personal triumph in having overstepped such racial boundaries. The enhanced feeling of freedom is also reinterpreted by the beachboy in terms of the benefits that association with whites can bring. It is no mere coincidence that he often accepts payment for his services in the form of luxury items or the promise of an immigration visa and job in the metropolis. The white tourist stands as a symbol of escape from the drudgery of the Third World and access to a better life. Finally, conquest of the white female is perceived in terms of acceptance and integration into the society she represents.[48]

In short, Karch and Dann represent the prostitute's behavior in this context as an act of resistance to forms of both local and global racial oppression and economic domination. And, as they argue, the possibilities for liberation afforded by these forms of prostitution are not so much different than those that existed in the colonial and slave past.[49]

Interestingly, Karch and Dann do not appear to derive their conclusions about the socially shaped motivations of these prostitutes and "jeans" directly from the interviews they conducted with them. For their conclusions are not offered as behavioral laws but as interpretations. And as interpretations, they represent one way the authors are able to make sense of the customers' and prostitutes' behavior in a particular case of sex commerce—a case whose cultural idiosyncrasies the authors emphasize by titling their essay "Close Encounters of the Third World." More specifically, Karch and Dann's interpretation that their customer-informants are not after mere sex but rather racially fantasized sex, and that their prostitute-informants are not after mere money but the concrete and symbolic advantages of racial privilege and equality,[50] does not appear to be grounded in any peculiarities or details of their interview data. Instead they ground their interpretation in the historical and cultural peculiarities of their case alone—whose strangeness to us consists, in part, in the customer's and prostitute's gender and race.

Yet this is not a problem in their research and analysis, for we can include as part of their "data" their own knowledge of the cultural backgrounds of these particular social actors. In other words, we should take their data to consist in their construals of the construals that others give to their actions. Moreover, in taking an interpretive approach to this case study, we look for the social origins of the client's and prostitute's motivations not in the literal things they say, but in the cultural associations and beliefs implicit in their many communicative behaviors. Having done this, Karch and Dann succeed in offering us a plausible, interesting, and supportable account of the social origins of the behavior of some North American sex clients and providers. In short, the behaviors of these women and men are partly intelligible in terms of the cultural presuppositions of North Americans regarding the sexuality of men of African descent, and the socially specific agendas and assumptions of Barbadian men with respect to white foreigners.

More importantly, this study points the way for many future studies of prostitution. For example, we might question whether the behavior of white American and European males who frequent female sex providers of African, Asian, Latin American, and Native American descent can be explained in part by culturally produced racial fantasies regarding the sexuality of these women. In general, this study encourages us to look at how cultural ideologies about race, nationality, ethnicity, class, age, and so on, intersect with those about gender in shaping the commercial sex industry in our contemporary world. Moreover, we can ask whether the cultural myths that have made sex trafficking a site of ethnic and racial "integration" are liberating ones or whether they involve pernicious and hostile racialized and gendered images, as West's comments suggest.

Furthermore, we need to understand the sexual myths a particular group entertains about itself, and its own women, in order to understand the sexual myths they entertain about others. Let me return to Rossiaud's case study of prostitution to explain why this is so. In commenting on the medieval john's tastes for foreign women, he notes that her foreignness could attenuate the gravity of his own sinful lust for her. Rossiaud explains how the prostitute's foreign status reduced the seriousness of the john's own sin by appealing to the Florentines' culturally shaped religious concerns about their own sexuality. These religious concerns in addition to the john's sexual tastes, he alleges, guided the staffing of the brothels with foreign women.

In the following passage, Rossiaud identifies the relevant concerns that Florentines had about the consequences of their sexual acts for themselves, individually and collectively. He states:

> this ethnic structure of *public* prostitution in Florence proves that the city fathers who organized the brothel in the early fifteenth century not only paid careful attention to the teachings of the Church, but saw to it that the *prostibulum* functioned smoothly and to the profit of Florentines. The clients ran no risk of committing an act of qualified fornication when the women were foreigners from outside Tuscany. Transgressing ties of spiritual parentage

(the godparental relationship, for example) or committing incest were made impossible as well, and the city officials avoided subjecting local girls to the sin of lust.[51]

One of the predominant religious concerns that conditioned the work force of the Florentine brothels, according to Rossiaud in this passage, pertained to imperatives against incest. This concern led the city "fathers" to design the brothels so that customers could avoid nonmarital sex with social and familial intimates, Rossiaud suggests. Rather than shut down the brothels because of these concerns, which was another way they could have been expediently addressed, Florentine city officials organized the prostitute work force in a way that allowed the customer to commit the sin of simple fornication (nonmarital sex), but not the more serious sin of qualified fornication (incestuous sex).

However, Rossiaud's appeal to the functional and religious expediency of importing foreign labor does not entirely explain the "rationality" of the city fathers' choice. For it does not explain why other equally functional constraints were not seen as expedient for these religious purposes. Why, for example, did they not shut down the brothels and thus deter both simple and qualified fornication? Or why did they not choose women from a different southern city or social class than the brothel's customers to insure that there were no ties of blood or spirituality between the prostitute and her client?

To explain why using prostitutes of foreign birth alone served the Florentines' religious ends it might help to explore Rossiaud's comment that the Florentines were concerned not to subject local girls to the sin of lust. More specifically, it might help to explore why the Florentines were concerned not to subject local girls to this sin when they were willing to subject local boys and foreign girls to it. Did the Florentines believe that a woman's moral or constitutional purity and innocence was somehow tied to her sexual purity and innocence? And were foreign-born women seen, perhaps, as already morally impure, because of their foreignness, so that corrupting their sexual innocence was less significant?[52] Such beliefs would explain why staffing the brothels with foreign women rather than women from other southern regions would be seen as more expedient, and why committing simple fornication with them might not be serious enough to close down the brothels. Moreover, such beliefs would also explain this mysterious Mediterranean male taste for foreign women. For perceptions of female purity and impurity might not only serve to construct sex with foreign women as less sinful, they would also serve to construct foreign women themselves as more sensual and sexually available. Thus, contrary to Rossiaud, the Florentines' religious scruples about lust and incest do not provide reasons in addition to the johns' sexual tastes for explaining the ethnic structure of the brothels, rather these scruples may provide reasons that explain their mysterious "catholic" tastes in women.

Without further knowledge of Rossiaud's sources, I can only offer this analysis as a kind of Weberian ideal type. For I have little first hand evidence that foreignness in medieval Florence would mark a woman as potentially morally impure, or that the Florentines associated sexual and moral innocence in women, although their religious teachings make the latter plausible. However, I do know that perceptions about racial identities in our contemporary world are often tied to perceptions of moral innocence and purity, and even perceptions of sexual innocence. In other words, in our contemporary world, perceptions of racial purity, moral purity, and sexual purity are somehow linked.[53] For this reason we may conjecture that the tastes of white North American and European males for racialized sexual others may stem from socially formed perceptions regarding the sexual and moral purity of white women—perceptions that may serve to construct racialized sexual others as morally impure, and thus as sexually available and sensual. That is, the ethnic structure of the prostitute work force in our contemporary world may be conditioned by racial fantasies white people have about themselves and others. I will explore this possibility in the next section.

Reflecting on the lack of open discussion by social theorists on the racialized sexual imaginations of white and black people in American society, West states that

> the paradox of the sexual politics of race in America is that, behind closed doors, the dirty, disgusting, and funky sex associated with black people is often perceived to be more intriguing and interesting, while in public spaces talk about black sexuality is virtually taboo.[54]

Though we do not confront our racialized sexual images of others in public political forums, commercialized exchanges of sex may offer some people the opportunity to confront and sample these exoticized sexualities and eroticized races in semi-public sex districts. However, recently a number of feminist writers of color have begun to explore the locally and globally dispersed eroticized and exoticized images of themselves, and thus their writings have initiated some productive, public political confrontations with our racialized sexual imaginations. In the next section, I will explore how some of these socially produced images of women of color may condition customers' tastes in the commercial sex industry in the U.S. and some contemporary urban centers where Americans tour for sex, and thus how they may partly explain the social origins of the high participation of women of color in this trade. In particular, I will explore the "sexual reputations" of African and Asian women, and of American women of African and Asian descent in Western culture, and I will speculate that these reputations have evolved from social perceptions that construct nonmarital sex with them as less sinful.

Butterflies and Jezebels[55]

"She was a brown-skin mole like a Chinese doll,
Walking up and down in sin.
Back and forth she'd trod with a wink and a nod
To the nearest whorehouse den . . .
She tricked with Frenchmen, torpedoes, and henchmen;
To her it was all the same.
With Japs and Jews, Apaches and Sioux,
And breeds I cannot name;
With Chinks and Greeks, with Arabs and freaks;
She tricked in the House of God.
No son-of-a-gun would this whore shun
Who could pay to use his rod."[56]

"By the old Moulmein Pagoda, lookin' eastward to the sea,
There's a Burma girl a-settin', and I know she thinks o' me;
For the wind is in the palm-trees, an' the templebells they say:
'Come you back, you British soldier; come you back to Mandalay!' . . .
Tho' I walks with fifty 'housemaids outer Chelsea to the Strand,
An' they talks a lot o' lovin', but wot do they understand? . . .
I've a neater, sweeter maiden in a cleaner, greener land!"[57]

In his discussion of racism in the gay male community, Daniel Tsang describes the sexual tastes of the "rice queen"—a term he suggests "was coined by white gays to describe and probably put down their fellow gays who were attracted to Asians."[58] According to Tsang,

The archetypical rice queen is a Caucasian male, in his 40's or older, attracted only to Asians, for very stereotypical reasons. He views Asians as a class lumping Chinese, Japanese, Koreans, Vietnamese etc., into one amorphous group. He is attracted to Asians for our youthfulness, our lack of body hair, and our perceived submissiveness, dependence, and dependability . . . He suspects we are desperate for white lovers and will have sex with him just because he is attracted to us.[59]

The "rice queen" has his counterpart in the nongay male community. For just as there are "boob" men and "leg" men, there also seem to be white men who like to play with exotic "dolls." But what are the characteristics that these white "doll" men prize in the amorphous category of "Asian" woman?

In her analysis of David Henry Hwang's M. Butterfly, Dorinne Kondo describes some Western fantasies about Asian women. According to Kondo, the Asian woman is imaged in Western culture as follows:

> she is humble, exotic, a plaything . . . a diminutive, delicate "flower" whose "exotic perfume" . . . intoxicates . . . [T]his child-woman with "long oval eyes" . . . makes her man her universe.[60]

Modesty, embarrassment, and timidity belong to her Oriental female essence, as well as submissiveness, docility, and even a predisposition for feeling inferior to Westerners.[61] She will cower to signs of strength and power and, ultimately, she wants to be dominated.[62] She is the image of the perfect woman, and with her a man can be a perfect man.[63] Similarly, according to Mark Berger, Asian women have been mythologized by Westerners as "more desirable and available than European women: [they are] the 'sexual other', the mysterious and sensual women of the exotic east."[64]

Kondo argues that M. Butterfly shows us how Orientalist images of power relations between the East and West are gendered. Just as Asian women are represented as humble and submissive, Asians in general vis-à-vis Europeans are represented as humble and submissive. In Orientalist discourse, to be "Asian" or "Eastern" is to be "feminine," while to be "European" or "Western" is to be "masculine." Thus, Asian women are seen as more purely feminine than European women, whose Western-ness taints them with some degree of masculinity. Moreover, "Oriental-ness" and "female-ness" are both forms of otherness for the European male. According to Kondo, "if the Orient is a woman, in an important sense women are also the Orient."[65] In European mythology, Asian women instantiate both forms of otherness, making them truly exotic.[66]

If the Asian woman is constructed in Western culture as super-feminine and hyper-hetero-sensual, then it is not difficult to see why she is desired as a sex provider, and sometimes as a "mail-order bride." A relationship with her promises greater sexual, gender, and racial complementarity, and thus it almost guarantees romance. To non-Asian men, for whom other avenues of social access to her may be rare, sex trading perhaps provides the easiest path to her sexual services.[67] This path may also be attractive because the customer can satisfy his racialized sexual fantasy without having to confront racial hostility itself. More significantly, we should infer from the globally dispersed constructions of Asian womanhood that the sexual desires and fantasies that propel the customer to the Asian prostitute are shaped by global racial politics rather than a universal male biology. As the above analysis of the role of the "Oriental woman" in Western culture suggests, johns who cross national and racial barriers for Asian prostitutes are typically acting upon principles that position Easterners as inferior to Westerners.

Furthermore, men who visit prostitutes may not always be driven by "amorous" racial fantasies. According to Symanski, around the turn of the century in San Francisco "hearsay that the Oriental women possessed vaginas with a peculiar slant created a 'lookee' trade among whites, boys and old men alike."[68] Whether the popularity of visiting Asian prostitutes by whites is sustained by explicitly hostile racist images, or implicitly paternalistic ones, this phenomenon reflects principles of social organization that are oppressive to all Asians, and especially Asian women.[69]

> All right. So now you know something 'bout me you didn't know! In these streets out there, any little white boy from Long Island or Westchester sees me and leans out of his car and yells—"Hey there, hot chocolate! Say there Jezebel! Hey you—Hundred Dollar Misunderstanding! YOU! Bet you know where there's a good time tonight . . . "
> Follow me sometimes and see if I lie. I can be coming home from eight hours on an assembly line or fourteen hours in Mrs. Halsey's kitchen. I can be all filled up that day with three hundred years of rage so that my eyes are flashing and my flesh is trembling—and the white boys in the streets, they look at me and think of sex. They look at me and that's all they think . . . Baby, you could be Jesus in drag—but if you're brown they're sure you're selling![70]

> hey
> is it really true what they say about colored pussy?
> come on now
> dont be trying to act like you dont know what i am talking about
> you have heard those stories about colored pussy so stop pretend-
> ing you havent
> you have heard how black and latina pussies are hot and uncon-
> trollable
> and i know you know the one about asian pussies and how they go
> from side to side instead of up and down
> and everybody knows about squaw pussies and how once a white-
> man got him some of that he wasnt never no more good . . .

... and you know that usually the ones who be doing all this vili-
fying abusing hating and fearing of colored pussy are the main
ones who just cant leave colored pussy alone dont you
they make all kinds of laws and restrictions to apartheid-ize colored pussy and then as soon as the sun goes down guess who is
seen sneaking out back to the cabins? ...
... the pimps say colored pussy is an untapped goldmine[71]

Sondra O'Neale claims that in the past 150 years "the black woman
has never been the feminine ideal."[72] Instead, according to O'Neale,

by the sixteenth century ... black women were presented in societal media as icons of evil rather than examples of divine beauty
... from the sixteenth century onward in Western culture, the
black woman has been the object of forbidden attention as the
symbol of devilish sensuality. From the position of queen, lover,
muse and pedestaled wife, she became a symbol of sexual excess in
the white mind. And if black men were made studs to procreate
slaves, black women became sexual receptacles for all men.[73]

O'Neale suggests that, unlike Asian women, the black woman is constructed in Western culture as having a somewhat unfeminine sexual
appetite or lack of sexual self-control. She is mythologized as being
sexually loose, wanton, and lustful: or, as bell hooks says, as "beasts"
—sexual savages who are unfit for marriage.[74] Patricia Hill Collins
states that, in commercial pornography, black women are often compared to or imaged as animals, and thus as "more openly carnal and
sexual."[75] According to Collins,

When they yell "Bet you know where there's a good time tonight,"
they expect commodified sex with Black women as "animals" to be
better than sex with white women as "objects."[76]

Represented as sexually untame pets, black women promise—to the
Western mind—sexual excitement. For this reason, they have been
sought, as O'Neale suggests, as "sexual receptacles for all men."
Yet physically, black women's bodies are degraded aesthetically.
According to West,

The dominant myth of black female sexual prowess constitutes
black women as desirable sexual partners—yet the central role of
the ideology of white female beauty attenuates the expected conclusion. Instead of black women being the most sought after
"objects of sexual pleasure"—as in the case of black men—white
women tend to occupy this "upgraded," that is, degraded, position

primarily because white beauty plays a weightier role in sexual desirability for women in racist patriarchal America. The ideal of female beauty in this country puts a premium on lightness and softness mythically associated with white women and downplays the rich stylistic manners associated with black women.[77]

West's comments may explain why black women are overrepresented in prostitution, but also overrepresented at the low end of the prostitute hierarchy. For the racialized and sexualized images we have of black women simultaneously render them as upgraded sexual partners and as downgraded aesthetic objects.

West's comments may also explain why biracial women have frequently been sought as prostitutes. According to Richard Symanski, "fancy girls," women of black and white parentage, were especially popular with white customers in Storyville, the notorious red-light district of New Orleans. Moreover, Symanski states that, "Octoroon women were a special favorite in the better houses and their names and addresses received prominence in the sporting guides."[78] Light-skinned "black" women may have been especially popular because they would be seen to possess both the sexual prowess mythically associated with black women and the fairness and softness attributed to white women. In other words, biracial women could conform to hegemonic white standards of physical beauty, while mirroring to the white customer his own salacious appetites.

Speculating about the origin of these sexual myths about black women, bell hooks argues

> As white colonizers adopted a self-righteous sexual morality for themselves, they even more eagerly labeled black people sexual heathens. Since woman was designated as the originator of sexual sin, black women were naturally seen as the embodiment of female evil and sexual lust.[79]

hooks's comments suggest that the construction of the black woman as hypersensual and sexually available depended on beliefs that colonizers had about themselves. If the perceived "racial purity" of white women served to construct them as morally and sexually pure, then these perceptions would also serve to construct nonmarital sex with white women as sinful and socially disruptive. Correspondingly, if the perceived "racial impurity" of black women served to construct them as morally and sexually impure, then these perceptions would serve to construct nonmarital and coercive sex with black women as fair play.

Such perceptions embodied what Gerda Lerner calls "the myth of the 'bad' black woman" and this myth conditioned a range of practices that socially oppressed and sexually victimized black women. Lerner describes the myth and its repercussions as follows:

> A myth was created that all black women were eager for sexual exploits, voluntarily "loose" in their morals and, therefore deserved none of the consideration and respect granted white women. Every black woman was, by definition, a slut according to this racist mythology; therefore, to assault her and exploit her sexually was not reprehensible and carried with it none of the normal communal sanctions against such behavior.[80]

Lerner also locates the origin of this myth in sexual ideologies that whites maintained about themselves. In imaging themselves as racially, morally, and sexually pure, they imaged all others in opposite terms. In this way, white men minimized the evils of their nonmarital sexual behavior, by confining a significant portion of their sexual relations to sexual partners conceived as somehow evil.

The sexual relations these racially and sexually pure selves had with racial and sexual others were characteristically coercive. For example, numerous writers have described the brutal sexual exploitation of female slaves of African descent by American slave owners. Yet, according to hooks, these same writers often overlook the fact that the sexual exploitation and degradation of black women did not end with slavery and has been "institutionalized by other oppressive practices."[81] These practices include the sexual harassment and rape of black women, the lenient legal sanctions applied to men who harass or rape black women, and the creation and enforcement of miscegenation laws.[82] Another such practice involves the commercial promotion and exploitation of black women's stereotyped sexuality for the benefit of white males. W. E. B. Du Bois comments on this phenomenon:

> I shall forgive the white South much in its final judgment day: I shall forgive its slavery, for slavery is a world-old habit; I shall forgive its fighting for a well-lost cause, and for remembering that struggle with tender tears; I shall forgive its so-called "pride of race," the passion of its hot blood, and even its dear, old, laughable strutting and posing; but one thing I shall never forgive, neither in this world nor the world to come: its wanton and continued and persistent insulting of the black womanhood which it sought and seeks to prostitute to its lust.[83]

As Du Bois's comments emphasize, the prostitution of women of African descent began but did not end with American slavery.

Symanski's research findings testify to the prevalence of commercial sexual transactions between parties who, in a previous century, might have been related as master and slave. He states:

The streets of the Western world are populated by significant numbers of black prostitutes. From their relatively high numbers, their persistence on the landscape and the small proportion of black males arrested for soliciting, it is safe to infer that much of their trade is with white males.[84]

And Roger Lane claims that, during the latter half of the nineteenth century, "Black prostitutes represented a fifth to a quarter of all those in [Philadelphia]" even though blacks averaged "4 percent of the city's population."[85] According to Lane,

[men] of all races visited prostitutes, but the number of adult black males . . . was not big enough to provide more than a fraction of the custom . . . Most male transients, such as sailors, salesmen, and other proverbially heavy customers, were also typically white.[86]

Describing prostitution around the turn of the century in the U.S., Symanski states that "In the south black prostitutes were available for white males, but the reverse situation was probably absent."[87] Furthermore, according to Symanski,

Chicago's Levee had two Japanese and two Chinese houses and at least one staffed only with black women—Black May's; all were said to have admitted only white males."[88]

Commenting on the demise of brothels that admitted white patrons only, in places like Chicago in the north and New Orleans (Storyville) in the south, Symanski states:

Although Storyville and districts like it are now a blurry part of American history, racism in brothels has changed less than one might have expected. Black prostitutes are commonplace in Nevada's legal brothels and they mix freely with their with coworkers. But in a few houses these women are available exclusively for white clients.[89]

Yet, what Symanski appears to find racist, however, is the exclusion of black men from the brothels and not the racially structured tastes of white males. He appears to believe that once black and white men have equal access to the bodies of black and white women, then we will have succeeded in eliminating racism. Yet as long as these unions are predicated on myths of black sexual impurity and aesthetic inferiority, and the corresponding myths of white sexual purity and aesthetic superiority, we will not have met the more fundamental challenge of humane interaction that West has articulated.

The trend that Symanski notes is corroborated by other observers of contemporary sex commerce. For example, Licia Brussa claims that, currently, "there is an increasing demand for black women in the West European [sex] market."[90] Carla Corso claims that "All over Italy there is a big migration from Third World countries; women from Asia and Africa are the 'latest fashion.'"[91] Since these historical and current "fashions" appear to derive less from mere ordinary sexual desire and more from socially constructed contempt, these fashions for sexual others represent only a continuation, perhaps, of a colonial rape mentality rather than a postcolonial mentality of mutual respect. Seen as less than fully human on two counts—both by race and by sex—women of African and Asian descent are regarded as inherently degraded, and thus the appropriate partners for degrading sex.

Toward Regulationism

Sex commerce in the U.S. and elsewhere appears to be produced and maintained by myths that serve to marginalize women of color. Therefore feminists and other political progressives should develop social policies that will challenge and subvert these myths, and that will deter practices like trafficking in the racialized and gendered sexualities of others. Criminalizing sex commerce, though, is neither practical for deterrence, nor does it place responsibility for sex commerce in the right place. For sex commerce comes about not from the deviant or criminal motives of sex clients and providers, but from their culturally formed values and beliefs. Thus to respond to sex commerce with punitive laws is in some ways to blame the victims.

Decriminalizing prostitution, without putting in place any positive social regulations, is also impractical for deterring prostitution, and it does not contribute to the subversion of the pernicious myths that serve to organize it in American society. For these reasons, as I argued in chapter 4, I support a policy of regulated prostitution. Such regulation should aim, as Roger Matthews has argued, to protect the sex worker's legal rights and minimize her exploitation by others, to eliminate corrupt business practices, and to protect society from any harms or annoyances caused by the industry. In addition, one of our primary aims, according to Matthews, should be to reduce the commercialization of prostitution. By this Matthews means that we should aim to prevent the industry in sex trading from being controlled by large scale commercial or capitalist interests. For just as we aim to protect the prostitute from exploitation by small-scale pimps and procurers, we should aim to protect her from exploitation by large-scale corporate pimps and procurers.

Previous regulatory models fail to protect the prostitute from powerful capitalist interests, or they do so at the expense of subjecting prostitutes to the arbitrary and paternalistic authority of governmental officials. In either case the prostitute is politically disempowered, and thus vulnerable to abuse and exploitation. Thus, we need a new kind of regulatory apparatus, one that avoids some of the problems apparent in systems built around publicly licensed private brothels, or in systems built on the public registration of prostitutes.

The system I propose utilizes elements of the two just mentioned. It would be a system where prostitutes would not be "registered" and brothels would not be "licensed," but where prostitutes themselves would be licensed, much like other professionals and semi-professionals. Since in the sex industry the primary productive assets are the bodies of sex providers, and the primary trade secrets are contained in their personal skills, knowledge, charm, and talent, sex providers should be given as much control as possible over the operation and use of these assets. In the same way that physicians are given authority to determine how healing is practiced, or in the same way that builders share authority with municipal and state governments to determine how buildings are built, sex providers should be granted the social authority—perhaps together with others—to determine how sex "entertainment" and "instruction" will be provided.

The standards for licensing sex providers should be established by public boards or commissions made up of service providers, community leaders, educators, and legal and public health experts. These commissions should especially include persons of color, women, persons who are economically disadvantaged, and gender and erotic nontraditionalists. Moreover, the standards these commissions impose should reflect the kinds of knowledge and skill required for the sex provider's work, and required to protect the society from any harm ensuing from her work. For example, candidates for this license could be expected to complete some number of college-level courses on human sexuality from the perspectives of biology, psychology, history, medicine, and so on. The aim of this requirement would be to make the sex provider more reflective about what she does, and more resourceful to meet the challenges she may encounter. Also, the presence of prospective sex providers in our institutions of higher learning, and in various communities as graduates from these institutions, will make it more difficult for society to treat them as social outcasts. In setting the requirements for obtaining a license to sex trade, though, license boards must make sure that the personal and material costs of obtaining a license do not outweigh the risks of operating without it. Thus, any required courses and tools must be available and affordable on a nondiscriminatory basis to qualified candidates for the license—something that might be accomplished by insuring that any necessary training or tooling would be available at public institutions. These institutions must also be willing to admit students identifying themselves as prospective sex providers, and to make available to them the usual forms of financial assistance.

Some of the main advantages of licensing individual service providers rather than commercial sex establishments by public boards are: first, that this would allow prostitutes to work for themselves, perhaps in workers' collectives or professional partnerships, making them less vulnerable to exploitation by large-scale capitalist interests. Second, by controlling how their services are offered, sex providers would be less vulnerable to abuse and harassment from patrons, small-scale entrepreneurs or pimps, and public officials. Third, sex providers would acquire the status of semi-professionals, giving them the social authority to lead certain kinds of business and sexual trans-actions. Fourth, by engaging in their profession profitably, female sex providers might challenge our cultural association between sex and harm to women. Fifth, by allowing advocates and representatives for sex providers to have a strong voice in designing the procedures for licensing, we would encourage the internal setting and monitoring of industry standards, and we would empower those who are likely to work to protect the sex provider's legal rights. Moreover, by includ-ing on licensing boards persons of color, women, working-class indi-viduals, and gender and erotic nontraditionals, we would give a voice to those who are able to recognize and contest racist, classist, sexist, and heterosexist practices. And sixth, a license would insure the con-sumer that the person so licensed had met certain professional stan-dards, and it would provide the public with a vehicle for addressing possible hazards that might result from the industry.

One of the notorious risks of prostitution is the spread of venereal disease. Especially when we are in the midst of an AIDS epidemic, it seems that the risks of this industry are particularly high. However, before regulators impose severe restrictions designed to curtail this risk, we should first attempt to estimate how much sex commerce contributes to the spread of AIDS. And if it should be determined that sex commerce, like noncommercial sexual activity, contributes to the spread of AIDS, we should not hold commercial sex providers more responsible for this health crisis than we hold other sexually active nonmonogamous people. To blame commercial sex providers for the spread of AIDS is like blaming commercial airline companies for the spread of terrorism. Instead, we need to respond by requiring that the industry take extraordinary precautions to abate this epidemic, just as we require commercial airline companies to take extreme precautions to abate terrorism; we do not shut them down.[92] Moreover, just as airline passengers feel safer when everyone is searched before boarding, perhaps it would be sensible to require that commercial sex clients are inspected for disease before they can visit a prostitute. And perhaps the easiest way to do this is to train prostitutes themselves to perform the necessary blood tests, etc., and to enforce the period of waiting for test results. Of course, it will also be of prime importance to keep sex workers drug- and alcohol-free.

In arguing for socialist and feminist regulationism in regard to prostitution, perhaps we provide a model for pressing for socialist and feminist regulation of other industries as well. If we no longer treat sex commerce as an evil produced by capitalism and patriarchy, but see the evil in the way sex commerce is produced and shaped in a classist, sexist, and racist society, then we should develop social policies that attempt to reshape it in anti-classist, anti-sexist, and anti-racist ways. Such policies should aim to contest the subordination of labor to more powerful commercial interests along class, gender or racial lines. Because even political conservatives are likely to see the need not to subordinate the sexuality of women to large-scale capitalist interests, we should exploit their sensibilities about sexuality and commerce to argue against subordinating the creativity and humanity of other workers to large-scale commercial interests. In short, perhaps in the future we can offer a more humane, feminist and socialist sex industry as a model for other kinds of labor reform.

7

Interpretive Ethics, Cultural Relativism, and Feminist Theory

---

Lingerie Féminine and L'écriture Féministe

The interpretive and pluralist, and even culturally relativist, approach to ethics that I have elaborated and defended in this book does not provide feminist theory any high and secure ground from which to insist on particular political positions. Yet this approach, as I have tried to show, does give us tools for shaping some new political agendas. Another advantage is that it gives us the tools to make sense of the cultural peculiarities of other women we know and love—even and especially women we sometimes see as anti-feminist. Let me provide one example of this from daily life.

Once when I was visiting my mother, we had the following confrontation.[1] The visit had been facilitated by my mother's offer to attend to my infant son so that I could attend the American Philosophical Association (APA) meetings in New York. Shortly before leaving her Manhattan apartment the day of the meetings, I noticed that my mother was becoming somewhat agitated as I assembled and put on my convention attire. Making my exit, I asked her what was bothering her, and with some exasperation she responded: "I'm surprised that you would even think of going off to a professional conference with underwear that do not match." These were her exact words, for I wrote them down in the taxi on my way to the APA—on my way, quite appropriately, to hear a session on Sandra Bartky's work.

There are numerous mysteries contained in my mother's utterance. For one, what does my mother think we do at philosophy meetings that requires matching undergarments? Actually, shortly out the door

I turned to my mother and pointed out what was obvious to both of us: that no one would see my underwear. My mother responded by raising a point she evidently wished was more obvious to me: that wearing matching, and also feminine, undergarments was something a woman did for herself. She started to take out some examples of underwear sets for my benefit, which I interrupted with a hasty and rude retreat.

The second mystery to me, revealed by her subsequent remarks, is why do women do for themselves just what my mother was describing? Why is it, especially when no one will notice, do women subject themselves to such extreme underwear "discipline" (a question Bartky's feminist uses of Foucault might lead us to ask)? Do we, at some level, believe that nonintimate others really notice our undergarments: that is, that men not only try but actually do see through our clothes? In other words, have we begun to take literally what began as a metaphor for the voyeurism of heterosexist men? But if we believe our underwear is surveilled by others, then wearing feminine underwear is not just something women do for themselves; and my retort to my mother was not as obvious as it then seemed.

Somewhat ironically, the underwear that offended my mother was expressly designed to make it easier for women like me to nurse, and thus do something for our infants—a service my mother should have been reminded of when we scrambled around her kitchen that morning looking for milk substitutes. Of course, this need not obviate my mother's concern, for we can imagine that our intimate apparel is visible to both grown as well as infant others, and measure it accordingly against different standards. Moreover, as I think my mother would point out, these standards are not necessarily incompatible. Could Victoria possibly have secrets to share even with lactating women? That morning I realized that there were mysteries and secrets about women's underwear, which, in my undisciplined pre- and post-pregnant states, I had never bothered to explore.

Since I was on my way to hear a session devoted to the work of Bartky, I began to think about how she would approach the underwear concerns of women like my mother. The confrontation between my mother and me seemed like the tip of an iceberg that the interpretive work of feminist writers like Bartky could help me explore. Bartky's work especially allows us to see how the habits and fantasies of women in our culture are shaped by larger societal institutions and political values. More specifically, in her book *Femininity and Domination,* she shows how femininity is "an artifice, an achievement" in our culture.[2] In the terms that I employed in chapter 3, she shows that the category "feminine" refers to an achieved rather than an ascribed status. And one achieves femininity, in part, by being able to achieve a particular kind of body.

In our current society, the woman who is regarded as feminine typically has a body that is thin, firm (though not muscular), soft in the right places, and pleasantly scented. This body has unblemished-looking skin, shaved limbs, manageable and shiny hair, enhanced facial color, enameled finger extensions, and delicate and soft hands and feet. Bartky describes, in ways that ring both humorous and true, the so called "beauty" routines and consumption habits that women develop, and which manifest their aspiration to, and even affirmation of, this bodily ideal. One such consumption habit involves clothing this real or imagined body in coordinated and pretty undergarments.

After describing these time- and money-demanding routines, Bartky raises the following mystery, "Why aren't all women feminists?"[3] Why, for example, don't women like my mother resist these excessively demanding ideals of femininity? The answer Bartky offers is a Foucaultian one: the above forms of feminine body discipline exemplify peculiarly modern and usually invisible forms of social power and authority. In Bartky's words,

> The disciplinary power that inscribes femininity in the female body is everywhere and it is nowhere; the disciplinarian is everyone and yet no one in particular.[4]

In Foucault's view, my mother's remonstrances about my underwear, and diligent upkeep of her own, are not expressions of any special or obvious social authority or power invested in her regarding matters of feminine appearance. Instead, my mother's remonstrances reflect more subtle and therefore less subvertible forms of social power: the power of particular social norms to shape our lives and our selves. People like my mother do not produce these norms, though they enforce and reproduce them, through self-surveillance and the monitoring of others.

The norms of femininity are especially powerful ones for women, because they are bound up with our conceptions of gender—of what it means to be a woman—and these conceptions are intimately bound up with our definitions of ourselves—what it means to be a person.[5] Moreover, because of the prevalence and authority of mass visual media in American society, our socially shaped norms of femininity can be enforced and reproduced on a massive scale. According to Bartky, mass visual media enable

> the spread of this discipline to all classes of women and its deployment throughout the life-cycle. What was formerly the speciality of

the aristocrat or courtesan is now the routine obligation of every woman, be she a grandmother or a barely pubescent girl.[6]

For instance, underwear tastes that were once the indulgence of courtesans and aristocrats are now the custom of middle-class grandmothers like my mother.

Bartky's analysis implies that women like my mother, who impose feminine underwear discipline on themselves and their female offspring, are merely succumbing to the power of socially hegemonic tastes and standards. Given this, her Foucaultian analysis of the patriarchal instruments of control and domination in American society provides some answer to the mystery of why women like my mother are not feminists about underwear: they have not resisted, for whatever reasons, the various insidious norms of femininity. Moreover, Bartky's analysis implies that my mother's underwear self-discipline does not require surveillance by others, or even the imagined surveillance by others through the literalizing of metaphors, for it is created by internalized social ideals. In other words, these internalized ideals produce both the disciplined behavior and the fantasy represented by taking literally certain metaphors about self-exposure, rather than the other way around.

But can we liberate ourselves from the control of these norms, on this Foucaultian model, and if so, how? Foucault's own interrogations of modern forms of political power often suggest that all social norms, and not just ones produced by the class structure of society (e.g., gender norms), create systems of power that illegitimately diminish our personal liberty. Yet if this is the case, then, as Charles Taylor argues, "there is no escape from power into freedom, for such systems of power are co-extensive with human society. We can only step from one to another."[7] That is, if there is no freedom from oppressive control and power in society, then Foucault must either place the possibility of freedom in the realm of nature, or accept some Nietzschean notion of freedom, where liberation consists of taking a critical, but detached stance toward competing systems of domination. Since Foucault rejects the former romantic view of a repressed and controlled nature needing to be liberated from the artificial human norms of society, he seems to be stuck with the Nietzschean view.[8]

To avoid Foucault's difficulty, we need to reject the idea that all social norms and ideals operate as instruments of domination and control. If we reject this idea—as Bartky indeed seems to do—then liberation can consist in identifying those norms that do operate this way, and finding ways to resist them and neutralize their power. This is what I have tried to do in analyzing the oppressive aspects of prostitution: to identify the insidious norms of gender, race, and sexuality that commerce in sex epitomizes in American society. Nevertheless, to do this, we need to have some way to distinguish oppressive social norms from nonoppressive ones. We need to ask: do these norms really render us unfree or unequal in particular ways? For example, do the norms of femininity in American society enable the domination and control of women by men?

In her descriptions of feminine body discipline, Bartky illustrates the ways that the norms of femininity disempower women. For one, they lead to feelings of inadequacy in virtually all women, even those who manage temporarily to conform to these norms. For all women age, and this process undoes even the greatest bodily achievements. Moreover, because of the relationship between femininity, gender, and personhood, women who do not feel completely feminine may feel inadequate as women and as persons. On the other hand, the women who do adequately fulfill our cultural ideal of femininity may feel shallow, decorative, and unproductive. In this way, femininity presents a double bind for women: they can be feminine, womanly, shallow and unproductive, and therefore nonpersons, or they can be unfeminine, unwomanly, and therefore nonpersons. Such feelings of inadequacy—as women and as persons—not only cause psychological and emotional tensions, they render some women helpless and unable to live creative and rewarding lives. Furthermore, the norms of femininity lead to consumption patterns that constrain women economically, and thus render them more dependent on others. These consumption habits deplete women of time and energy they may need to pursue other things—children, occupations, recreations, and so on. In sum, Bartky has made a strong case that women would be better off if we could both resist these norms in our own lives and develop political strategies that might neutralize their social authority in all our lives.

Yet, in resisting these norms, we have to remember that the problem is not in the frivolous underwear, the make-up, the aerobic routines, or the perfumes themselves, but in what these things symbolize, as Bartky emphasized at the APA session I attended. In American society, their obsessive use by women reflects standards of bodily grooming that can debilitate women. But their use in, for example, contemporary Iran by women may have a very different social meaning.[9] There their use may symbolize resistance to religious authority, just as the adultery in *Ju Dou* symbolized resistance to oppressive marital traditions. Moreover, there may be some subcultural contexts in our own society where apparent conformity to feminine body discipline fails to have its usual meaning or consequences. Certainly the feminine body discipline of transvestite men may represent one such subcultural context. Also, I suspect that the feminine body discipline of so-called "lipstick lesbians" does not have its usual social meaning, and may moreover serve to subvert some of the heterosexist aspects of these norms. These examples, at least, show us that we need to make sense of feminine body discipline enacted by gender nontraditionalists and members of sexual minorities.

To make sense of outwardly similar behaviors of bodily grooming that nevertheless may have different social meanings and consequences, we need to uncover the cultural assumptions, values, and ends constitutive of the contexts and institutions in which these behaviors occur. To do this we need to collect and study the narratives of social actors from different groups both within and without the U.S. Such narratives might reveal whether all women who engage in feminine body discipline have interiorized the debilitating norms of femininity that Bartky has described, or whether all women who engage in my mother's underwear discipline inevitably reflect the same norms. But collecting and studying these narratives requires further ethnographic and interpretive work.

The stories we collect and study, through ethnography and interpretation, will prompt us to create spaces in our feminist texts for the voices of other women. Some theorists have argued that postmodern, nonauthoritative texts must be polyvocal, and feminist moral and political texts with postmodern concerns should consider this narrative option. This option, for example, is well illustrated in Maria Lugones and Elizabeth Spelman's paper "Have We Got a Theory for You! Feminist Theory, Cultural Imperialism and the Demand for 'The Woman's Voice,'" and thus this paper provides us with a model for future polyvocal feminist moral and political texts.[10] In this essay, Lugones and Spelman take some license with the monological and authoritative narrative formats of traditional theorizers, and develop a textual style that works well to challenge the assumption that there is a single "woman's voice" or even a single "feminist voice" that can be recovered for feminist theory. Their textual style also allows two distinct voices—an "inside" feminist voice and an "outside" one—to be heard together and to challenge each other's distortions. Moreover, as "they" argue, "only when genuine and reciprocal dialogue takes place between 'outsiders' and 'insiders' can we trust the outsider's account."[11] If feminist accounts are intended to render "nonfeminist" women intelligible to both "us" and "them," then we need to open "our" theories to "their" voices. In doing this we also challenge the hierarchy that Lugones and Spelman note between theorizers and those theorized about, while retaining the distinctness and irreducibility of each voice.[12]

Lugones and Spelman demonstrate how polyvocal texts can be achieved through collaborative writing, but such texts can also be created to some extent by using the "traditional" skills of ethnographic interpretation and translation, as Faye Ginsburg does. For example, feminists writing on feminine body and underwear discipline might open dialogues with women who shop at Victoria's Secret or Frederick's of Hollywood in order to reflect their ideals and assumptions about underwear. Though ethnography places our collaborators within a hierarchy of researcher and informant, good interpretive work disrupts our propensity to theorize about our informants in our own terms. Instead it requires that we respectfully work at presenting their own self-understandings. For example, had I sought my mother's self-understandings or even authorial collaboration in writing this section, I might have been able to create a space for her voice here to articulate the ideals of feminine underwear in her own terms. And soon my daughter's voice may push its way into this conversation. This is a child who, at six years old and despite her mother's underwear, playfully aspires to the norms of Barbie glamour, though she seriously prefers the more "realistic" body of her "happy-to-be-me-doll." She is now the second biggest critic of my relatively drab apparel.[13]

Interpretation and Resistance

Feminists have resisted pluralist and nonreductionist approaches to ethics because they often fear that such approaches will not provide us with sufficient resources to resist our oppression as women. The bottom line for a feminist theory is its usefulness for guiding feminist political practice. Lugones and Spelman elaborate this meta-theoretical criterion:

> Theory cannot be useful to anyone interested in resistance and change unless there is reason to believe that knowing what a theory means and believing it to be true have some connection to resistance and change.[14]

Moreover, Lugones and Spelman describe how nonimperialist feminist theories should inform resistance and change:

> a theory that is useful will provide criteria for change and make suggestions for modes of resistance that don't merely reflect the situation and values of the theorizer. A theory that is respectful of those about whom it is a theory will not assume that changes that are perceived as making life better for some women are changes that will make, and will be perceived as making, life better for other women.[15]

By taking an interpretive and pluralist approach to abortion and prostitution, we develop political agendas that express the incommensurable values of differently situated social actors. And we do not assume that the changes we bring about as the result of these agendas will improve, or be perceived as improving, the lives of all women. For the agendas we develop on an interpretive approach involve compromise, which implies feelings of both loss and gain, differently configured in different social actors. For example, in proposing the policies of conditional and socially regulated access to abortion and prostitution, I expect some women, including many feminists, will feel these policies are too restrictive, while others will feel they are not restrictive enough. Yet, they meet the aim of an interpretive analysis, which is to fashion policies that take account of different social constructions of reality—policies that may also challenge aspects of these constructions or render them more visible. Let me give one final example of how an interpretive and pluralist ethics can promote the formation of nonimperialist, feminist practical political agendas. This last issue that I will pursue is in many ways similar to the issues of access to commercial sex and medically assisted abortions, for it involves access to commercial and medically assisted pregnancy.

Parallel to the debate that has raged between socialist and liberal feminists over prostitution, is a debate taking place between socialist and liberal feminists over surrogate motherhood. Socialist feminists see the practice of "womb commerce" as another form of prostitution—a distortion of human procreative processes brought on by the excesses of capitalism and patriarchy. Liberal feminists, on the other hand, see gestational surrogacy as a legitimate option for procreatively disadvantaged couples and for some "good Samaritan" (and often economically disadvantaged) women. Yet, these socialist and liberal feminist analyses of surrogacy manifest weaknesses similar to socialist and liberal feminist analyses of sex commerce. For the socialist feminist approach illegitimately assumes that the market alienation and commodification of some forms of labor—procreative labor, sexual labor—is universally more oppressive than the alienation of other forms of labor. And the liberal approach overlooks how the practice of surrogacy is produced by and reproduces questionable cultural ideals about families and parenting, and pernicious ideologies about race and gender. I will elaborate some of these ideals below.

In his examination of gestational surrogacy, Richard Arneson identifies many of the problems that plague liberal and socialist accounts.[16] Arneson attempts to resolve some of the differences between them by defending a policy of liberal regulationism—a policy that would legally permit, but allow the government to regulate the sale or rental of womb space. In defending this policy, Arneson especially attempts to meet the socialist feminist objection that commercial access to pregnancy would lead not only to the degradation of women, but to the degradation of all persons. For such access, according to some socialist feminists, would lead to the assignment of monetary values to commercially and medically assisted pregnancies and the babies produced. And this assignment would be made not merely in terms of the health of the product or the convenience of the service, but in terms of the predicted personal attributes of the product (for example, eye color, sex, intelligence, and so forth).[17] Such assignments of monetary value to individual traits may affect the way we value people: that is, we may come to value not only commercially produced babies in proportion to their possession of these traits, but we may come to put a price tag on all people.

Moreover, commercial and medically assisted access to pregnancy may reinforce the social hegemony of oppressive racialized and gendered tastes in persons. For example, Arneson speculates that the

> market pricing bound up with commercial surrogacy ... might result in a higher price for blond, blue-eyed babies than for others, [which] would tend to decrease people's willingness to accord proper respect to the individual rights of all persons or to believe that the proper goal of governmental policy is the good of all citizens regardless of race, creed, ethnic origin, or the market price of their labor power.[18]

If male babies were to command a higher price in this market, then commercial and medically assisted access to pregnancy would reinforce the social devaluation of women in ways other than, or in addition to, the industry's symbolic treatment of women as mere breeding stock. In short, preferences or tastes may be expressed in this market that would serve to perpetuate racism, sexism, and so on.

Arneson argues that none of these foreseeable consequences of commercially available gestational surrogacy provide a reason to criminalize it, they only provide reasons for carefully regulating it. According to Arneson, "A suitably regulated market in adoption and gestational services would [not] allow market pricing to run amok."[19] In short, if pricing mechanisms were controlled, then we could contain the kinds of consequences of commercial surrogacy that would overshadow its potential benefits. And the possible benefits are not insignificant, as Arneson points out.

> Many couples want their own children but are infertile. Besides heterosexual married couples, one should count infertile lesbian and

gay couples. If the cause of the infertility is the inability of either member of the couple to become pregnant or to carry a fetus to term, surrogacy can help.[20]

Arneson rightly points out that more conventional forms of adoption are not available or suitable for some would-be parents. They are typically not available to lesbian and gay couples, or other nontraditional families, and thus commercial or informal forms of surrogacy may be especially helpful for assisting, creating, and gaining greater social tolerance for nontraditional families.

While I agree with Arneson that criminalizing commercial access to pregnancy is not justified, I seriously doubt that instituting liberal price controls will be sufficient to regulate it. Price controls will only address the monetary, symbolic, and social value we attach to the products of such services; they will not address the symbolic and social value we attach to the providers of such services. To address the potential social devaluation of women brought on by the price-tagging of women's wombs, we need to develop socialist and feminist forms of regulationism. We need to develop regulations that can contest the demeaning jobs and roles we create and define for women, which requires that we investigate the social origins of these roles through interpretive social analysis.

For example, Arneson rightly points out that the aims of individuals who seek the services of gestational surrogates need not be morally suspect, but he overlooks how their aims may be socially shaped by forces that produce and perpetuate the marginalization of women.[21] To understand the social origins of these aims, I will briefly compare gestational surrogacy with AID (Artificial Insemination by Donor).[22] AID enables women whose partners have some procreative problem (low sperm count, carriers of genetic disorders), and women without a male partner or mate, to become impregnated without the hassle or awkwardness of engaging in impersonal, and possibly manipulative sex. Significantly, since men can easily be separated from their sperm (legally and physically) in American society, AID allows a woman to become impregnated by a man with whom she has no social relationship, and with whom her future child will have no social relationship. In a society where men were thought to have the same interest in their sperm that women have vis-à-vis the fetal contents of their uteruses, then legal and physical separation would probably be more difficult. Yet, in the U.S., men freely give up sperm to women, or to sperm "banks."

"Surrogate motherhood" is supposed to provide to men and their procreatively disabled partners the same advantage that AID provides to women and their procreatively disabled or nonexisting mates. In the typical case, it is supposed to enable a man whose wife cannot or should not carry a fetus for the full term of a pregnancy to produce a baby that is genetically related to him in a manner relatively under the couple's control. However, while men can be easily separated from their sperm in American society, the "surrogate" mother cannot be easily separated from her womb, which the desired offspring will inhabit for roughly forty weeks. And this constraint has two significant consequences: (1) the contracting couple must establish a social relationship with the womb (and possibly egg) "donor," and (2) there is sufficient time for the womb donor to establish a "social" relationship with the contents of her womb. That is, the "surrogate's" pregnancy will have a social as well as biological reality and dimension that she and others must negotiate.

The whole point of the surrogacy "business" contract is to establish a way to terminate the social relationships initiated by the "surrogate's" pregnancy for the benefit of the procreatively disadvantaged couple and, presumably, for the child. Indeed the social practice of drawing up contracts that define and relegate the "womb donor" or "mother surrogate" to the status of "donor" and "surrogate" merely reflects the greater social power of the parties that initiate the contract—parties whose interested perspectives obscure the meaning that a woman's pregnancy, and the relationships it establishes, may have to her. Our practice of creating surrogate contracts also reflects our own social ideologies about families and parenting. More specifically, the practice assumes "surrogate" pregnancies provide us with two options—that the child together with the procreatively disadvantaged couple can constitute a "family," or that the child together with the "gestational" or "egg" mother can constitute a "family." Yet "surrogate" pregnancies provide options involving other ways to configure families that we often fail to see, such as families with two mothers. In short, what makes the kind of surrogate contract we now have seem like an appealing option to "us" are the dominance of social perspectives that ignore the meaning of pregnancy for women in the U.S., and the widespread social assumption that motherhood has to be unambiguous and singular for effective parenting.

What if instead of "surrogacy" contracts, couples with a procreatively disadvantaged female partner were to seek joint-parenting contracts. This would be the sort of custody contract that people typically seek in the case of divorce, only in this case these contracts would be drawn up prior to the formation of any social tie between the prospective parents, and prior to the creation of their offspring.[23] In this kind of arrangement, a couple would seek a woman who was willing to bear a child with them, and possibly share with them some of the parental rights and responsibilities for the child. In this sort of case, the procreatively disadvantaged couple would probably not secure exclusive rights to a child, but they would nonetheless have the possibility of gaining a shared right in a child that they would not otherwise have. Of course, the womb mother may relinquish her parental or custody rights to the child (just as parents sometimes do in the case of divorce or adoption), but the contract would not require this in advance. Instead, with joint-parenting contracts, the relinquishing of parental rights would be decided as social relationships develop or fail to develop.

With joint-parenting contracts, one might care about other aspects of "the womb and egg parent" than her mere physical characteristics. For the source and value of the services that this parent provides are recognized in this contract by not treating her as a mere procreative subordinate, but rather as a potential co-parent. Consequently, by restructuring in this way the kind of business or social relationships infertile couples have to fertile "surrogates," we encourage the establishment of more humane relationships between people who exchange precious human labor and capacities. For example, by redefining the "prostitute" as an erotic artist or therapist, we hope to alter the kinds of qualities people seek and see in her, and to socially define her as a person that one can say hello to on the streets. Similarly, by elevating the womb mother to a potential co-parent, we encourage precious human goods and services to be exchanged only between social parties who can establish respectful, nondegrading social relationships. With co-parenting contracts, money and human fertility are exchanged not as commodities between a buyer and seller, but as gifts between those who have the opportunity to establish ongoing social relationships as a result of those precious gifts.

Given the social and biological parameters imposed by pregnancy, socially regulated joint-parenting agreements, unlike commercial "surrogacy" contracts, attempt to balance the competing interests of procreatively disadvantaged couples and "good Samaritan" women who may help them. And by having such contracts, we balance these interests not by restricting the liberty of procreatively disadvantaged couples, or treating women paternalistically, but by giving each party new procreative options to consider. Yet to invent and elaborate these contracts, we need to understand the meaning of pregnancy in American society and its meaning for differently positioned social actors, and we need to examine our parochial notions about proper families. These are needs that a comprehensive and interpretive moral, social, and political philosophy can help us with.

Pluralism and Relativism

Feminists have avoided pluralist and other postmodern approaches to ethics because such approaches are seen to commit us to an impotent, relativist politics of tolerance. In this book, I have tried to show that this is not the case. However, as I argued in chapter 1, pluralism does steer us away from universalist and ultimately ethnocentric ethics, and thus may commit us to some form of cultural relativism. In this section I will explore the kind of relativism to which we are committed, and whether it is necessarily politically debilitating.

As I see it, there are at least three distinct theoretical strategies we may choose among to deal with the spectre of helpless relativism. First, we can reject moral pluralism and take a more formalist, reductionist approach to ethics—a strategy embodied in the following kinds of ethics: discourse ethics, care ethics, entitlement ethics, consequentialist ethics, and virtue ethics. Second, we can accept moral pluralism, but argue that it does not commit us to any form of relativism.[24] Or third, we can accept moral pluralism and acknowledge its relativistic aspects, but argue that the forms of relativism to which we are committed are not problematic.[25] I will adopt this third strategy. More specifically, I will try to show that the implications of cultural relativism for ethics have been largely misunderstood by philosophers.

Cultural relativism refers to a school of thought that emerged in American anthropology around the turn of the century, and which was articulated in the work of Franz Boas and, later, Ruth Benedict. Cultural relativists claim that the differences between the isolated, nonindustrialized societies that anthropologists study and the industrialized Western societies that produce anthropologists should not be interpreted as superficial variations of a common human nature. Nor are these differences to be understood in evolutionary terms—as representing earlier and later stages of a single path of human development—as they were by a previous generation of anthropologists. Instead, cultural relativists see the differences between European societies and human groups not descended from Europeans as representing diverse and equally good possibilities for human social organization and cultural achievement. This is the fundamental thesis of cultural relativism.

Importantly, cultural relativism is a view that arose historically in opposition to intellectually entrenched views that treated non-European societies as primitive and inferior versions of ourselves. As a radical departure in anthropological theorizing about difference, cultural relativism supported a radical politics. For it could be used (and was used) to oppose both racial notions of inferiority and the economic exploitation of Third World societies. Since cultural relativists regarded the brown-complexioned people Europe colonized as possessing cultural achievements and social systems comparable in worth to their colonizers, cultural relativism provided additional resources for debunking European racial prejudices and rationales for colonial domination.

Ironically, cultural relativism is seen within philosophy as supporting an ineffectual politics and an "anything goes" morality (i.e., a morality of accommodation).[26] For philosophers have reasoned that, if no culture or race is superior to any other, then each culture or race can be judged only by its own moral principles and social norms. Consequently, if moral justification can only appeal to the customs and moral beliefs of the culture in question, it becomes impossible to oppose morally any behaviors or practices that are the status quo in the cultural context in which they occur. Therefore, a moral relativist, it is alleged, must be tolerant and accommodating toward any culturally entrenched practice or belief, no matter how offensive to her it may be. Paradoxically, a moral relativist, according to the standard philosophical view, must even accommodate European racism and cultural chauvinism where these attitudes, and the practices they support, are embedded in particular cultural systems and social formations.

There are some fundamental mistakes in this picture of the theoretical implications of cultural relativism. Yet because this distorted picture is entrenched in American and British academic philosophy, Anglo-American moral philosophers have generally avoided serious discussion of cultural relativism.[27] And to declare oneself a cultural relativist in academic philosophical circles, is simply to mark oneself as a theorist not to be taken seriously. Indeed relativism is often dismissed with wry academic humor. For example, in his presidential address to the American Philosophical Association (Pacific Division) in 1990, John Searle remarked: "if there were no universal truths, then doing philosophy would no longer be fun!" Because it is presumably absurd to think that philosophical inquiry should fail to generate the usual pleasures, the implication we are supposed to draw from Searle's remark is that there must be universal truths and philosophers must continue to search for them.

Searle's *reductio ad absurdum* of all relativistic theories was offered somewhat as a caution against a growing interest on the part of American philosophers in critiques of the European Enlightenment that have been generated by continental philosophers. In particular, Searle was responding to the increasing rejection of positivist models of science by philosophers, and the rejection of realist notions in metaphysics and epistemology. This rejection of "scientism" and "naturalism," in the social sciences at least, has coincided with increasing acceptance of hermeneutical or interpretive models of human understanding. However even with the acceptance of anti-positivist accounts of knowledge, many philosophers still reject "relativism." I will try to show that relativism is a philosophical bogeyman, one associated with nonsensical and frightening ideas that no respectable cultural relativist really holds. Indeed, perhaps only some students, after taking a class in moral philosophy, hold the ideas philosophers attribute to cultural relativists.[28]

Pluralism without Objectivity

Susan Wolf characterizes moral pluralism as a meta-ethical view intermediate between relativism and absolutism.[29] Absolutism is usually understood to be the view that "there is a single, uniquely best moral position on every issue."[30] Moral relativism is presumably the view that there is no best or even better moral position on any issue; all positions are equally good. By contrast, moral pluralists hold that while there are rational methods for distinguishing between better and worse moral positions, these methods may not yield a best position for every moral issue. In other words, pluralists maintain (contra absolutists) that there is no one rational or objective method for adjudicating all ethical disagreements, but (contra relativists) that we have some apparently universal or widely shared intellectual resources for adjudicating some ethical disagreements. Thus, moral pluralism avoids moral subjectivism or skepticism, which some forms of relativism entail, while at the same time it avoids dogmatic appeals to moral universals required by absolutist accounts. As an intermediate view then, moral pluralism appears to possess the virtues of the more extreme meta-ethical views while avoiding their faults. For, according to Wolf, pluralism makes possible some form of objectivity in ethics, without resorting to the extremes of absolutism.

Yet while Wolf's "pluralism" does not dogmatically appeal to any *moral* universals, her account does appeal to the existence of some *epistemic* universals. According to Wolf, we should

> associate moral objectivity with the position that *some* actions and attitudes are morally intolerable, that *some* things are morally required, that, in other words, there are limits and constraints on what constitute acceptable moral thought and action, and that these limits and constraints are to be found and justified by the exercise of intellectual and imaginative skills—by means, for example, of reflection and dialogue, logic, argument, perception, experience . . .[31]

But if moral judgments are to be constrained by "the exercise of intellectual and imaginative skills" and by "logic," "perception," and "experience," rather than by universal values, then we might ask—à la MacIntyre—whose intellectual skills, whose logic, whose perception, and whose experience?[32] Wolf seems to assume that our experiences and perceptions, and that our logical instruments and intellectual skills are free of cultural and historical shaping, and thus provide a final court of appeal for—i.e., impose an ultimate constraint on—our subjectively irresolvable moral prejudices. Yet what if all our perceptions and thoughts, including moral ones, reflect cultural prejudices? Can we hold consistently and without arbitrariness that moral principles vary across cultures but epistemic ones do not?

Certainly, a more thorough and consistent pluralism would hold that there are neither epistemic nor moral universals, (e.g., as pluralists like Charles Taylor do). This does not mean, though, that practices can only be judged in terms of the epistemic and moral ideals constitutive of them, as we saw in chapter 1. For the irreducibility of distinct principles and practices does not render them incomparable. Nor does it mean that when someone's actions conform to the ideals of her society, her actions are right. For pluralism based on an interpretive model of knowledge rejects such formalist and reductionist principles, and instead commits us to trying to see the distortions in our own moral customs and practices by comparing them with the irreducibly different practices of others. Indeed, on a pluralist and culturally relativist view, the person who unreflectively conforms to the social norms of her society reflects parochial narrowness, and her actions may fail to realize many worthy ideals that make the lives of others, and even her own life, meaningful.

But Wolf seems to think that without epistemic universals we are committed to forms of relativism that lead to subjectivism. Thus she tries to find some common epistemic ground on which to have moral objectivity, while avoiding moral absolutism. For example, she states,

> I suggest that we think of the question of objectivity in terms of the questions, Does the conjunction of reason and empirical fact constrain value judgments? and Does reason (in conjunction with empirical fact) allow us to ascertain that certain positions are better than others? As debates about the best hitter in the major leagues can illustrate, reason, in conjuction with empirical fact, can constrain judgment even if it does not dictate a single objectively best answer. If we understand the distinction between objectivist and subjectivist ethical stances in these terms, then pluralism can be a form of objectivism.[33]

As this passage makes evident, to reconfigure questions about objectivity as she does, Wolf must resort to some ahistorical and acultural conception of human rationality and "reason," and to some decontextualized perceptions or "empirical facts." But by invoking this positivist model of "reason" and "fact"—a model that requires detached, unencumbered *epistemic* selves, if not *moral* selves—Wolf manages to reach her theoretical objectives. For Wolf, "reason" provides a foundation for objective, if not universal, moral truths:

> As reason can constrain moral judgments within a moral system, it can also constrain moral assessments of the systems themselves, providing a basis for comparison among different systems as well as a basis for criticism and revision within these systems.[34]

In sum, Wolf's unencumbered "reason" provides the basis for the critical comparison and frequent adjudication of multiple and incompatible moral judgments—a multiplicity that results from the existence of a plurality of moral standards in any single social context and across multiple social contexts.

To have a thorough and consistent pluralism, though, we should locate our capacity for critical comparison in our human capacity for hermeneutical and ethnographic dialogue, rather than in some unembedded faculty of rationality. For a pluralism that rests our capacity for moral judgment on "reason and fact" is a shallow pluralism: it is a pluralism grounded on a singular and unitary view of human rationality. More specifically, Wolf's variety of moral pluralism assumes an anti-pluralist conception of rationality, where human knowledge in ethics, as in other areas, proceeds by assuming a single godlike or scientific perspective located in some faculty "reason." By contrast, Taylor's hermeneutically inspired moral pluralism takes a pluralist view of human rationality, where human knowledge is created by assuming multiple embedded human perspectives and rendering actions that are intelligible in one way intelligible in another. And though, on this epistemic account, we do not achieve moments of objectivity, nevertheless we achieve mutual intelligibility, which serves equally well to constrain our subjective human prejudices.

In sum, instead of achieving a robust pluralism that avoids subjectivism, Wolf has achieved a tenuous and shallow moral pluralism—one that can easily turn to more absolutist forms of objectivism. For if "reason" together with "empirical fact" allow us to compare different moral principles and different moral systems, there is no reason to think that "reason" is not capable of showing us some ultimate way of ordering these systems and principles—that is, "the rational foundation" of all moral practice. In short, searches for objectivity contain a logic that generates absolute dogmas, such as the dogma of "reason"—a dogma we might do better to put to rest.[35]

To avoid the dogma of "reason," we should try to fashion a moral pluralism without epistemic objectivity. For pluralism without objectivity does not commit us to subjectivism or the emotivism that MacIntyre fears.[36] Subjectivism and emotivism are often both conceived as the apparently individualist view that what is right or wrong depends upon an individual's own tastes or emotions.[37] Nor does it commit us to the view that most philosophers, including Wolf, associate with moral relativism—the view that what is right or wrong, good or bad, for an individual in any situation depends upon the moral customs, rules, and principles of that individual's culture or group. For, as I noted above, pluralism based on interpretive models of knowledge eschews such simplistic formalist catechisms. And, rather than promote unreflective conformity with one's culturally formed prejudices, thoroughgoing pluralism promotes greater familiarity with the great arc of human possibilities in order to educate our perceptions.[38]

Pluralism without objectivity commits us to a normative view much closer to a form of cultural relativism that some ethnographers endorse. This is a view that acknowledges that our actions can be assessed from multiple cultural perspectives and, thus, in any situation we must determine which perspectives or norms are dominant. Because any social situation is structured by a set of variable norms and assumptions that determine the meanings and consequences our actions have for others, we need to be aware of the norms and assumptions constitutive of our interactions with others as we strive to behave well and be good. Thus it would be wrong for someone to practice "penis-feeding" or "post-partum abortion" in the U.S. because, given the meaning of these behaviors in American society, they would be constituted as acts of exploitation and cruelty, and they would be experienced in terms of harm and pain. Moreover, to engage in these practices in this cultural context would reflect ethnic chauvinism or ignorance, and it would violate numerous moral ideals whose successful realization can be appreciated by others (to borrow Taylor's notion), such as the ideals of universal human dignity, humility, sensitivity, care, responsibility, peaceful coexistence with others, and so on.[39] In short, cultural relativism does not imply that it is always right for penis-feeders to penis-feed their children, or the absurd conclusion that it is allowable for Nazis to impose their Nazi practices on others, because they are merely conforming to their cultures.

Since cultural relativism arose as an intellectual movement aimed at making us more respectful of human others and appreciative of their virtues as well as vices, it is ironic and even somewhat sad that philosophers have twisted this view into one that states that it is always right to do what one's own culture dictates. For this is a view that rationalizes and sanctions cultural chauvinism, parochialness, and even ignorance and contempt toward human others. What cultural relativism implies for moral analysis is that when penis-feeders penis-feed members of their own society, then we might not have any qualms with them. Or at least, to have qualms with them, we would need to find out whether some penis-feeders themselves had grounds for opposing penis-feeding, that is, whether some penis-feeders felt that they were being oppressed, degraded, exploited, or treated with hostility and contempt, when penis-feeding occurred. But if no one in this society holds such views, then our intervention to prevent penis-feeding in these situations would reflect ethnic arrogance, hostility, and unjustified paternalism, and it would violate many other moral ideals that render our lives meaningful and intelligible to ourselves—humility, tolerance, respect, understanding, generosity, kindness, and so on. Similarly, if Nazis imposed Nazi practices only on those who shared their Nazi constructions of reality in Nazi social contexts, then we might not have any qualms with them. But this is not what Nazis do, and which is why we can criticize their actions with full force and still be cultural relativists.

Susan Sherwin argues we are sometimes justified on moral relativist grounds to intervene with customs that we think oppress people even if no group in the society objects to them. Our intervention is justified, according to Sherwin, when the power structures in a society are oppressive. While Sherwin stresses the need for feminist ethics to embrace cultural relativism, she holds,

> we cannot treat all communities the same . . . in ethics we need to be assured of a community worthy of trust if we are to accept its moral standards as adequate.[40]

But how can we determine whether penis-feeders, for example, are worthy of trust?

Sherwin argues that to determine whether a community is morally trustworthy, and thus

> To be confident about the moral worth of a community's standards . . . we need to evaluate moral decision-making within the community itself and be assured that it is not achieved through oppressive forces . . . The process of reaching moral agreements should be democratic . . .[41]

One problem with this view is that there may be few societies, including our own, whose moral credentials we can be confident about. For example, is a society genuinely democratic when there are, and have always been, racial and class barriers to voting, even though technically all adults are eligible to vote? Or, are societies in which there are large inequalities in wealth and power ones where we can be confident that the processes for reaching moral agreements and setting policies are democratic?

Moreover, there is the danger in Sherwin's moral relativism that we will tend to see societies that are more similar to our own as more democratic and trustworthy than those which are more dissimilar. Indeed, the very existence of practices in a society that are disturbing to Westerners may lead us to question the democratic character of a society. Sherwin seems aware of this danger and argues that when we evaluate communities radically different from our own,

> Western feminists need to be careful that they are not simply engaged in the familiar exercise of imposing Western global power and values on other communities.[42]

To demonstrate the advantage of the analytical safeguard she has developed, Sherwin focuses on a practice common in some nonindustrial and non-Western societies: the practice of female circumcision or clitoridectemy.

Sherwin concludes that societies where female circumcision is practiced cannot be morally trustworthy, even when there appears to be universal approval of the practice. Her reasons are that:

> Genital mutilation is linked to interests associated with male dominance—assurances of sexual fidelity, tight vaginas for male pleasure, protection against women's demands for sexual satisfaction, and cruelty to women. Unless there is evidence that women would agree to this practice if they were free of patriarchal coercion, we cannot treat it as an acceptable local custom, even if the majority of citizens in areas where it is customarily practiced now approves of it.[43]

Unfortunately, Sherwin's assumption that female circumcision generally involves the coercion and exploitation of women by men is not based, as she admits, on an ethnographic investigation of this practice or the societies in which it occurs. She states,

> It should be stressed, however, that this argument is made from outside the culture, where it is sometimes difficult to understand the complex dimensions of the power structures. The moral criticism offered here is conditional, based on the assumption that women's consent to this practice has been coerced. If that interpretation turns out to be wrong, unlikely though that seems, then the grounds for criticism would dissolve.[44]

Yet what leads Sherwin to assume, with confidence, that women's participation has been coerced, when, as she admits, she is viewing this practice from "outside the culture"? Sherwin's assumption of coercion here seems to be based both on her own culturally shaped perceptions of a culturally unfamiliar practice—variously described by her and others as genital mutilation, female circumcision, and clitoridectemy—and on her consequent lack of trust in a community constituted by values and assumptions different than those with which she is familiar.

In other words, Sherwin's assumption of coercion and her consequent distrust is grounded on her opposition to a particular practice rather than on some independent evidence of a lack of democratic decision-making. Nevertheless she argues that,

> Western feminists are morally entitled to offer support as it is requested by feminists within the societies where an oppressive practice continues, even though the majority of the population, including many women, in the society in question may express support for the practice.[45]

What Sherwin is licensing here is the displacement of the authority of cultural others by the authority of Western feminists when we deem it necessary to protect women. In short, since Sherwin's cultural relativism challenges the moral authority of each community, but provides no independent or culturally unbiased criterion of what an acceptable community is, it may end up promoting ethnocentric attitudes and the imperialist treatment of others.

To determine whether feminist intervention against the practice of "female circumcision"[46] is justified or not, we should not examine the power structures in another society from our own cultural perspectives, as Sherwin recommends, but rather we should try to examine the problematic practice itself from the perspectives of those within the particular societies in which it occurs. We should not assume but try to find out, through dialogue with others, whether this practice is linked to male dominance—whether it is linked to attempts to control women's sexuality or to appropriate women's bodies for male uses. And should it turn out, as we found with sex commerce in some cases, that clitoridectemy is produced and perpetuated by beliefs that serve to socially degrade and marginalize women, then we might consider strategies to deter it.

It should be noted, however, that the only way we can find out whether a particular practice degrades and oppresses women is by communicating with people from societies where it occurs, and by studying their communicative acts with each other. We cannot infer the oppressive nature of a practice from our own perceptions of and reactions to it. Moreover, in attempting to deter a particular practice, we need to keep in mind how our actions are likely to be perceived by those whom we intend to aid. For we do not assist people very well if our actions are perceived by them as aggressive and culturally elitist. Furthermore, if our actions are perceived this way, we do little to challenge the assumptions on which their problematic practice rests. In short, though cultural relativism can approve some interventions in other societies, our first interventions must involve serious, extensive, and careful ethnographic work, and any subsequent interventions must take account of the assumptions and cultural prejudices on both sides that structure such intercultural negotiations.

To conclude, when moral pluralism is informed by hermeneutical models of knowledge, we do not end up with a Cole Porter "anything goes" relativism.[47] For a thoroughgoing pluralism inspired by interpretive practice is consistent with the critical comparison and assessment of our individual actions and collective customs. Yet, because this pluralism rejects all claims to objectivity, moral insight must be gained, not by the privileged perspective of the unencumbered self, but from the educated perspective of one who has been exposed to a great variety of human possibilities. And since no moral critic can consider all possibilities, moral knowledge is always limited and tentative. Consequently, though like the art critic, we can sometimes give serious, inspired, educated, and self-aware criticism, there are no final or complete assessments. In brief, rather than endorsing an "anything goes" relativism, we should accept a "one never knows do one" (Fats Waller) variety of relativism.

The Place of Prejudice in a Feminist Ethics

Feminist theory often aims to eliminate irrational prejudices against women, and male or masculine biases in general, from our thinking.[48] Implicit in this project is a view that all socially shaped biases or prejudices are harmful and need to be exposed, so that we may free ourselves of their influence. Male biases are seen as simply a subset of the myriad distortions we unwittingly accept. One problem with this conception of feminism is that, in some sense all our socially formed beliefs represent biases of some sort. Moreover, if we accept an antipositivist account of human understanding, all our beliefs are socially formed. Thus to liberate ourselves from all our biases we might need to liberate ourselves from all beliefs, which, though probably not impossible, is to subscribe to some form of epistemic nihilism.

In his book *Truth and Method,* Hans-Georg Gadamer argues that the desire to rid ourselves of all historically and culturally formed biases and prejudices stems from Enlightenment notions about human knowledge. According to Gadamer,

> What is necessary is a fundamental rehabilitation of the concept of prejudice and a recognition of the fact that there are legitimate prejudices, if we want to do justice to man's finite, historical mode of being. Thus we are able to formulate the central question of a truly historical hermeneutics, epistemologically its fundamental question, namely: where is the ground of the legitimacy of prejudices? What distinguishes legitimate prejudices from all the countless ones which it is the undeniable task of the critical reason to overcome?[49]

The central question for an interpretive and pluralist feminist ethics is what distinguishes prejudices and norms that oppress women from those that do not? Which norms and prejudices do we need to resist and which ones can we get by with? For example, are all social norms that differentiate men and women—norms that produce and reproduce genders—oppressive? Are all sexualized or racialized social identities oppressive? Or are there ways that these norms and identities bring joy and love to our lives, make the stars smile, and enrich the universe, to echo Cornel West?

The danger in promoting an approach to moral analysis that draws our attention to the meanings and assumptions we share, and which shape our interactions, is that it may make us somewhat over-zealous to challenge each and every assumption we find. For we may realize, as Jeffrey Weeks notes, that "We cannot unilaterally escape the grid of meaning that envelops us,"[50] and thus we may entertain many multilateral transformations and reconfigurations of our grid in order to enable some collective escapes. Yet not all changes in our grid will improve the lives of women, or challenge our social domination by men. For though we are enveloped by our grid, we are not imprisoned by it—and without it we would have no way to communicate and render our lives intelligible to others. Thus, whatever alterations we attempt, they should be chosen carefully.

Notes

Preface

1. The talk I helped to organize occurred on February 27, 1982 in La Jolla, California.

2. Catharine MacKinnon, *Toward a Feminist Theory of the State* (Cambridge: Harvard University, 1989), pp. 188–189.

3. Laurie Shrage, "Should Feminists Oppose Prostitution?" *Ethics* 99 (1989): 347–361.

1. Eschewing Ethnocentric Ethics

1. Caryn James, "What's Adultery? A Little Sex, A Lot of Politics," *New York Times*, October 14, 1990.

2. Richard Wasserstrom, "Is Adultery Immoral?" in R. Baker and F. Elliston, eds., *Philosophy and Sex* (Buffalo, NY: Prometheus, 1984), pp. 93–106.

3. Ibid., p. 106.

4. I tend to share Bernard Williams's skepticism about the efficacy of moral theorizing here. See his *Ethics and the Limits of Philosophy* (Cambridge: Harvard University Press, 1985), p. 74.

5. Alasdair MacIntyre, *After Virtue: A Study in Moral Theory*, 2d ed. (Notre Dame, IN: University of Notre Dame Press, 1984), p. 45.

6. Kathryn Pyne Addelson, "Why Philosophers Should Become Sociologists (and Vice Versa)," in *Impure Thoughts: Essays on Philosophy, Feminism, and Ethics* (Philadelphia: Temple University Press, 1991), pp. 108–132.

7. Ibid., p. 122.

8. See especially Clifford Geertz, "Thick Description: Toward an Interpretive Theory of Culture," in *The Interpretation of Cultures* (New

York: Basic Books, 1973). For a succinct and clear discussion of Geertz's contribution to the development of this approach, see Richard Handler, "Clifford Geertz," in R. Turner, ed., *Thinkers of the Twentieth Century*, 2d ed. (Chicago: St. James Press, 1987), pp. 279–281.

9. See especially Charles Taylor, *Philosophy and the Human Sciences: Philosophical Papers, 2* (Cambridge: Cambridge University Press, 1985), and *Sources of the Self: The Making of the Modern Identity* (Cambridge: Harvard University Press, 1989). See also Hans-Georg Gadamer, *Truth and Method* (New York: Continuum, 1975).

10. Geertz, p. 5.

11. Ibid., p. 14.

12. Ibid., p. 5.

13. Ibid., p. 9.

14. Ibid., p. 14.

15. See ibid., pp. 27–30.

16. Taylor, *Philosophy and the Human Sciences,* pp. 123–124.

17. Wasserstrom might reply here that though we might evaluate the counterculture from the perspective of the dominant culture, the dominant culture does not really provide us with a critical perspective from which to evaluate the counterculture, but only a conventional perspective on marriage and adultery. To a certain extent I agree with this. Since we are all familiar with the dominant culture's perspective on marriage (this is, in part, what makes it the dominant perspective), taking this perspective does not allow us the kind of distance that might afford certain insights into the practices of others or our own practices. But it does not follow from this that there is no cultural group that can offer us a critical perspective on the sixties counterculture. Certainly viewing the sixties countercultural values about sex and marriage from the perspectives of societies that practice arranged marriage, marriage by capture, or polygamous marriage would provide us with critical vantages from which to gain insights about the sixties.

18. According to Francis Fukuyama, "it matters very little what strange thoughts occur to people in Albania or Burkina Faso, for we are interested in what one could in some sense call the common ideological heritage of mankind." "The End of History?" *The National Interest* (Summer 1989): 9. Fukuyama dismisses the possibility that beliefs, practices, or institutions in such "strange" contexts might offer interesting counterexamples to our political and moral theories. In the same year that *Ju Dou* was made, another politically charged film about adultery was produced in Burkina Faso (*Tilai*). If Fukuyama is correct, then these films may be irrelevant to our analysis of adultery. But how can such arrogant dismissal of other societies be correct?

19. Michael Wreen questions whether societies in which prohibitions on extramarital sex are weak approve extramarital sex. Wreen entertains

the common anti-relativist idea that though behavior can vary cross-culturally, the underlying values may remain constant. I agree with Wreen that societies are not transparent with respect to widely shared values and beliefs, and that we should not take the widespread indulgence in a particular behavior as our only evidence of widespread moral approval of that behavior. In addition to observing what people do, we need to examine authoritative social texts to see which doings are valorized or condemned, (e.g., legal texts, religious texts, popular culture, etc.). However, this more cautious approach should not give us license to read our own values into other societies. Unfortunately, contra Wreen, even a casual glance at the historical and cross-cultural literature on marriage and sexuality seems to support Wasserstrom's contention that the sexual values and ideals underlying different marital practices vary significantly. For example, many societies appear to approve sexual relations between a married person and some of her/his affinal relatives. See Philip Lampe, ed., *Adultery in the United States: Close Encounters of the Sixth (or Seventh) Kind* (Buffalo, NY: Prometheus Books, 1987), p. 6. Michael Wreen, "What's Really Wrong With Adultery" in Alan Soble, ed., *The Philosophy of Sex* (Savage, MD: Littlefield Adams, 1991), pp. 179–192.

20. Seyla Benhabib, *Situating the Self: Gender, Community and Postmodernism In Contemporary Ethics* (New York: Routledge, 1992).

21. MacIntyre, p. 39.

22. Benhabib, p. 9.

23. Ibid., p. 62, note 48.

24. Uma Narayan, "The Project of Feminist Epistemology: Perspectives from a Nonwestern Feminist," in A. Jaggar and S. Bordo, eds., *Gender/Body/Knowledge: Feminist Reconstructions of Being and Knowing* (New Brunswick: Rutgers University Press, 1989), pp. 256–269.

25. Ibid., pp. 264–265.

26. Benhabib, p. 45.

27. See for example the documentary film *Maasai Women*, Odyssey Series, Public Broadcasting Associates, Inc., Boston, 1980. In this film, ethnographer Melissa Llewelyn-Davies asks several Maasai women (Kenya) whether they are jealous when their husbands take other wives. The women respond that they are not jealous like European women, and one woman states "To us, a co-wife is something very good because there is much work to do. When it rains the village gets mucky and it's you who clears it out. It's you who looks after the cows. You do the milking and your husband may have very many cows. That's a lot of work. You have to milk and smear the roof [the Maasai waterproof their roofs by smearing cow dung on them] and see to the calves. If your children are small they can't help. Can they? No, they're too silly. So when you give birth and it rains who will smear the roof if you have no co-wife? No one. Who will clear the muck from the village? No one.

So Maasai aren't jealous because of all this work." I am grateful to Susan Seymour for suggesting this film to me.

See also *A Wife Among Wives: Notes on Turkana Marriage,* produced and directed by David and Judith MacDougall, 1981. In that film the narrator states, "I once asked Naingiro if there wouldn't be fighting and jealousy among co-wives in a large family. She answered me this way: 'You're basing your question on your own society where other people build your houses for you. Your women just come and live in them; they have only a little work to do ... In our society a woman can decide about her husband's second wife ...'" While the practice of polygyny is not merely a function of the quantity of work in a given society, the remarks of the women in these films suggest that not all women experience polygamy as an unfair or unequal arrangement.

28. Narayan, p. 263.

29. Benhabib, pp. 42–43.

30. Stephen Toulmin similarly comments on the incomparability of these marital institutions:

> it is questionable whether the practices compared [of Christian and Muslim marriage] can be regarded as "alternatives" at all. The ramifications, both in Christian and in Muslim societies, of the institution of marriage, its relations to the institutions of property, of parenthood and so on, are so complex that there is no question of simply replacing the one institution by the other. Such different parts does the institution of "marriage" play in the ways of life of a Christian society and of a Muslim one that we might even feel it hardly right to describe Christian and Muslim marriage as being instances of the "same" institution at all.
>
> The question, "Which of these institutions is 'right'?", is therefore an unreal one, and there is no conceivable way of answering it—as it stands. (pp. 152–153)

In other words, these institutions are to a large extent incommensurable, and thus need to be understood in terms of their own cultural ideals—presuppositions not shared by all—before they can be subject to moral evaluation. See Stephen Toulmin, *An Examination of the Place of Reason in Ethics* (Cambridge: Cambridge University Press, 1970).

31. Narayan, p. 263.

32. See especially Rita Manning, *Speaking From the Heart: A Feminist Perspective on Ethics* (Lanham, MD: Rowman & Littlefield Publishers, 1992).

33. See, for example, Tan Tai Wei, "Morality and the Love of God," in G. Kessler, ed., *Voices of Wisdom* (Belmont, CA: Wadsworth Publishing Company, 1992), pp. 104–107.

34. Sandra Lee Bartky, *Femininity and Domination: Studies in the Phenomenology of Oppression* (New York: Routledge, 1990), p. 113.

35. Patrocinio Schweickart, "In Defense of Femininity: Commentary on Sandra Bartky's *Femininity and Domination*," *Hypatia* 8 (Winter 1993): 186–187.

36. See Manning, pp. 61, 128, 159.

37. Bartky, pp. 111–113.

38. Virginia Warren notes the similarity between the notion of "connection" in care ethics and the notion of "connection" in Christianity: "We are all God's children; we are all related to God and to each other." Virginia Warren, "Comment on Rita Manning's Book," paper read at the Pacific American Philosophical Association Meetings, March 1993 (p. 12). Such notions of connection can give rise to feelings of responsibility, as the Christian notion gave rise, of course, to the idea of the "white man's burden."

39. Ibid., p. 15.

40. Taylor, *Philosophy and the Human Sciences*, p. 236. Taylor, *Sources of the Self: The Making of the Modern Identity*, p. 62.

41. Taylor, *Philosophy and the Human Sciences*, p. 236.

42. Ibid., p. 4.

43. Ibid., pp. 9–10.

44. Taylor, *Sources of the Self*, p. 63.

45. See ibid., pp. 53–90.

46. Taylor, *Philosophy and the Human Sciences*, p. 120.

47. Lynn M. Morgan, "When Does Life Begin?" A Cross-Cultural Perspective on the Personhood of Fetuses and Young Children," in W. Haviland and R. Gordon, eds., *Talking About People: Readings in Contemporary Cultural Anthropology* (Mountain View, CA: Mayfield Publishing Company, 1993), p. 33. I will consider "post-partum abortion" in somewhat more detail in chapter 3.

48. This example involves the male initiation rites of the Sambia and the Etoro, which I will take up again in chapter 6. David Gilmore suggests that describing such acts as "homosexual" may distort them, and regards the term "ritualized masculinization" as less ethnocentric. See David Gilmore, *Manhood in the Making: Cultural Concepts of Masculinity* (New Haven: Yale University Press, 1990), p.151.

49. Richard Handler and Daniel Segal, *Jane Austen and the Fiction of Culture: An Essay on the Narration of Social Realities* (Tucson: University of Arizona Press, 1990), pp. 137–148. Handler and Segal critique Evan-Pritchard's well-known discussion of Azande witchcraft. Charles Taylor also discusses Evan-Pritchard's work on Azande witchcraft in order to demonstrate what nonethnocentric readings of the practices of others involve, but he does not question Evan-Pritchard's provisional identification and description of Azande beliefs, as do Handler and Segal.

50. Taylor, *Philosophy and the Human Sciences,* pp. 4–5.

51. Benhabib, p. 43.

52. MacIntyre calls this view of the self that "is totally detached from all social particularity" the "democratized self." On this view, "Anyone and everyone can thus be a moral agent, since it is in the self and not in social roles or practices that moral agency has to be located." Benhabib locates practical reason outside of particular social roles and cultural practices. Thus, her discursive interactions occur between "democratized selves" not "situated selves." In this way her ideal conversations are formally democratic—anyone is eligible to participate—though not genuinely inclusive of diverse perspectives. See MacIntyre, p. 32.

53. Compare Williams, *Ethics and the Limits of Philosophy,* p. 110.

54. Maria Lugones and Elizabeth Spelman, "Have We Got a Theory for You! Feminist Theory, Cultural Imperialism and the Demand for 'The Woman's Voice,'" in *Women and Values: Readings in Recent Feminist Philosophy,* 2d ed. (Belmont, CA: Wadsworth, 1993), pp. 23–24.

55. Ibid., pp.28–29.

56. Judith DeCew, for example, argues that the existence of plural non-orderable moral standards is consistent with objectivity in ethics. By recognizing multiple goods, DeCew admits, we may not be able to arrive at uniquely right answers in all cases, though there can be uniquely right answers in some cases. DeCew makes this logical point in the process of interpreting what she takes to be the apparently contradictory remarks of Stuart Hampshire, who claims that irresolvable moral conflicts are inescapable but who also claims that moral relativism and skepticism must be rejected. DeCew resolves the apparent contradictions in Hampshire's remarks by construing his moral theory as a fundamentally nonrelativist, objectivist one that only allows for there being competing "right" answers in a limited range of cases. I will discuss anti-relativist, objectivist versions of pluralism in chapter 7. See Judith DeCew, "Moral Conflicts and Ethical Relativism," *Ethics* 101 (October 1990): 27–41.

57. Williams, *Ethics and the Limits of Philosophy,* p. 219, note 2.

58. Taylor, *Philosophy and the Human Sciences,* p. 123.

59. Ibid., p. 123.

60. Williams, *Ethics and the Limits of Philosophy,* p. 162.

61. Taylor, *Philosophy and the Human Sciences,* p. 145.

62. MacIntyre, p. 50.

63. Rosalind Hursthouse, "Virtue Theory and Abortion," *Philosophy and Public Affairs* 20 (Summer 1991): 240.

2. Interpreting Adultery

1. Clifford Geertz, *The Interpretation of Cultures* (New York: Basic Books, 1973), p. 27.

2. Ibid., p. 13.

3. Ibid., p. 12.

4. Ibid., p. 7.

5. Charles Taylor, *Philosophy and the Human Sciences: Philosophical Papers, 2* (Cambridge: Cambridge University Press, 1985), p. 36.

6. Ibid., p. 38.

7. Geertz, p. 13.

8. Ibid., p. 12.

9. Taylor, p. 39.

10. For a brief discussion of the origin of this distinction see Richard Handler, "Clifford Geertz," in R. Turner, ed., *Thinkers of the Twentieth Century,* 2d ed. (Chicago: St. James, 1987), p. 280.

11. Geertz, p. 12.

12. Ibid., p. 9.

13. See ibid., p. 15.

14. Ibid., p. 23.

15. See ibid., p. 21.

16. Richard Wasserstrom, "Is Adultery Immoral?" in R. Baker and F. Elliston, eds., *Philosophy and Sex* (Buffalo, NY: Prometheus, 1984), p. 97.

17. Given the frequency of insincerity in these matters, something girls are cautioned against, deception is not only a common feature of adultery in our mainstream society, but a feature of many more ordinary heterosexual encounters. Perhaps, the adultery of married men—and the consequent deception of women it involves about the state of the husband's affection—is, in many cases, merely an extension of earlier premarital male sexual behavior. Wasserstrom does not address the fact that the emotional deception of women on the part of men is a culturally sanctioned game played in many nonadulterous situations, and the implications this fact might have for our moral assessment of adultery.

18. Wasserstrom, p. 97.

19. Gayle Rubin, "Thinking Sex: Notes for a Radical Theory of the Politics of Sexuality," in Carole Vance, ed., *Pleasure and Danger: Exploring Female Sexuality* (Boston: Routledge, 1984), p. 279.

20. Taylor, p. 124.

21. Wasserstrom, p. 99.

22. Stuart Hampshire, *Morality and Conflict* (Cambridge: Harvard University Press, 1983), pp. 163–164.

23. Taylor, p. 125.

24. See ibid., p. 150.

25. Ibid., pp. 148–149.

26. Rebecca Kukla and Andre Kukla refer to the idea that all descriptive systems are commensurable as "conceptual colonialism." See "Davidson's Conceptual Colonialism," unpublished manuscript.

27. Nancy Davis, "The Abortion Debate: The Search for Common Ground, Part 1," *Ethics* 103 (April 1993): 520–521.

28. Nancy Davis, "The Abortion Debate: The Search for Common Ground, Part 2," *Ethics* 103 (July 1993): 773.

29. Steven Seidman, *Embattled Eros: Sexual Politics and Ethics in Contemporary America* (New York: Routledge, 1992).

30. Ibid., pp. 187–189.

31. Ibid., p. 194.

32. Ibid., pp. 194–195.

33. Ibid., p. 195.

34. Ibid., p. 196.

35. Ibid., pp. 199–200.

36. When he says things like "We—contemporary adult Americans—would agree . . ." (quoted above) he seems to be suggesting that there are criteria that are universally held and given the same importance by all Americans. By viewing these ideals as universal, he may be obscuring important differences between similar but ultimately incommensurable ideals (e.g., different cultural conceptions of responsibility). It would be better to consider whether the successful realization of the libertarian ideal of consent can command the appreciation of sexual romanticists and whether the successful realization of the romanticist ideal of responsibility can command the appreciation of libertarians.

37. In another great example of cinematic adultery, Billy Burke passively endures pain as Katharine Hepburn carries on with Burke's husband (*Christopher Strong*).

38. Think of Alex in *Fatal Attraction*.

39. Seidman, pp. 200–201.

40. Ibid., p. 201.

41. If the "common meanings" that were the basis of this libertarian community were partly a response to oppressive romanticist ideologies that stigmatized certain sexual minorities, then it may be good to question the reproduction of this libertarian ideology through collective behavior.

42. Ibid., p. 202.

43. Ibid., p. 200.

44. For an interesting discussion of the role of intuition in moral philosophy, see Bernard Williams, *Ethics and the Limits of Philosophy* (Cambridge: Harvard University Press, 1985), pp. 93–95.

45. For an interesting discussion by men and boys in the "man/boy love" movement see Daniel Tsang, ed., *The Age Taboo: Gay Male Sexuality, Power and Consent* (London: Gay Men's Press, 1981).

3. Fetal Ideologies and Maternal Desires: A Post-Enlightenment Account of Abortion

1. For feminist critiques of defenses of abortion that rest on a right to privacy see Mary Poovey, "The Abortion Question and the Death of Man," in J. Butler and J. Scott, eds., *Feminists Theorize the Political* (New York: Routledge, 1992), pp. 240–41; and Catharine MacKinnon, *Toward a Feminist Theory of the State* (Cambridge: Harvard University Press, 1989), pp. 184–194. For a critique of the libertarian notion of autonomy and Judith Thomson's classic defense of abortion which rests on it, see Elizabeth Mensch and Alan Freeman, *The Politics of Virtue: Is Abortion Debatable?* (Durham, NC: Duke University Press, 1993), pp. 130–132; and also Nancy Davis, "The Abortion Debate: The Search for Common Ground Part, 2," *Ethics* 103 (July 1993): 750–755. For feminist critiques of the liberal notion of equality, see the various articles included in the section on Sexual Difference and Equality Theory in K. Bartlett and R. Kennedy, eds., *Feminist Legal Theory: Readings in Law and Gender* (Boulder, CO: Westview, 1991).

2. Poovey, p. 250.

3. See Poovey, p. 246.

4. Judith Butler, *Gender Trouble* (New York: Routledge, 1990).

5. Mary Anne Warren argues that

   > because even late-term fetuses are not yet persons, and because all persons have a basic moral right to "control their own bodies,"— i.e., to defend, and make decisions affecting, their own physical integrity—a woman has a moral right to choose even late abortion for any reason which she regards as sufficient. (p. 104)

   Warren also argues that abortions for sex selection are morally objectionable because they "deprive a sentient human being of its life because of its sex" (p. 104). Yet she concludes that this is not a sufficient reason either to morally criticize women who seek abortion for sex selection or to restrict access to abortions sought for sex selection (pp. 189–191). In this way, Warren carries to their logical extreme the premises of her liberal rights approach. Yet this "all abortions are equal before the state" approach does not allow for a nuanced and complicated response to women's demands for abortion. Mary Anne Warren, *Gendercide: The Implications of Sex Selection* (Totowa, NJ: Rowman and Allanheld, 1985).

6. Mensch and Freeman, p. 132.

7. Faye Ginsburg, *Contested Lives: The Abortion Debate in an American Community* (Berkeley: University of California, 1989). See also Nancy Davis's review of Ginsburg in *Ethics* 103 (April 1993): 516–539.

8. T. M. Scanlon, "Partisan for Life," *New York Review of Books* 40, no. 13 (July 15, 1993): 45.

9. Dworkin escapes the radical implications of his idea by detaching our discourses about rights and justice from their historical and religious origins and representing them as a neutral or common basis for adjudicating "religious" and other conflicts. But if feminists are not willing to endorse liberal Enlightenment ideologies about rationality, we cannot take the out Dworkin offers.

10. Compare Scanlon, p. 46.

11. In her insightful critique of Lawrence Tribe's *Abortion: The Clash of Absolutes* (New York: Norton, 1990), Nancy Davis shows that Tribe (like Dworkin) avoids the deeper implications of recognizing that appeals to abstract rights have obscured the real issues behind the abortion debate. Tribe's argumentative manoeuvers take a somewhat more libertarian twist than Dworkin's. See Davis, "The Abortion Debate: The Search for Common Ground, Part 1," *Ethics* 103 (April 1993): pp. 527–528.

12. Ibid., pp. 527–528.

13. Kristin Luker, *Abortion and the Politics of Motherhood* (Berkeley: University of California Press, 1984).

14. Davis, p. 528.

15. Faye Ginsburg, "The Body Politic: The Defense of Sexual Restriction by Anti-Abortion Activists," in Carole Vance, ed., *Pleasure and Danger: Exploring Female Sexuality* (Boston: Routledge and Kegan Paul, 1984), p. 173.

16. Luker, p. 193.

17. See Mensch and Freeman, p. 129.

18. Ginsburg, "The Body Politic," pp. 173–174.

19. Luker seems less committed than Ginsburg to all aspects of this approach. Indeed, Luker seems to be interested in exposing the cultural presuppositions of "pro-life" women in order to show that they are really not concerned to protect life so much as to protect traditional gender roles for women. In doing this, Luker may be encouraging us to discount the belief systems of "pro-life" women, and to see them as self-deceived. That is, in some parts of her book, Luker appears to be uncovering the cultural assumptions of "pro-life" women through the distorting lenses of "pro-choice" women. Because she does not appear to attempt the reverse, I see her as ultimately striving for the total victory of one side in this debate. Ginsburg is much more successful in both enabling the distinct and coherent voices of "pro-life" and "pro-choice" women to be heard together, and in identifying a diversity of incommensurable ideals that shape women's lives. In reviewing Ginsburg's book, Nancy Davis seems to be more sympathetic to Luker's approach, and thus criticizes Ginsburg's work for what I see to be its greatest strength. That is, Davis seems to mistake Ginsburg's anti-ethnocentrism for reflecting her own "credo" through these women's

voices. And because Davis seems to miss the significance of Ginsburg's relativising strategy, she ends her essay by expressing skepticism toward the search for less complete victories in the abortion conflict. See Davis, Parts 1 and 2, especially pp. 533–39.

20. Luker, p. 214.

21. Ginsburg, "The Body Politic," p. 174.

22. Ibid.

23. See Luker, p. 176.

24. Compare Davis, Part 1, p. 531.

25. Kathryn Pyne Addelson states:

> The dominant philosophic definitions . . . analyze abortion as a conflict of rights. Academic feminists (including Gilligan) rightly complain that this silences women. Other academics complain it silences Christians. By the results of Kohlberg's test, it silences nonwhites, members of lower classes, and citizens of Third World nations—to say nothing of the clients of our prisons, mental institutions, and elementary schools . . . The ethical theories that support the definition of abortion as a conflict of rights are implicated in all these things.

See K. P. Addelson, *Impure Thoughts: Essays on Philosophy, Feminism, and Ethics* (Philadelphia: Temple University Press, 1991), p. 104.

26. Here I am in some agreement with feminist theorists who take a "care" approach. What we agree on is that the notion of caring for others provides an extremely important moral ideal. What we disagree on is that this insight can provide a principle for developing "an ethics of care": that is, a reductionist approach to ethics that treats care issues as the most fundamental or basic. As I argued in chapter 1, without appealing to other "basic" notions, care ethics cannot help us make responsible decisions about whom and what we should care for. To avoid the problems of care ethics in particular, and reductionist approaches in general, I advocate a pluralist approach.

27. This way of putting it may seem to ignore the social pressure on some women and couples to bear sons in some cultural contexts, but I am primarily thinking of the American context here.

28. In one of the earliest essays by a feminist philosopher to question the standard liberal defenses of abortion based on the rights to privacy and "to control one's body," Alison Jaggar argues that women in our society should be granted the sole authority to decide whether to terminate their pregnancies. But Jaggar grants this social authority to women only contingently and not absolutely, and argues that their having this authority should be contingent upon the kinds of social resources a society makes available to women and their children. Jaggar argues that in a society where the responsibility for pregnancy and children was more widely shared, it would be acceptable for the state to limit women's access or

right to abortion. Jaggar bases her conclusion on two universal moral principles: that only those who are significantly affected by a decision have the right to participate in making it, and that a right to life means a right to the necessities for sustaining life. In a society where the burden of supporting and caring for children is placed almost entirely on individual women who, in some cases, may not be able to guarantee their offspring the necessities for sustaining life, women should be able to have abortions on demand. But in a society where all children were guaranteed the necessities for life, and where the responsibility for child care was more equitably distributed, women would not be able to demand abortions, though through some collective decision making procedure they might sometimes get them. Though my argument for restricting abortion on demand is not based on the universal principles Jaggar articulates, I share some of her more basic unarticulated assumptions. For one, like Jaggar, I assume that the abortion practices of women affect others besides themselves. Second, like Jaggar, I assume that the reasons a woman chooses abortion are relevant to assessing the moral value of her decision. Third, like Jaggar, I do not see social life as necessarily in conflict with pre-existing human desires and needs, but rather our recognition of our needs and desires depends upon forms of social life. While Jaggar makes access to abortion contingent on what a society materially contributes to the support of children, I make access to abortion contingent on the cultural beliefs constitutive of the meaning of pregnancy and its termination in a particular society. See Alison Jaggar, "Abortion and a Woman's Right to Decide," in C. Gould and M. Wartofsky, eds., *Women and Philosophy: Toward a Theory of Liberation* (New York: Capricorn Books, 1976), pp. 347–360.

29. See Mensch and Freeman, p. 150.

30. See Daniel Segal, "A Patient So Dead: American Medical Students and Their Cadavers," *Anthropological Quarterly* 61 (1988): 17–25. Of course, in order to discuss in a sensitive way the moral ambiguities regarding abortion, physicians would need to be trained differently than they are now. Perhaps, given the inequality in social power that often exists between the physician and patient, in order to avoid physicians imposing their own views on their patients, physicians should merely direct their patients to confer with the latter's own moral and spiritual counselors prior to obtaining an abortion. I am grateful to Jacqueline Glover for this suggestion.

31. I have heard from some Wisconsin residents that some communities there are experimenting with this, but I have no first-hand material to back this up.

32. Ginsburg, *Contested Lives,* pp. 219–220.

33. See Davis, Parts 1 and 2.

34. Mensch and Freeman, p. 151.

35. Ibid., p. 153.

36. Ibid., p. 140.

37. Ibid., p. 147.

38. On the way Tribe overestimates, see Davis, Part 2, p. 775.

39. Mensch and Freeman, p. 157.

40. See Lynn M. Morgan, "When Does Life Begin? A Cross-Cultural Perspective on the Personhood of Fetuses and Young Children," in W. Haviland and R. Gordon, eds., *Talking About People: Readings in Contemporary Cultural Anthropology* (Mountain View, CA: Mayfield Publishing Company, 1993), pp. 28–38.

41. Ibid., p. 29.

42. See ibid., p. 34.

43. Ibid., p. 35.

44. Ginsburg, *Contested Lives*, pp. 217–218.

45. Morgan, p. 31.

46. See Morgan, throughout.

47. Ibid., p. 30.

48. Ibid., p. 31.

49. Ibid., p. 33.

50. Ibid.

51. Ibid., p. 30.

52. Ibid.

53. Mensch and Freeman, p. 149. Mensch and Freeman may be offering this as a pragmatic compromise between religious and secular forces in our society, though it does seem to privilege the latter.

54. Morgan, p. 31.

55. Ibid., p. 29.

56. I offer these accounts without the cultural distance and ethnographic field experience that may be necessary for getting them "right," and thus I hope that others will correct, if not excuse, my mistakes.

57. The relationship between the fetal gift view and the "pro-life" view of motherhood is a complex one. Kristin Luker at times in her book appears to hold that one's views about the place of motherhood in a woman's life somehow determine which fetal account one subscribes to. In other places, she seems to suggest that these views are independent, but mutually determining of one's views on abortion. To understand the relationship between them, we need to separate the questions of the place of motherhood in any woman's life and the place of motherhood in a pregnant woman's life, as I argued above. The fetal gift ideology clearly conditions the "pro-life" view of the latter relationship, rather than the other way around.

58. According to Barbara Duden, neither English nor American common

law prior to the nineteenth century recognized the existence of a fetus until quickening occurred. And because quickening was the criterion that determined the existence of a fetus, pregnancy was a condition that only a woman could sense and publicly establish. Thus the concept of "abortion" did not apply to the early stages of pregnancy. This changed when, according to Duden,

> Physicians attacked quickening as a criterion because they wanted to challenge the court's reliance on women and jury matrons. They sought to promote themselves as medical experts.

Duden suggests that the replacement of quickening with medical-scientific criteria of pregnancy contributed historically to the diminishment of women's authority and control over the processes of reproduction. Barbara Duden, *Disembodying Women: Perspectives on Pregnancy and the Unborn* (Cambridge: Harvard University Press, 1993), p. 82.

59. Morgan, p. 36.

4. Feminism and Sexuality

1. See Faye Ginsburg, *Contested Lives: The Abortion Debate in an American Community* (Berkeley: University of California Press, 1989).

2. See especially David Halperin, *One Hundred Years of Homosexuality* (New York: Routledge, 1990).

3. Gayle Rubin, "Thinking Sex: Notes for a Radical Theory of the Politics of Sexuality," in C. S. Vance, ed., *Pleasure and Danger: Exploring Female Sexuality* (London: Pandora, 1989), p. 277.

4. Ibid., pp. 298–99.

5. Ibid., p. 298.

6. Ibid., p. 304.

7. For an interesting discussion of the emerging split between feminists on abortion, see Sidney Callahan, "A pro-life feminist makes her case," *Utne Reader,* no. 20 (March/April 1987): 104–108; and Kathleen McDonnell, "Pro-choice feminists must open up the abortion debate," *Utne Reader,* no. 20 (March/April 1987): 109–115.

8. The latter position is held, for example, by the prostitute civil rights organization COYOTE (Call Off Your Old Tired Ethics). See Valerie Jenness, *Making It Work: The Prostitutes' Rights Movement in Perspective* (New York: Aldine De Gruyter, 1993), p. 67. The former position is exemplified by Kathleen Barry, *Female Sexual Slavery* (New York: Avon Books, 1979).

9. See Elizabeth Mensch and Alan Freeman, *The Politics of Virtue: Is Abortion Debatable?* (Durham, NC: Duke University Press, 1993), p. 135.

10. Philippa Levine is one of the few who advocate reform, rather than removal, of existing criminal prohibitions by redistributing moral respon-

sibility for prostitution from the prostitute to her male clients and managers. This would be accomplished, for example, by increasing the criminal penalties imposed on clients and managers while diminishing the social and criminal sanctions imposed on prostitutes. See Philippa Levine, *Prostitution in Florida* (A Report Presented to the Gender Bias Study Commission of the Supreme Court of Florida, 1988).

11. See for example, Barbara Meil Hobson, *Uneasy Virtue: The Politics of Prostitution and the American Reform Tradition* (Chicago: University of Chicago Press, 1990), pp. 234–235.

12. See for example, Priscilla Alexander, "Prostitution: A Difficult Issue for Feminists" in F. Delacoste and P. Alexander, eds., *Sex Work: Writings by Women in the Sex Industry* (Pittsburgh, PA: Cleis Press), pp. 210–211. Prostitute advocates generally refer to systems of legally regulated prostitution as "legalized prostitution" or the "legalization" of prostitution. Legalization in this sense means that the state treats prostitution as a special kind of industry, imposing special regulations: such as the registration of workers, mandatory health exams, special zoning and curfews limiting places and times of operation, special licenses and taxes, and so on.

13. For example, see the "World Charter for Prostitutes' Rights: International Committee for Prostitutes' Rights, Amsterdam, February, 1985," in Gail Pheterson, ed., *A Vindication of the Rights of Whores* (Seattle, WA: Seal Press, 1989), pp. 40–42. I believe that social policies very similar to those described in this document are still endorsed by NOW (National Organization for Women).

14. Roger Matthews, "Beyond Wolfenden?: Prostitution, Politics and the Law," in R. Matthews and J. Young, eds., *Confronting Crime* (London: Sage, 1986), p. 198.

15. Ibid., p. 199.

16. Ibid., p. 204.

17. Ibid.

18. Ibid.

19. Ibid.

20. Ibid., p. 205.

21. Ibid., p. 209.

22. Hobson, pp. 214–215. See also Laurie Bell, ed., *Good Girls, Bad Girls: Feminists and Sex Trade Workers Face to Face* (Seattle, WA: Seal Press, 1987), and Gail Pheterson, ed., *A Vindication of the Rights of Whores*.

23. Seidman characterizes anti-pornography feminists as sexual romanticists, and by extension, I am characterizing anti-prostitution feminists in this way. See Steven Seidman, *Embattled Eros: Sexual Politics and Ethics in Contemporary America* (New York: Routledge, 1992), pp. 108–109, 133–135.

24. See Hobson, p. 221.

25. For a discussion of the philosophical and political differences between WHISPER and COYOTE, see Jenness, pp. 76–81. This book primarily focuses on the group COYOTE, and thus is also useful for an introduction to the views and political agendas of this group.

26. See Hobson, p. 220.

27. The first half of this section is a slightly revised version of my paper "Comment on Overall's 'What's Wrong with Prostitution: Evaluating Sex Work,'" *Signs* 19:2 (Winter 1994). Copyright © 1994 by The University of Chicago. All rights reserved.

28. For example, the socialist feminist position is articulated in or derived from the following writings: Gayle Rubin, "The Traffic in Women: Notes on the 'Political Economy' of Sex," in Rayna Reiter, ed., *Toward an Anthropology of Women* (New York: Monthly Review Press, 1975); Friedrich Engels, *The Origin of the Family, Private Property and the State* (New York: Penguin, 1985); Emma Goldman, "The Traffic in Women," in Alix Kates Shulman, ed., *Red Emma Speaks* (New York: Schocken, 1983); Alison Jaggar, "Prostitution," in Alan Soble, ed., *The Philosophy of Sex* (Totowa, NJ: Rowman & Allanheld, 1985); and Gerda Lerner, *The Creation of Patriarchy* (New York: Oxford University Press, 1986). The libertarian feminist view has been advanced by spokespersons for various prostitute civil rights groups (such as Margo St. James of COYOTE), and has been taken up and defended in the following essays: David Richards, "Commercial Sex and the Rights of the Person: A Moral Argument for the Decriminalization of Prostitution," *University of Pennsylvania Law Review* 127 (May 1979): 1195–1287; and Lars Ericsson, "Charges Against Prostitution: An Attempt at a Philosophical Assessment," *Ethics* 90 (1980): 335–366. See also Janet Radcliffe Richards, *The Sceptical Feminist* (London: Routledge and Kegan Paul, 1980), pp. 197–202.

29. Christine Overall, "What's Wrong With Prostitution?: Evaluating Sex Work," *Signs* 17 (Summer 1992): 705–724.

30. Ibid., p. 724.

31. Some feminists distinguish prostitution from other demeaning occupations by the prostitute's intimate use of her body. This has numerous problems though. For one, there are non-demeaning occupations that appear to involve intimate, though perhaps less sexual, uses of one's body: the occupations of an actor, athlete, dancer, model, etc. Second, if the intimate or sexual use of one's body is what makes prostitution degrading, then we need to explain why such uses of one's body in one's work are degrading. Carole Pateman suggests that it has something to do with how our bodies and our sexuality are constitutive of our identity as women and as persons. I will discuss and critique this part of Pateman's account in chapter 6. See Carole Pateman, "What's Wrong With Prostitution?" in *The Sexual Contract* (Stanford, CA: Stanford University Press, 1988), pp. 206–207.

32. Overall, pp. 716–717.

33. Ibid., p. 717.

34. Ibid.

35. Ibid., p. 718.

36. Ibid., pp. 717–18.

37. See Cecilia Karch and G. H. S. Dann, "Close Encounters of the Third World," *Human Relations* 34 (1981): 249–268.

38. See Luise White, *The Comforts of Home: Prostitution in Colonial Nairobi* (Chicago: University of Chicago Press, 1990).

39. Ibid., p. 175.

40. Ibid., p. 57.

41. Indeed it appears that sexual services were bought and sold in many precapitalist societies, e.g., ancient civilizations in Mesopotamia, Greece, India, and China.

42. White, p. 11.

43. See Marcel Mauss, *The Gift,* trans. Ian Cunnison (Glencoe, IL: Free Press, 1954). Alison Jaggar states "We need to understand the relationship between 'the traffic in women' and other forms of exchange in our society; in other words, we need to understand the political economy of prostitution." See Jaggar, "Prostitution," p. 364. I am arguing, contra Overall, that while prostitution, as it occurs in our society, is closely related to other kinds of commodity (rather than gift) exchange, the capitalist character of this exchange is not inherent to prostitution. I believe this account of the political economy of prostitution, as suggested by Luise White, will help us better understand it, and to distinguish it from other forms of sexual activity.

44. Overall, p. 706.

45. See especially Luise White, *The Comforts of Home*; Donna Guy, *Sex and Danger in Buenos Aires: Prostitution, Family, and Nation in Argentina* (Lincoln, NE: University of Nebraska Press, 1991); Mary Gibson, *Prostitution and the State in Italy, 1860–1915* (New Brunswick, NJ: Rutgers University Press, 1986); Sue Gronewold, *Prostitution in China 1860–1936* (The Institute for Research in History and The Haworth Press, 1982); Leah Otis, *Prostitution in Medieval Society* (Chicago: University of Chicago Press, 1985); Thanh-Dam Truong, *Sex, Money, and Morality: Prostitution and Tourism in South-East Asia* (London: Zed Books, 1990); Judith Walkowitz, *Prostitution and Victorian Society: Women, Class, and the State* (Cambridge: Cambridge University Press, 1980); Barbara Meil Hobson, *Uneasy Virtue: The Politics of Prostitution and the American Reform Tradition* (Chicago: University of Chicago Press, 1990); and Philippa Levine, *Prostitution in Florida* (A Report Presented to the Gender Bias Study Commission of the Supreme Court of Florida, 1988).

46. For a refutation of this general liberal assumption, see Marshall Sahlins, "The Original Affluent Society," in *Stone Age Economics* (Chicago: Aldine-Atherton, 1972).

47. See especially Ericsson, "Charges Against Prostitution."

48. Janet Richards, p. 200.

49. Ericsson, p. 355.

50. David Richards, "Commercial Sex and the Rights of the Person: A Moral Argument for the Decriminalization of Prostitution," *University of Pennsylvania Law Review* 127 (May 1979): 1269–1270.

51. Compare Ericsson, "Charges Against Prostitution."

52. Janet Richards, p. 199 and 200.

53. Ibid., p. 200.

54. Jaggar, "Prostitution," p. 351.

55. This assumption, which Ericsson appears to make, is somewhat ethnocentric. In one of the least violent human societies known, that of the Semai, men and women are expected to submit peacefully to the sexual requests of others, for to refuse a sexual advance is considered an act of aggression. See David Gilmore, *Manhood in the Making: Cultural Concepts of Masculinity* (New Haven: Yale University Press, 1990), p. 211.

56. Ericsson, p. 360.

57. See Karl Heider, "Dani Sexuality: A Low Energy System," *Man* 11 (1976): 188–201.

5. Comparing Prostitutions

1. Three recent essays on prostitution have the title "What's Wrong with Prostitution?": Christine Overall's in *Signs,* Carole Pateman's in *The Sexual Contract,* and Igor Primoratz's in *Philosophy* 68 (1993), although the last author thinks there isn't much wrong with it.

2. Alison Jaggar, "Prostitution," in A. Soble, ed., *Philosophy of Sex* (Totowa, NJ: Rowman and Allanheld, 1985), p. 349.

3. Ibid., p. 365.

4. Ibid.

5. Quoted in Gerda Lerner, *The Creation of Patriarchy* (New York: Oxford University Press, 1986), p. 129.

6. Lerner, p. 126.

7. Emma Goldman, "The Traffic in Women," in Alix Kates Shulman, ed., *Red Emma Speaks* (New York: Shocken, 1983), p. 180.

8. Lerner, p. 125.

9. Ibid.

10. Ibid., p. 130.

11. Ibid., p. 132.

12. Ibid., p. 125.

13. Ibid., p. 130.

14. Ibid., p. 124.

15. Ibid., p. 133.

16. Ibid., p. 134.

17. Ibid., p. 135.

18. Ibid., p. 137.

19. Ibid., p. 134.

20. Luise White, *The Comforts of Home: Prostitution in Colonial Nairobi* (Chicago: University of Chicago Press, 1990), pp. 1–2.

21. Ibid., p. 39.

22. Ibid., p. 171.

23. Ibid., pp. 226–27.

24. Ibid., p. 11.

25. According to Friedrich Engels, "Marriage of convenience turns often enough into the crassest prostitution—sometimes of both partners, but far more commonly of the woman, who only differs from the ordinary courtesan in that she does not let out her body on piecework as a wage worker, but sell it once and for all into slavery." *The Origin of the Family, Private Property and the State* (New York: Penguin, 1985), p. 102.

26. Compare Simone de Beauvoir, *The Second Sex* (New York: Vintage, 1974), p. 619.

27. White, p. 19. The extraordinariness of this, from our cultural perspective, is perhaps reflected in the recent movie *Pretty Woman*. In this movie it took an exceptionally pretty prostitute—and one capable of adopting fairly readily the consumption habits, cultural ideals, and personal demeanor of her betters—to bring about a client/prostitute marital union, and thus to bring about the class elevation that this union achieved for the prostitute in this context. Ironically, when prostitutes married their clients in Colonial Nairobi, their class status may have been lowered from petty-bourgeois to working class. Perhaps because of the possibility for downward mobility, exceptional prettiness does not seem to have been required to create marriage opportunities for prostitutes, and to erase the social memories of their previous class identities.

28. Ibid., p. 2.

29. Ibid., p. 19.

30. See ibid., p. 176.

31. Ibid., p. 7.

32. Ibid., p. 20.

33. Tom Cox, *The Badi: Prostitution as a Social Norm Among an Untouchable Caste of West Nepal* (Kathmandu, Nepal: Asian Ethographer Society Press, 1993), p. 3. I am grateful to Don Brenneis for bringing this work to my attention. (All page references are to an unpublished draft.)

34. Ibid., p. 1.

35. Ibid., p. 2.

36. Ibid., p. 7.

37. Ibid., pp. 3–4.

38. Ibid., p. 11.

39. Ibid.

40. Ernestine McHugh, another ethnographer of Nepali society, suggested to me that this may be another reason Badi men marry out of caste.

41. Cox, p. 9.

42. Ibid., p. 10.

43. Cox briefly describes three castes in India whose primary income generating activity is prostitution, and whose customs and laws also discourage their female members from marrying. Thus the Badi are not alone in favoring prostitution as an occupation for their women.

44. Jacques Rossiaud, *Medieval Prostitution,* Lydia Cochrane, trans. (New York: Basil Blackwell, 1988), p. 166. See also ibid., p. 59.

45. Ibid., p. 105.

46. Leah Otis, *Prostitution in Medieval Society* (Chicago: University of Chicago Press, 1985), pp. 102–103.

47. Rossiaud, pp. 65–66 and p. 68.

48. Otis, p. 67.

49. Rossiaud, p. 69.

50. Ibid., p. 70.

51. Otis, p. 68.

52. Rossiaud, p. 12.

53. Ibid., p. 18.

54. Ibid.

55. See ibid., especially pp. 160–162.

56. Ibid., p. 48.

57. Otis, p. 101.

58. Ibid., p. 104.

59. Ibid.

60. Rossiaud also mentions that women's natures were seen as weak, and that this was thought to explain "why they respond to solicitation or consent to brutality" (ibid., p. 76). Though Rossiaud connects this cultural belief to the propensity of medieval society to hold women responsible for their own seduction or even rape, he does not connect it to the policy of institutionalizing prostitution.

61. Otis, p. 104.

6. **Exotic Erotica and Erotic Exotica: Sex Commerce in Some Contemporary Urban Centers**

1. According to Carole Pateman,

    The claim that prostitution is a universal feature of human society relies not only on the cliché of the "oldest profession" but also on the widely held assumption that prostitution originates in men's natural sexual urge. There is a universal, natural (masculine) impulse that, it is assumed requires, and will always require, the outlet provided by prostitution.

    Pateman, *The Sexual Contract* (Stanford, CA: Stanford University Press, 1988), pp. 197–198. In this chapter I will consider how this assumption, made by many liberals, shapes prostitution in our society.

2. For a philosophical articulation of this general line of argument, see Michael Walzer, *The Spheres of Justice* (New York: Basic Books, 1983). Walzer states that "we can buy and sell universally only if we disregard real values; while if we attend to values, there are things that cannot be bought and sold" (p. 97). Walzer refers to goods that ought not be exchanged for money as "blocked exchanges." According to Walzer, "Sex can be sold only when it is understood in terms of pleasure and not exclusively in terms of married love or religious worship" (p. 103). Walzer argues, though, that we need to resist the tyranny of money and the dominance of the market, which tend to distort and undermine other distributive principles and social goods. He states "[money] corrupts distributions without transforming them; and then corrupt distributions coexist with legitimate ones, like prostitution alongside married love. But this is tyranny still, and it can make for harsh forms of domination" (p. 317).

3. This section and the following are largely based on my previous paper "Should Feminists Oppose Prostitution?" *Ethics* 99 (January 1989): 347–361.

4. We see the provider as deviant, but not the buyer because, as Mary McIntosh points out, we assume that love and romance are more important to women, or are a more important part of sex for them. See Mary McIntosh, "Who Needs Prostitutes?: The Ideology of Male Sexual Needs," in C. Smart and B. Smart, eds., *Women, Sexuality and Control* (London: Routledge & Kegan Paul, 1978), p. 63.

5. See Gayle Rubin, "Thinking Sex: Notes for a Radical Theory of the Politics of Sexuality," in Carole Vance, ed., *Pleasure and Danger: Exploring Female Sexuality* (London: Pandora, 1989), p. 304.

6. Carole Pateman, "Defending Prostitution: Charges against Ericsson," *Ethics* 93 (1983): 563.

7. According to Pateman,

    Once the story of the sexual contract has been told, prostitution can be seen as a problem about *men*. The problem of prostitution then becomes encapsulated in the question why men demand that women's bodies are sold as commodities in the capitalist market.

Pateman, *The Sexual Contract,* p. 194. By telling the story of the sexual (as opposed to the "social") contract, Pateman attempts to shed light on the origins of patriarchal authority. Here we get an origin story about prostitution that includes elements of both the socialist and liberal ones I discussed in chapter 4.

8. The term "penis-feeding" is a translation developed by Daniel Segal for the purposes of teaching this material to college students. For information on the Etoro and Sambia, see Gilbert Herdt, ed., *Rituals of Manhood* (Berkeley: University of California Press, 1982); Harriet Whitehead, "The Varieties of Fertility Cultism in New Guinea: Part 1," *American Ethnologist* 13 (1986): 80–99; and David Gilmore *Manhood in the Making: Cultural Concepts of Masculinity* (New Haven: Yale University Press, 1990).

9. Clifford Geertz, *The Interpretation of Cultures* (New York: Basic Books, 1973), p. 27.

10. In the preface to *Spheres of Justice,* Michael Walzer states "My argument is radically particularist. I don't claim to have achieved any great distance from the social world in which I live . . . Another way of doing philosophy is to interpret to one's fellow citizens the world of meanings that we share" (p. xiv). Actually I think Walzer achieves quite a bit of distance, and he seems to have done this by reading the writings of anthropologists and other social theorists. Though we may be more familiar with the world of meanings we share than the worlds of meanings shared by others, we often do not have the concepts to articulate these meanings. Comparing and contrasting worlds of meanings can help us identify useful concepts for describing our own cultural common sense.

11. Arthur Schopenhauer, "The Metaphysics of the Love of the Sexes," in W. Durant, ed., *The Works of Schopenhauer* (New York: Simon & Schuster, 1928), p. 333.

12. Karl Heider, "Dani Sexuality: A Low Energy System," *Man* 11 (1976): 188–201.

13. Gayle Rubin, "The Traffic in Women: Notes on the 'Political Economy' of Sex," in R. Reiter, ed., *Toward an Anthropology of Women* (New York: Monthly Review Press, 1975), p. 172.

14. Ibid., p. 174.

15. Claude Lévi-Strauss, *The Elementary Structures of Kinship* (Boston: Beacon, 1969), p. 132. A culture in which men are gifts in a ritual of exchange is described in Michael Peletz, "The Exchange of Men in Nineteenth-Century Negeri Sembilan (Malaya)," *American Ethnologist* 14 (1987): 449–469.

16. Rubin, "The Traffic in Women," p. 177.

17. Ibid., p. 179.

18. McIntosh, p. 55.

19. Compare, for example, Gail Pheterson, ed., *A Vindication of the Rights of Whores* (Seattle, WA: Seal Press, 1989), pp. 23 and 194.

20. Robert Baker, "'Pricks' and 'Chicks': A Plea for 'Persons,'" in R. Baker and F. Elliston, eds., *Philosophy and Sex* (Buffalo, NY: Prometheus, 1984), pp. 260–266.

21. Andrea Dworkin, *Intercourse* (New York: Free Press, 1987), p. 122.

22. Igor Primoratz argues, in response to this part of my argument, that the metaphors Dworkin uses are not used by most people, and this is because they are silly. I agree that Dworkin's metaphors are not in wide use, and that they may appear to us as "silly." But their perceived silliness may be due to their taking what is more "obvious" to us—that women are "penetrated" in sexual intercourse with men—to its logical extreme. We still accept the more obvious "fact" of "penetration," which, as I am arguing, is also a cultural image. Primoratz also argues that the vulgarisms Baker identifies do not necessarily reflect "standard" (i.e., universal or pervasive) images of heterosexual intercourse but only "vulgar" images. While I believe these vulgar images are quite pervasive in our culture, Primoratz is right to point out that they are not the only images we have. Indeed, for some in our society, the dominant images of heterosexual intercourse may be those of "love-making," "intimate caressing," "fondling," "genital kissing," "adult play," and so forth. I doubt, however, that there are two separate groups of people in our society, one under the sway of the images of hostility and one under the sway of the romantic metaphors. Instead, I suspect we are influenced by both types of images, though to a lesser or greater extent in different people. Unfortunately, this is not the sort of thing either I or Primoratz can settle by speculation, rather it requires social linguistic research and analysis. See Igor Primoratz, "What's Wrong with Prostitution?" in *Philosophy* 68 (1993): 177–181.

23. Ann Garry, "Pornography and Respect for Women," in R. Baker and F. Elliston, eds., *Philosophy and Sex*, p. 318.

24. Describing prostitution in ancient Athens, David Halperin states,

> It was understood . . . that a man went to prostitutes partly in order to enjoy sexual pleasures that were thought degrading to the person who provided them and that he could not therefore easily obtain from his wife or boyfriend (insertive oral sex, for instance). The liability to be subjected to degrading sexual acts made prostitutes impure in the Athenian imagination—hence, unfit to perform sacred duties on behalf of the city . . .

Halperin's comment suggests that, perhaps even in our society, it may be the kind of sex that prostitute women have—i.e., the sexual acts they perform—rather than their being known and exploited sexually by numerous men, that leads us to view prostitutes as impure and contaminated. See David Halperin, *One Hundred Years of Homosexuality: and Other Essays on Greek Love* (New York: Routledge, 1990), p. 96.

25. A "high class" call girl once told me that she was only able to work at her job for six months of the year, for the work exacted a large psychological toll. When I asked her if she thought there was anything wrong with what she was doing, she replied that it wasn't wrong, for she wasn't hurting anyone but herself.

26. Pateman, "Defending Prostitution," p. 562. See also, Pateman, *The Sexual Contract*, pp. 206–207.

27. Elizabeth Spelman asks:

> What is it I know if I know that I am a woman or a man, Black or Hispana or white, Jewish or Christian, straight or gay or lesbian? Could I be wrong? If others disagree with me, is there a way of deciding which of us is right?

See *Inessential Woman: Problems of Exclusion in Feminist Thought* (Boston: Beacon, 1988), p. 143. To address these questions Spelman asks us to imagine a series of doors marked with labels for our gender and ethnic identities. She then asks, what conditions our going through one door or another? (p. 147) And do some people have the authority to refuse us admission through some doors and direct us through others? (p. 151) Whether I walk through the door marked "Jewish" seems to me partly a choice that I make, partly an opportunity that others offer or deny me, and partly a result of inter-subjective and common meanings I share or fail to share with others.

28. Sander Gilman, *The Jew's Body* (New York: Routledge, 1991), p. 123.

29. Ibid., p. 123.

30. Ibid., p. 122.

31. Ibid., p. 2.

32. Cornel West, *Race Matters* (Boston: Beacon Press, 1993), pp. 83–84.

33. Patricia Hill Collins, *Black Feminist Thought: Knowledge, Consciousness, and the Politics of Empowerment* (Boston: Unwin Hyman, 1990), p. 164.

34. Sarah Pomeroy states "It is no accident that the most famous woman in fifth-century Athens was the foreign-born Aspasia, who started as a *hetaira* and ended as a madam . . ." See *Goddesses, Whores, Wives, and Slaves: Women in Classical Antiquity* (New York: Schocken Books, 1975), p. 89. While it may be no accident, due to the social prestige of some courtesans, Pomeroy's remark suggests that it is somewhat of a surprise that the most popularly known woman in this context was a foreigner. However, Pomeroy does not attempt to analyze further such social characteristics of prostitutes, she merely notes them.

35. Jacques Rossiaud, *Medieval Prostitution*, Lydia Cochrane, trans. (New York: Basil Blackwell, 1988), p. 112.

36. *Far Eastern Economic Review*, January 9, 1976. See also Thanh-Dam Truong *Sex, Money and Morality: Prostitution and Tourism in South-East Asia* (London: Zed Books, 1990).

37. *Los Angeles Times Magazine*, November 8, 1992, p. 22. I have heard the term "silk whores," used to describe sex workers of Asian descent, in a way that similarly emphasizes some culturally stereotyped ethnic-racial-national feature. While this term may seem more repugnant to us, the term "blond geisha" is equally repugnant, as it trivializes the possibly racist meanings of the phenomenon it describes.

38. Cecilia Karch and G. H. S. Dann, "Close Encounters of the Third World," *Human Relations* 34 (1981): 249–268.

39. Richard Symanski, *The Immoral Landscape: Female Prostitution in Western Societies* (Toronto: Butterworth, 1981), p. 67.

40. Ibid., p. 67.

41. Ibid., p. 92.

42. Licia Brussa, "Migrant Prostitutes in the Netherlands," in G. Pheterson, ed., *A Vindication of the Rights of Whores*, p. 231.

43. West, p. 85.

44. Rossiaud, p. 112.

45. See Karch and Dann, "Close Encounters of the Third World."

46. Male prostitutes appear to be studied most when they serve a gay male clientele.

47. Karch and Dann, p. 263.

48. Ibid., p. 257.

49. Ibid., p. 256.

50. In my own discussions with white American prostitutes, one theme that I hear repeatedly is how prostitution affords women entry into an apparently glamorous world of economic and gender privilege.

51. Rossiaud, pp. 112–113.

52. Compare Gail Pheterson "The Social Consequences of Unchastity" in F. Delacoste and P. Alexander, eds., *Sex Work: Writings by Women in the Sex Industry* (Pittsburgh, PA: Cleis Press, 1987), p. 215.

53. Gail Pheterson explores some of these links in her article "The Social Consequences of Unchastity." Pheterson also considers religious and class difference as social marks of impurity.

54. West, p. 83.

55. This section is largely based on my paper "Is Sexual Desire Raced?: The Social Meaning of Interracial Prostitution," *The Journal of Social Philosophy* XXIII (Spring 1992): 42–51.

56. From "The Fall," Dennis Wepman, Ronald Newman, and Murray Binderman, eds., *The Life: The Lore and Folk Poetry of the Black Hustler* (Philadelphia: University of Pennsylvania Press, 1976).

57. Rudyard Kipling, quoted in the *Far Eastern Economic Review*, January 9, 1979.

58. Daniel Tsang, "M. Butterfly Meets the Great White Hope," *Informasian* 6 (March 1992): 3.

59. Ibid., p. 3.

60. Dorinne Kondo "M. Butterfly: Orientalism, Gender, and a Critique of Essentialist Identity," *Cultural Critique* 16 (1990): 10.

61. Ibid., p. 16.

62. Ibid., p. 24.

63. Ibid., p. 17.

64. Mark Berger, "Imperialism and Sexual Exploitation: A Response to Ronald Hyam's 'Empire and Sexual Opportunity.'" *Journal of Imperial and Commonwealth History* 17 (1988): 87.

65. Kondo, p. 25.

66. Compare Thanh-Dam Truong, pp. 178–180; and Cynthia Enloe, *Bananas, Beaches, and Bases: Making Feminist Sense of International Politics* (Berkeley: University of California Press, 1990), p. 36.

67. See Symanski, p. 67.

68. Ibid., p. 133.

69. Wendy Lee argues that these racist images of Asian women also condition the behavior of Japanese male sex tourists. According to Lee:

    > Racist stereotypes of the exotic, sexually licentious oriental woman fuel the sex tourist industry in South-East Asia. It is partly "the subconscious feelings of sexual and racial superiority of Japanese males," former colonizers of South Korea, which account for Korea's popularity as a tourist destination.

    Wendy Lee, "Prostitution and Tourism in South-East Asia," in N. Redclift and M. Sinclair, eds., *Working Women: International Perspectives on Labour and Gender Ideology* (New York: Routledge, 1991), p. 91.

70. Lorraine Hansberry, *To Be Young, Gifted and Black*, quoted in bell hooks, *Ain't I A Woman: black women and feminism* (Boston: South End Press, 1981), p. 58.

71. Hattie Gossett, "is it true what they say about colored pussy?" in C. S. Vance, ed., *Pleasure and Danger: Exploring Female Sexuality* (Boston: Routledge and Kegan Paul, 1984), pp. 411–412.

72. Sondra O'Neale, "Inhibiting Midwives, Usurping Creators: The Struggling Emergence of Black Women in American Fiction," in T. de Lauretis, ed., *Feminist Studies/Critical Studies* (Bloomington: Indiana University Press, 1986), p. 143.

73. Ibid., p. 142.

74. hooks, p. 65.

75. Collins, p. 172.

76. Ibid., p. 175.

77. West, p. 90.

78. Symanski, p. 137.

79. hooks, p. 33.

80. Lerner, quoted in hooks, p. 59.

81. hooks, p. 59.

82. See hooks, pp. 56–65.

83. W. E. B. Du Bois, "The Damnation of Women," in *Du Bois: Writings* (New York: Library of America, 1986), p. 958.

84. Symanski, p. 67.

85. Roger Lane, *Roots of Violence in Black Philadelphia 1860–1900* (Cambridge: Harvard University Press, 1986), p. 131.

86. Ibid., p. 132.

87. Symanski, p. 136.

88. Ibid., p. 137.

89. Ibid., p. 143.

90. Brussa, p. 231.

91. Carla Corso, "Migrant Prostitutes in Northeast Italy," in G. Pheterson, ed., *A Vindication of the Rights of Whores*, p. 242.

92. I do not believe this recommendation reflects the "panic logic" that Linda Singer identifies, since I am ultimately arguing for removing statutes that criminalize prostitution and putting in their place more sensible regulations. Importantly, the regulatory apparatus I recommend does not privilege the nuclear, bourgeois and patriarchal family as the only site of "safe" sex. See Linda Singer, *Erotic Welfare: Sexual Theory and Politics in the Age of Epidemic* (New York: Routledge, 1993).

7. Interpretive Ethics, Cultural Relativism, and Feminist Theory

1. My mother read an earlier draft of this section and has given me her permission to use it.

2. Sandra Bartky, "Foucault, Femininity, and the Modernization of Patriarchal Power," in *Femininity and Domination: Studies in the Phenomenology of Oppression* (New York: Routledge, 1990), p. 65.

3. Ibid., p. 75.

4. Ibid., p. 74.

5. See ibid., p. 77.

6. Ibid., p. 80.

7. Charles Taylor, "Foucault on Freedom and Truth," in *Philosophy and the Human Sciences: Philosophical Papers, 2* (Cambridge: Cambridge University Press, 1985), p. 153.

8. Margaret McLaren, in her discussion of Bartky's book, also comments on the difficulties of imagining liberation given Bartky's Foucaultian framework. See Margaret McLaren, "Possibilities for a Nondominated Female Subjectivity," *Hypatia* 8 (Winter 1993): 153–158.

9. Lila Abu-Lughod claims that purchases of lingerie and cosmetics by some young Bedouin women currently "are directed pointedly at, and are a form of resistance to, their elders of both sexes." See Lila Abu-Lughod, "The Romance of Resistance: Tracing Transformations of Power Through Bedouin Women," *American Ethnologist* 17 (1989): 50. And Chandra Talpade Mohanty argues

   > While there may be a physical similarity in the veils worn by women in Saudi Arabia and Iran, the specific meaning attached to this practice varies according to the cultural and ideological context ... For example, as is well known, Iranian middle-class women veiled themselves during the 1979 revolution to indicate solidarity with their veiled working-class sisters, while in contemporary Iran, mandatory Islamic laws dictate that all Iranian women wear veils. While in both these instances, similar reasons might be offered for the veil (opposition to the Shah and Western cultural colonization in the first case, and the true Islamicization of Iran in the second), the concrete *meanings* attached to Iranian women wearing the veil are clearly different in both historical contexts. In the first case, wearing the veil is both an oppositional and a revolutionary gesture on the part of Iranian middle-class women; in the second case, it is a coercive, institutional mandate ... To assume that the mere practice of veiling women in a number of Muslim countries indicates the universal oppression of women through sexual segregation not only is analytically reductive, but also proves quite useless when it comes to the elaboration of oppositional political strategy.

   What Mohanty describes here about the veil—its contextually shifting significance—probably holds true for any bodily ornamentation or covering. See Chandra Talpade Mohanty, "Under Western Eyes: Feminist Scholarship and Colonial Discourses," in C. Mohanty, A. Russo, and L. Torres, eds., *Third World Women and the Politics of Feminism* (Bloomington: Indiana University Press, 1991), p. 67.

10. Maria Lugones and Elizabeth Spelman, "Have We Got a Theory for You! Feminist Theory, Cultural Imperialism and the Demand for 'The Woman's Voice,'" in *Women and Values: Readings in Recent Feminist Philosophy*, 2d ed. (Belmont, CA: Wadsworth, 1993), pp. 18–29.

   For an interesting analysis of Maxine Hong Kingston's works as exemplary postmodern texts, see Patricia Lin, "Clashing Constructs of

Reality: Reading Maxine Hong Kingston's *Tripmaster Monkey: His Fake Book* as Indigenous Ethnography," in *Reading the Literature of Asian America* (Philadelphia, PA: Temple University Press, 1992), pp. 333–348. According to Lin,

> As the "writer" of *Tripmaster Monkey,* Maxine Hong Kingston extends the continuum of making meaning not through use of the totalizing strategies of the novel but through deliberated disjunctions of language and texts. Less novelist than ethnographer, she performs the postmodern ethnographic role of producing a "cooperatively evolved text consisting of fragments of discourse." (p. 346)

Lin argues that the hybridized and creolized lives of ethnic Americans requires that they negotiate daily conflicting constructions of reality, and thus they are well-positioned to take on tasks of ethnographic description. Lin's essay suggests that the writings of ethnic American women writers like Kingston might also serve as models for cooperative and polyvocal feminist moral texts.

11. Ibid., p. 24.

12. Ibid.

13. Though my mother, whose underwear concerns I have caricatured in this section, has never been an activist for feminist causes, she has been an activist for civil rights. When I was my daughter's age, my mother belonged to CORE (Congregation of Racial Equality) and helped set up legal cases against landlords who would not rent to blacks. When I was a few years older, she took me with her to stand on picket lines to protest the racist hiring practices of local businesses. Later, my mother helped to integrate local community theater in San Jose, California, among other things. Thus, as Ginsburg's studies of pro-life women well demonstrate, many of the women whom we are inclined to regard as anti-feminist are social activists in ways that we admire. It is partly because of this that we might try to understand life as these women see it.

14. Lugones and Spelman, p. 26.

15. Ibid., p. 25.

16. Richard Arneson, "Commodification and Commercial Surrogacy," *Philosophy and Public Affairs* 21 (Spring 1992): 132–164.

17. Ibid., p. 141.

18. Ibid., p. 144.

19. Ibid., p. 142.

20. Ibid., p. 145.

21. See ibid.

22. One might also compare our commercial surrogacy practices with outwardly similarly practices involving paid pregnancy in other societies in order to understand the range of social ideals and presuppositions that produce such practices.

23. I am grateful to Wynne Furth for suggesting this idea to me.

24. This strategy is taken, for example, by Susan Wolf, whose work I will discuss below.

25. This is the approach taken by Charles Taylor and Bernard Williams, as I discussed at the end of chapter 1.

26. For a sympathetic articulation of this view, see David Wong, "Coping With Moral Conflict," *Ethics* 102 (July 1992): 763–784. Wong defends a morality based on a principle of accommodation, which he sees as a normative consequence of meta-ethical relativism. Also see Wong, *Moral Relativity* (Berkeley: University of California, 1984).

27. Compare Philippa Foot, "Moral Relativism," reprinted in J. Meiland and M. Krausz, eds., *Relativism: Cognitive and Moral* (Notre Dame, IN: University of Notre Dame, 1982), p. 152.

28. Bernard Williams also comments on the possibly pernicious effects of moral theory. He states:

> Many people draw a distinction between killing an early fetus and killing newborn child. Not everyone does. A good many people, in particular Catholics, equate abortion with infanticide and regard both as evil. A very few people equate infanticide with abortion and see both as permitted. In the modern world, the latter seem to consist mostly of enthusiasts for ethical theory . . . (p. 112)

However, contra Williams, there are others besides Catholics and moral theory enthusiasts who equate killing a neonate with killing a fetus, as we saw in chapter 3. Though such folks do not equate "abortion" with "infanticide," as both are concepts belonging to our conceptual scheme. Nevertheless, the criticism of ethical theory that Williams is articulating here is similar to my own above. It concerns the tendency of philosophers to ignore the social and historical sources of our moral distinctions and patterns of reasoning. In doing this we misrepresent the intellectual and reflective habits of others, including other theorizers, and these misrepresentations then take on a life of their own.

29. Susan Wolf, "Two Levels of Pluralism," *Ethics* 102 (July 1992): 788.

30. Ibid., p. 791.

31. Ibid.

32. See Alasdair MacIntyre, *Whose Justice? Which Rationality?* (Notre Dame, IN: University of Notre Dame Press, 1988).

33. Wolf, p. 791.

34. Ibid. p. 796.

35. Sandra Harding attempts to rethink and redefine objectivity from a feminist perspective, and argues that

> in a society structured by gender hierarchy, "starting thought from women's lives" increases the objectivity of the results of

research by bringing scientific observation and the perception of the need for explanation to bear on assumptions and practices that appear natural or unremarkable from the perspective of the lives of men in the dominant groups. Thinking from the perspective of women's lives makes strange what had appeared familiar, which is the beginning of any scientific inquiry. (p. 150)

By thinking from the perspectives of women's lives and also from the perspectives of other societies, in the last chapter I tried to render strange aspects of prostitution that had appeared natural and unremarkable to previous, predominantly male, social scientists. For example, I tried to render strange the supposed Mediterranean male desire for women who are physically novel that Jacques Rossiaud finds unproblematic, and I tried to render strange the desires of men in our society for the services of prostitutes, especially prostitutes of color. Yet, unlike Harding, I do not see the need to rehabilitate claims to objectivity.

One of the ways my view differs, perhaps, from Harding's is that, for me, it is equally important to recover the perspectives of persons from different societies—especially non-Western, nonindustrial ones—in order to render visible problematic assumptions. But the primary disagreement I have with Harding is this: if we accept the idea that our thoughts, perceptions, experiences, conceptions, and so on, are culturally and historically shaped, and that even within a given society they are shaped by the social identities we inhabit, and if we also accept that there is no thought procedure that can allow us to have thoughts, perceptions, experiences, or conceptions which are free of all such shaping, then knowledge must come about, as Harding describes, by defamiliarizing the familiar and understanding it in new ways. But any new way of understanding must still exist relative to some historical and cultural context and, thus, there is no possibility of understanding something "as it is in-itself" apart from some human perspective. Though we can "educate" our perceptions and conceptions by gaining both exposure to other human possibilities and some distance from and critical self-awareness of our own socially formed prejudices, this does not engender understanding of objects as they exist in some nonhumanly ordered space. Now, given this picture of human understanding and knowledge which Harding to a large extent accepts, and given its rejection of traditional objectivist and realist notions, it seems somehow awkward and distorting to describe our capacity for rendering other human worlds, lives, practices, and artifacts intelligible to ourselves and others as "increasing objectivity." Rather than resuscitate "objectivity," I am suggesting that we rethink our notions about "relativism," and also question the basis of the subjective/objective distinctions we make. See Sandra Harding, *Whose Science? Whose Knowledge? Thinking from Women's Lives* (Ithaca, NY: Cornell University Press, 1991). For an interesting discussion of the objective/subjective distinction, and also the relationship between relativism and subjectivism, see Lorraine Code, *What Can She Know? Feminist Theory and the Construction of*

Knowledge (Ithaca, NY: Cornell University Press, 1991), especially pp. 27–28, and 3.

36. See Alasdair MacIntyre, *After Virtue: A Study in Moral Theory*, 2d ed. (Notre Dame, IN: University of Notre Dame Press, 1984), pp. 6–35.

37. Compare Wolf, p. 786.

38. See Ruth Benedict, *Patterns of Culture* (Boston: Houghton Mifflin, 1934 [1959]), p. 24.

39. In saying this I do not mean to imply that we should respond to such actions with harsh and punitive legal measures. For we need to consider whether the culturally transported persons who engage in such "alien" practices are aware of their meaning and potential consequences in their new social setting. Recently we have seen cases of African immigrant mothers in France circumcising their daughters, and Hmong residents in California practicing bride-capture on more Americanized Hmong women. In both cases prosecutors, urged on by feminists, pursued rather punitive sentences for these misplaced social actors. If punishment is to fit the crime, then we need to understand the "crime," which in these cases are not "genital mutilation" or "rape," but cultural ignorance and contempt, and provincialism and ethnic arrogance.

40. Susan Sherwin, *No Longer Patient: Feminist Ethics and Health Care* (Philadelphia: Temple University, 1992), p. 67.

41. Ibid., p. 69.

42. Ibid., p. 74.

43. Ibid.

44. Ibid., p. 249, note 10.

45. Ibid., p. 74.

46. Since I have not studied the ethnographic literature on this, I remain somewhat unsure of this translation.

47. This formulation of the epistemic commitments of cultural relativism was suggested to me by Richard Handler.

48. Alison Jaggar states that "feminist ethics may be identified by its explicit commitment to challenging perceived male bias in ethics. Approaches that do not express such a commitment should be characterized as nonfeminist . . ." See her "Feminist Ethics: Projects, Problems, Prospects" in Claudia Card, ed., *Feminist Ethics* (Lawrence, KS: University Press of Kansas, 1991), p. 97.

49. Hans-Georg Gadamer, *Truth and Method* (New York: Continuum, 1975), p. 246.

50. Jeffrey Weeks, *Sexuality and Its Discontents: Meanings, Myths and Modern Sexualities* (London: Routledge, 1985), p. 226.

Index